KENNESAW

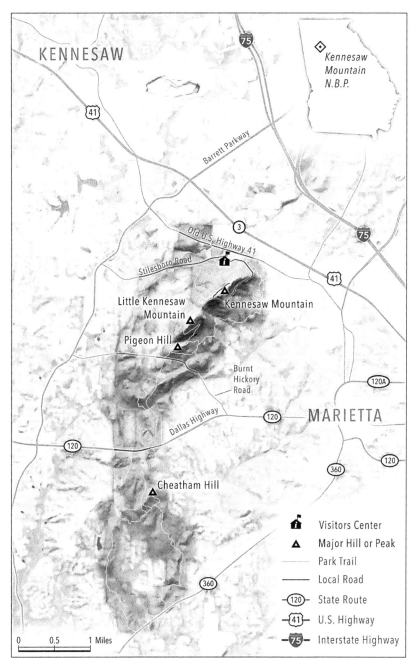

Frontispiece. Map of Kennesaw Mountain National Battlefield Park. Inset: location of Cobb County, Georgia.

# KENNESAW

*Natural History of a Southern Mountain*

Sean P. Graham

THE UNIVERSITY OF ALABAMA PRESS
Tuscaloosa

The University of Alabama Press
Tuscaloosa, Alabama 35487-0380
uapress.ua.edu

Typeface: Scala Pro

Cover image: Kennesaw Mountain National Battlefield Park; photo by Brandon Westerman
Cover design: David Nees

Cataloging-in-Publication data is available from the Library of Congress.
ISBN: 978-0-8173-5999-7
E-ISBN: 978-0-8173-9344-1

The author acknowledges the many folks at UA Press whose contributions and editorial suggestions greatly enhanced this book, especially Claire Evans Lewis, Laurel Anderton, and Joanna Jacobs, as well as Craig Remington and the UA Cartography Lab.

For Tom Patrick, Georgia Department of
Natural Resources Botanist, 1944–2019.

# Contents

# Figures

# Preface

"In early days (1844), when a lieutenant of the 3rd artillery, I had been sent from Charleston, South Carolina, to Marietta Georgia ... we remained in Marietta about six weeks, during which time I repeatedly rode to *Kenesaw Mountain*, and over the very ground where afterward, in 1864, we had some hard battles. Thus by a mere accident I was enabled to traverse on horseback the very ground where in after-years I had to conduct vast armies and fight great battles. That the knowledge thus acquired was of infinite use to me, and consequently to the Government, I have always felt and stated."
—William Tecumseh Sherman, *Memoirs of William T. Sherman*

THE MOUNTAIN'S NAME IS SUPPOSED to derive from the Cherokee word *ga-ni-sa*, which means "burial place." But this seems almost too appropriate to be true, and the Cherokee were forced from this place too long ago to know for sure how it got the name or what exactly it means. Little prehistoric archaeology has been done on Kennesaw. In any case, mountains aren't good places to reconstruct the ancient past because they are sites of erosion, rather than places where artifacts get buried. Kennesaw Mountain lies on the divide between the Chattahoochee and Etowah Rivers, along whose valleys Native Americans settled and built towns. The woods near Kennesaw were once the frontier between Creek and Cherokee land and were probably visited only occasionally for the purpose of hunting or perhaps gathering medicinal plants. But we can be certain the mountain had some significance for Native Americans, since most noteworthy places did.

Although it is certainly striking, Kennesaw is hardly a mountain. Somebody from Colorado or Alaska would understandably scoff at the idea of calling this lovely, camel-humped hill a mountain. And if we're going to be completely honest, even by Georgia standards it's not very impressive. Compared to mountains of the Blue Ridge in northern Georgia it's just a pile of rocks. It's no Brasstown Bald, Hightower Bald, Rabun Bald, Blood Mountain, Rich Mountain, or Fort Mountain. Even though it's as tall as some of the ridges of northwest Georgia—like Taylor's Ridge, Johns Mountain, or Rocky Face—it's not nearly as long. Geologically, it has little similarity to the ridges of

Figure 1. Kennesaw Mountain National Battlefield Park. Photograph by Sean P. Graham.

northwest Georgia or to the mountains of the Blue Ridge. It's a monadnock, or, if you prefer, an inselberg, which are fancy words for a large, isolated, solid rock outcrop. In this way Kennesaw is more similar to nearby Stone Mountain. But even there the similarity is superficial because Stone Mountain is made of a different kind of rock than Kennesaw, and the two mountains had very different beginnings.

The mountain's two humps are known locally as Big and Little Kennesaw, and the rocks that make up the mountain continue on, with diminished height, as Pigeon and Cheatham Hills. At 1,808 feet above sea level, the peak of Big Kennesaw rises a mere 608 feet above the floor of old farmland and subdivisions below. Its length stretches all of a mile before it disappears again below the surrounding Georgia red clay. The only thing that makes it stand out is how utterly ordinary the Piedmont terrain surrounding the mountain is. The mountain breaches from the plain, rolling hills like a humpback whale. From the top you can see all around for miles, a view that includes a few other knobby peaks like Blackjack Mountain, Sweat Mountain, and Lost Mountain, which in combination someone once had the gall to call the Kennesaw Range. But these are clearly just hills.

Despite clamoring for a measly six hundred feet of altitude, the mountain is special. The peak accumulates the faintest bit more rain each year than the surrounding oak-hickory forests and has been doing so on a cumulative basis for thousands of years. Kennesaw Mountain's forests are just a tad cooler and moister, and its soils richer than those of other forests nearby. The mountain is noticeable enough from the air that it beckons the arrival and departure of thousands of migrating birds from all points during spring and fall. Its 1,808 feet above sea level has made more of a difference than it rightfully should have. And it was for this reason it became the site of a great human tragedy in the summer of 1864.

In 1864 the American Civil War was reaching its crescendo. U. S. Grant took over command of all federal forces and left Chattanooga for Virginia to tackle the army of Robert E. Lee. He left his friend William T. Sherman to deal with Confederate forces in Tennessee and Georgia. Sherman was already familiar with the terrain. He fought a series of battles across the rugged ridges and valleys of northwestern Georgia, mostly tactical draws wherein Sherman outflanked the Confederates but failed to capitalize on his tactical advantage and entrap the enemy. The mission was to destroy Joseph E. Johnston's army, but Sherman would eventually change his strategy, taking the war to the South's industrial and agricultural production capacity. Sherman would attack not armies, but the South's civilian centers. Sherman set his sights on Atlanta.

Kennesaw Mountain is the highest peak in the Atlanta area and stands like a fortress on its northwestern approach. It stood in the way of Sherman's army heading toward Atlanta, and in his memoirs he referred to it as "the key to the whole country." He first sighted the mountain on June 9, 1864, observing that the "summits were crowned with batteries, and the spurs were alive with men busy in felling trees, digging pits, and preparing for the grand struggle impending." With artillery placed on the heights, you couldn't go around it without getting shelled. And you couldn't flank Kennesaw without the rebels seeing your moves. It was the last great naturally fortified position before you got to the Chattahoochee River, and beyond that, there were only the outer fortifications of Atlanta itself. The rebels dug in. Something would happen here.

Most soldiers in 1864 probably viewed Kennesaw Mountain with feelings ranging from dread to a shrewd, tactical indifference. Northern soldiers, especially, would have viewed it as an imposing obstacle, bristling as it was with cannons. According to William Key, a Pennsylvania captain wrote home that he was "on the fringes of Hell, a mountain called on the maps Kennesaw." The Southern troops—excepting those who had to lug artillery to the top— may have had a slightly more fond view, for such a ridge was a fortified position. In his memoirs, Sherman gave it the most pleasant description, writing, "Kennesaw, the bold and striking twin mountain, lay before us, with a high range of chestnut hills trending off to the northeast . . . the scene was enchanting; too beautiful to be disturbed by the harsh clamor of war." Mountains and other natural environments would not become objects of beauty for most Americans for some time yet. The soldiers were mostly farm boys whose idea of a handsome landscape was one with good, dark soil fit for the plow. People were just beginning to have romantic notions about nature. The transcendentalists and their views were by no means mainstream, and at the time, Thoreau was likely considered a bit odd because of his love affair with the Concord woods. *Walden* was published just before the war broke out, and it is doubtful that it was among the books soldiers carried with them. Noted author Ambrose Bierce—who was nearly killed near Kennesaw—described his generation's changing attitudes toward mountains in his essay "On a Mountain." He wrote, "Modern literature is full of evidence that our great grandfathers looked upon mountains with aversion and horror. The poets of even the seventeenth century never tire of damning them in good, set terms."

Despite having such an imposing natural fortress at his front, Sherman tried something different at Kennesaw. Instead of the careful flanking maneuvers that characterized the earlier battles for Georgia, Sherman decided on a frontal assault on the center of the Confederate positions. The main assault was not on the tallest peaks of Big or Little Kennesaw, but farther down the line at Cheatham Hill. The assault failed, resulting in a lopsided Confederate defensive victory. Although estimates range widely, most sources (for example, the National Park Service's historical outline by Robert Hellman, as well as Earl Hess's and Albert Castel's battlefield histories) put the Union losses on June 27 at three thousand, most of whom were killed or wounded during the main assaults on Pigeon and Cheatham Hills, and a large percentage of whom were killed within twenty minutes of reaching Johnston's defensive works. Confederate losses were only about five hundred.

The Battle of Kennesaw Mountain was the only frontal assault Sherman attempted during his campaign for Georgia, and after flanking the rebels again after the main battle, his army was on the move again, eventually besting the Confederates in a series of decisive battles around Atlanta. The city was evacuated in September after Sherman cut the last railroad line supplying it from Jonesboro, south of town. The fall of Atlanta was considered a major contribution to the reelection of Abraham Lincoln and was among a number of Northern successes in late 1864 that seemed to indicate that Union victory was possible. In the spring of 1865 the war was finally over.

●

The goal of this book is to introduce general readers to another side of Kennesaw Mountain. It is not a tedious list of regiments and battalions and the strategic and tactical decisions made in 1864, and not a rehashing of postwar letters and memoirs. There are plenty of books about all that. I will not help you reimagine the carnage of the storming of the Dead Angle—a defensive salient that became the focus of the Union attempt to break the Confederate lines—in which hundreds of young men died in twenty minutes. I will not try to transport you over 150 years in the past to help you understand the motivations of the men and women on either side, or the reasons they were trying to kill each other. Things are different now. No matter their motivations, what happened on June 27, 1864, led ultimately to the establishment of a national battlefield park. Their sacrifice inadvertently created a quiet, forested island within a sea of highways, subdivisions, office parks, and strip malls.

Kennesaw Mountain National Battlefield Park exemplifies both the rich culture and natural history of the South. Without knowing anything about what happened here in 1864 you can still enjoy its magnificent forests, trails, flowers, and birds. But I wonder whether that is possible. I wonder whether anyone can visit the mountain without briefly thinking about the industrial-scale murder that went on there, and why. Ironically, the mountain would by now be changed irrevocably if thousands hadn't died here during the Civil War. The battle that took place ensured the park's protection as hallowed ground when the National Park Service began setting aside public lands not only to protect iconic landscapes but also to establish memorials to the fallen during the Civil War. Because of its topographical prominence and its former military strategic importance, Kennesaw Mountain simultaneously encompasses a treasured historical monument and an exceptional green space.

This book is for visitors interested in this accidental natural area. I will describe the natural history of the mountain from the ground up, beginning with its fascinating geology. We'll next explore the mountain's vegetation and forests, as well as some interesting animals that call Kennesaw home. The book culminates with a description of what is arguably the park's most important attribute from an ecological and conservation perspective: its status as a globally important hot spot for migratory birds. The final chapters describe the uncertain future of Kennesaw as a historical site and green space for all Americans. The result, I hope, is a thorough and engaging treatment of the value of one of the South's most accessible natural and historical sites.

KENNESAW

# 1
# Unfortunate Rocks

L OOK AT THE ROCK OUTCROPS on top of Kennesaw Mountain, up where the bus road terminates, or farther up the trail at the summit. You'll see blocky gray rocks with obvious wavy bands of dark material and lighter stripes of quartz: the telltale indication of metamorphism. One of my favorite rock outcrops is just up the road from Kennesaw Mountain on I-75, where an impressive road cuts through a gigantic hulk of migmatite that is almost one hundred feet tall and one hundred feet long. This cut reveals more of this characteristic banding, but on a much larger scale than what can be seen on the mountaintop: enormous bands of light and dark, grading through all shades of gray, some bands shiny black, curving and intertwining among thick swarms of confused quartz. The outcrop takes on the aspect of a finger painting made by a feral child or a madman. It has faults cutting between the layers, and evidence of brutal folding. These rocks have been subjected to intense pressures and relentless shearing, pushed together in a geological vise like punching together two sets of knuckles, so hard they have undergone

Figure 2. Kennesaw gneiss, the metamorphic rock that makes up Kennesaw Mountain. Photo by Sean Graham.

changes to their very chemical structure in a sad process of hellish destruction and torture.

I truly do feel pity for metamorphic rocks.

I imagine them buried down there, deep underground, under the crushing weight of thousands of feet of younger rocks. I imagine the slow, steaming, gradual pressure and the incremental rise in heat. Imagine being squashed flat from three sides over millions of years.

Igneous rocks, born from the fires of volcanism, may at first consideration seem to be produced from a more extreme process. But they begin as molten lava or magma—born bright, sparkling, and fresh—and after cooling they can lie comfortably and unmolested for millennia. Sedimentary rocks form by the slow precipitation of tiny fragments of other rocks deposited as distinctive layers laid flat. They look like the pages of a book, and geologists can read them that way. Pages buried down deep in the earth under younger layers are the oldest. Those on top were deposited more recently and are the youngest. Sedimentary rocks can be folded and faulted, sometimes exhibiting confusing patterns, but they can still be interpreted easily with a little practice. They also have fossils, allowing correlation among layers and interpretation through time. They are a godsend to geologists, and happy geologists—those who know best—spend their time studying sedimentary rocks. Metamorphic rocks, by contrast, are formed when either igneous or sedimentary rocks experience slow, deep heat and pressure. They are then bent and deformed, their structure reworked, their fossils and layers obliterated. Their very minerals recrystallize into strange new ones. Geologists shudder in fear in their presence, knowing the difficulty in interpreting rock that has been completely renovated.

Examine metamorphic rocks more closely and you'll see peppery minerals within each grayscale band aligned in obvious order. They have obediently aligned themselves perpendicular to the direction of the wicked pressure that formed them. You would have too if you'd experienced the kind of heat and pressure that caused the minerals to align. Unlike sedimentary rocks, which can also contain layers of minerals, the large-scale structure of metamorphic rocks is not uniform. It's a warped mess.

Sedimentary rocks are formed from deposition and later solidification of minerals by familiar weathering processes: beaches become sandstone, marine ooze becomes limestone, and mud becomes shale. Igneous rocks are formed from cooled magma or lava: rhyolite, granite, basalt, or gabbro. Metamorphic rocks are formed when you take either of these and torture them— put them under immense heat and pressure, but not enough heat to melt them, because then they would become molten: quartzite, marble, schist, and gneiss. All these rocks have the potential to become one of the other types, depending on their particular fortune: granite can erode to sand, wash to the sea, and become sandstone. Sandstone can be brought under the brutal strain of metamorphism and change to quartzite, its gritty grains becoming pulverized to a solid sheen. Or, sandstone can be buried deep in the crust, become molten, and become granite again. This same granite can be smashed slowly until it recrystallizes as gneiss. Since nothing is permanent and no rock will remain one kind forever, this is referred to as the rock cycle.

Now step back—very, very far back—and examine a geological map of the Kennesaw Mountain area—the Georgia Piedmont region. You'll immediately notice a similar tortured, banded pattern to the rock units—miles upon miles of entire rock groups thrown over each other, banded around each other, and shot through with younger material and foreign rock types. The colored geological map might suggest a diverse provenance for these rocks, but many are still the gray-white-black banded metamorphic rocks you saw on top of the mountain. Each rock unit is squeezed and faulted upon another, with each composed of waves of the gray-black-white squiggled texture, and within each of these bands, minerals are aligned against the source of the pressure. These metamorphic rocks have been twisted and smashed, but smashed slowly—not like having your finger smashed in a door, but rather like having it smashed in a vise, with someone cranking it once per day, day after day—during a nightmarish scenario of low, prolonged, throbbing regional metamorphism.

Feel very sorry for these rocks.

Despite the challenges rife in interpreting the geological history of metamorphic rocks, and despite this directly resulting in fewer geologists willing to take on such a problem, there is a tantalizing hint at what has gone on here at Kennesaw Mountain. This fascinating story has been pieced together from others' research completed over decades; for more information, consult the list of primary research provided at the back of the book. The story begins far back in the dimmest earth history, when life was a hit-or-miss proposition, and involves the very basement of North America—the continental root of our country. It involves the construction of the Appalachian Mountains. The youngest rocks involved were formed when dinosaurs were first getting their start.

To the northwest of Kennesaw Mountain, just east of Cartersville, is an obvious contact between unrelated rocks: to the west of this boundary are those easy, happy sedimentary rocks—limestone in the valleys with gurgling springs, and ridges capped with pebbly sandstone and layers of thin, papery shale. To the east are the Talladega Uplands—rugged, folded, unruly, and composed of dusty old Corbin gneiss. Gneiss is the result of very long, intense metamorphism. This particular gneiss appears to be composed of the same material as rocks from the very bottom of Tallulah Gorge near Clayton, Georgia, one of the deepest and oldest canyons of the East. This gorge cuts straight down to the core of Georgia: what geologists call the craton. The craton is the foundation of the continent, the continental shield. It formed before complex life began, when the earth was still cooling, when it was still loose and raw. Geologists love verbosity, so they also call this the basement. They also like to name rock units after places, so it's called the Grenville Basement, after an exposure in Grenville, Quebec. This is the floor of our continent, with rare exposures running from central Georgia to Canada.

Corbin gneiss is similar to the basement exposed at the bottom of Tallulah Gorge, which is overlain by a tortured, metamorphosed chunk of oceanic crust. There is a similar section of metamorphosed oceanic crust just east of the Corbin gneiss—the New Georgia Group—which is exposed to the west of Kennesaw in Cobb County. This analogy allows geologists to draw a time line between the old rocks of the basement and those of the Corbin gneiss. Dating techniques have confirmed that the Corbin gneiss is over a billion years old. Lying smooshed on top and to the east are long, streaming bands of metamorphic rocks: sandstone turned to quartzite, limestone turned to marble, shale turned to slate, and more unlucky rocks pounded to schist.

These bands continue in ropy units for hundreds of miles diagonally to the northeast, and the Blue Ridge Mountains and Piedmont are composed of them. To the northwest are sedimentary rocks, ranging in age from the Cambrian (500 million years ago) to Pennsylvanian (350 million years ago) periods. These sedimentary rocks have not gotten away completely unscathed—they are warped into curving, banded hills like corduroy and have eroded into the characteristic ridges and valleys that trend northeast from Georgia all the way to Canada. To the west of the Ridge and Valley region, sedimentary rocks of the same age and composition lie flat, comfortable, and untrammeled: the Cumberland and Allegheny Plateaus. The rocks are progressively less punished the farther northwest you go, all the way to the top of Lookout Mountain, where you can see just how happy, flat, and parallel rocks can be.

The metamorphic zone, which Kennesaw Mountain is part of, has more surprises. The contorted, suffering metasedimentary rocks have had some unexpected, and presumably unwanted, visitors. Giant blobs of magma seeped up from the hot depths of the earth and injected themselves into the sedimentary sequence. When the first of these intrusions took place, the sandstones, shales, and limestones surrounding the Kennesaw area were still untouched, still unwarped. Then, a massive volcanic pluton crept from the depths (it's helpful to imagine this as the rising goop of a giant lava lamp) and cooled slowly, without producing an external nuisance like a volcano. Then the metamorphic event happened—the big squeeze—pressing the sedimentary units near Atlanta together, crushing them under such intense pressure that their very minerals recrystallized and in some cases completely changed into new ones. The pluton didn't escape the squeeze, and so it became metamorphosed as well. To the west of this compression, a massive fault snapped, thrusting an enormous section of the sedimentary rocks over themselves, ripping open a hole that exposed the deep craton. West of the Cartersville Fault, rocks were spared metamorphism but were thrust into ripples—the ridges and valleys—like kicking up a carpet. These snapped and faulted but did not experience the intense pressures and heat of regional metamorphism. Farther to the northwest, rocks were not affected at all and still lie flat, as in the Cumberland Plateau.

As metamorphism continued, additional magma intrusions appeared, forming the Austell, Sand Hill, and Mulberry Rock gneisses found elsewhere in the Atlanta area, which became metamorphosed almost before they were even done cooling. Finally, after the metamorphism, more pressure was relieved, and new intrusions percolated up from the depths, which were completely spared from metamorphism. Insertions of magma shot like beams of light into rocks formed during all these earlier events, creating the youngest rocks around—the diabase dikes of the Triassic period. The magma intrusions that occurred after the metamorphism never became gneiss and include the famous—and, as it were, lucky—Stone Mountain granite.

Younger rocks are found much farther to the southeast of all this great geological upheaval, and they are actually composed of the eroded remains of the mountains it formed: the Coastal Plain of Georgia is made of fine, unconsolidated erosive remnants of the Appalachians, which were deposited around them like a skirt during periods of high seas.

Evidence of this ancient violence can be found all over Kennesaw Mountain and the Atlanta area. Kennesaw was formed originally as a deep magma intrusion into what were then sedimentary rocks like the ones in northwest Georgia. It never exploded as a volcano but simply lay there and cooled in place, deep under the crust. Some of the limestone that dissolved into this pluton as it gurgled up from the depths can be found intact as inclusions—skarns—in the Kennesaw gneiss on the mountain's summit. After the magma cooled, the metamorphic event occurred, changing the pluton and all the rocks around it (and in it) into metamorphic ones—the quartzites of Blackjack Mountain and the Chattahoochee Palisades, the marbles of Pickens County, and the gneiss of Kennesaw Mountain. The Kennesaw gneiss is migmatitic, displaying those extremely warped bands. Migmatite forms at temperatures and heat so extreme that you can't even have more metamorphism, because more heat and pressure will simply melt the rock and then you'll have magma.

Try to imagine what those poor rocks went through. Buried so deep and pressed so hard they nearly melted, so burdened their minerals began to bend and ripple into those bands while still solid. Rocks don't have it any worse.

What kind of catastrophe could cause such a major metamorphic event on such a spectacular scale? Where does this kind of deep pressure come from? To understand this, one must imagine what the earth actually looked like when all of this was going on. Our continent was much different then, and there were no Appalachian Mountains—not yet. This is what happened: The shield rocks formed a definite continent, albeit a smaller one, but the landmass was centered far to the northwest of Atlanta, in Canada. Where Atlanta is now there was just ocean. Another continent approached and when it contacted the shield it dove under it like a porpoise. This was during the Ordovician period, when fish were a crude joke and hadn't even experimented with limbs yet. Volcanoes and highlands formed along the margin of the continent where the Appalachians would eventually rise, and over the next two hundred million years erosion wore them down to nothing, creating massive sedimentary deposits to the west, which would eventually become the Ridge and Valley and Cumberland Plateau. During the rest of the Paleozoic, the roots of this ancient mountain range and the craton were smashed with wave after wave of small continents, culminating with the collision of a substantial portion of Africa that careened slowly into North America. This event pushed up the Appalachians as we know them now: it lifted and metamorphosed the Blue Ridge, furrowed the Ridges and Valleys, snapped the long faults along the East Coast, and created the gash through which you can see the Corbin gneiss. During the successive accumulation of small island arcs, volcanic events occurred, and three cycles of magma intrusions appeared. The massive pressure involved in the collision metamorphosed the eastern sedimentary beds beyond recognition. It changed them into new rocks, squeezed the old magma chamber into Kennesaw gneiss, and lifted the entire sedimentary region to the west of the Piedmont several hundred feet above sea level, clean out of the ocean. The Appalachians would have been much taller then, more like the Andes or Himalayas, both of which are currently caught between colliding continents.

Understanding this explanation depends in no small part on whether you can fathom something that at first seems as counterintuitive as the idea that the earth is spherical rather than flat, or that the earth is speeding around the sun rather than the sun racing around the earth. You must imagine continents slowly shifting around the surface of the earth, riding on the warm, plastic mantle, unfurling from midocean ridges and peeling off on top of each other at subduction zones. But plate tectonics is now as established and necessary an explanation for the way the world works as the other previously doubted theories of heliocentrism and the round earth. A skeptic can look at a world map—those nice ones that show the texture of the earth with the oceans removed—and see how obviously the plates are arranged like a giant quilt, the midocean ridges like stitches. Where the plates meet, there are mountains. Where they are spreading, there are rift zones.

The gneiss of Kennesaw Mountain has low levels of silica and is instead composed mostly of very heavy, dark, so-called mafic materials. The Kennesaw gneiss is a formation within the Laura Lake mafic complex, just one part of a larger metamorphosed intrusion extending all the way out of Cobb County. The fact that the material is mafic indicates the magma formed deep inside the earth's crust, almost down to the mantle. Light-colored, silica-rich granites accumulate a lot of lighter material on their way up to the surface, becoming fine, pale domes like Stone Mountain. The slower these magma chambers cool, the coarser the grain of their minerals. Very coarse, slowly cooled magma—with crystals as big as or bigger than a marble—are known as pegmatite. Pegmatites with isolated, very large crystals are known as porphyroblasts. Some of the Kennesaw gneiss displays this texture, indicating the original igneous rock of Kennesaw was gabbro, a mafic pegmatite. From this we can infer the remarkable fact that Kennesaw Mountain originally formed very deep in Georgia's crust, and it took a long, long time to cool, and an agonizingly long time to eventually be exposed at the surface. Large crystals formed during this slow cooling, before becoming metamorphosed into entirely new minerals: amphibole, plagioclase, garnet, pyroxene, and magnetite.

The mountain is also riddled with tiny specks of gold—another mineral forged deep in the earth—and an enterprising and completely unscrupulous company could argue that tearing down the mountain, grinding it up, and sifting the gold out would be good business practice. Surely it would provide jobs, which everyone knows is the ultimate litmus test of good environmental practice.

The large magnetite crystals, some of which are porphyroblasts, are noteworthy and are so prevalent that the whole mountain gives off a loud magnetic signature that can be picked up by aerial magnetic mapping equipment as a bright peak. But more on that later.

The gneiss that formed Kennesaw Mountain was finally left alone by the powerful forces of metamorphism, and during the Triassic period a rift formed between Africa and North America, and they began to slowly move apart. This rift is now positioned along the midocean ridge in the middle of the Atlantic. Release of pressure during this time allowed diabase to creep into the Piedmont and released the Stone Mountain magma, which never experienced metamorphism. Then, after all of this geological agony, the mountains and distorted rocks were left to slowly decompose and wash away, their minerals steadily eroding over the next one hundred million years to the sea, while dinosaurs, glyptodonts, and Carolina parakeets came and went. Eventually, as the easily eroded rocks sagged and melted down to nothing, lumps of the most resistant rock began to appear—imagine pouring hot coffee on a fruitcake—exposing the old granite domes and the deep gneissic chambers that had long ago quietly inserted themselves into the Piedmont during the Appalachian orogeny.

Kennesaw Mountain was born.

It is possible to estimate when rocks formed, but not when they became exposed on the surface for the first time, so we have no idea when the rocks of Kennesaw actually became a mountain. We can determine when mountain-building events occurred, because they are associated with crystallization of minerals, and minerals can now be absolutely dated using radioactive decay methods. According to Keith McConnell and Charlotte Abrams, the metamorphic rocks near Kennesaw Mountain are 250–300 million years old, the time when the metamorphic event occurred. But we don't know exactly when the magma originally intruded into the Piedmont, because the clock is reset when metamorphosis occurs. And nobody has yet tried to absolutely date the rocks of Kennesaw Mountain. Even if we had such a date, it would be only for when the minerals formed, not when they became exposed through erosion.

We will therefore probably never know when Kennesaw first appeared, but for it to do so required a lot of the Piedmont rind atop it to erode away, and this must have taken quite some time. The mountain itself is still wearing away and won't last too much longer, geologically speaking. However, like an iceberg, the mountain has more material below it, and more gneiss and granite intrusions will appear as the Piedmont washes away even more, eventually wearing all the way down to the basement, all the way to nothing, until someday it is reborn again.

# 2
# Ancient Forest

IN THE 1850S A NETWORK of professional botanists scoured North America collecting plants. These included men of some education, like ministers and physicians, and also more adventurous sorts who would climb unknown mountains in search of new botanical treasures. Most had some idea about which plants were interesting and possibly new to science, although many would simply collect local plants that were unknown to them and send them to authorities for identification. This was during a time when, biologically, most of the country was still terra incognita. The untapped potential of plants was then becoming unlocked and their importance widely recognized. Plants new to science had actual monetary value. Rather than collecting useless objects like baseball cards, coins, or stamps, gentlemen of sound financial standing would pay good money for seeds, pressed specimens, and live plants for their gardens. A trading system developed, whereby botanists would swap collections for rare plants they wanted, and a trickle of cash from wealthy sponsors—most of whom were from rich European families—fueled the whole market.

Figure 3. Tulip tree. This ancient species has only one close relative, which lives in China. Photo by Sean P. Graham.

At the center of this botanical commerce in America was Harvard botanist Asa Gray. He had begun along the periphery collecting plants as a mere hobbyist in New York, but he eventually became a major authority on plant taxonomy. Logistically it was too difficult to lead expeditions and also sit down for the time necessary to describe new species. A division of labor developed: most collectors were only too happy to stay in the field and do the actual discovering, leaving the tedious job of diagnosing new species to Gray. And he was the perfect man for the job. His work ethic was absolutely outstanding: while simultaneously describing hundreds of new species, he published several editions of botanical handbooks and textbooks. Twenty-seven plants known from Kennesaw Mountain bear his name as describer. For Gray this was a small number, reflecting the fact that the eastern United States was already well known when he was in his prime. In other areas of the country, the number of plants he was responsible for identifying is much higher.

This botanical vortex in North America can be imagined as streams of plants picked and packaged by dozens of collectors fanning out into the landscape, their contributions trickling back across the young country's lanes and railroads—down mountains only then named, from the West to St. Louis, across oceans by ship to New Orleans, up rivers by steamer to Cincinnati—eventually back to Asa Gray in Boston. This stream was then integrated into a worldwide network of botanists, with material from North America sent to large private collections and museums in Europe. Gray encouraged his most skilled collectors to gather additional specimens of interesting plants, which could be used to satisfy patrons across the Atlantic. He forwarded collections from places outside his expertise to authorities overseas.

By the late 1850s Gray had seen enough plants from around the Northern Hemisphere that he began detecting patterns. Because he was the leading expert on North American plants and had recently received small but irreplaceable collections from Japan and China, he was the first botanist able to analyze the distribution of plants over such a large portion of the world. Being so busy working on so many other things, Gray put off such work until he received gentle and clever encouragement from a colleague in England best known at the time for a travelogue about his circumnavigation of the world aboard the *Beagle*.

Charles Darwin himself needed no small amount of encouragement to work on his own book, which would ultimately explain how life changes into new forms, and he wanted to bounce an idea off Gray, whose familiarity with plants far exceeded his own. He wrote to Gray and asked him whether he had ever considered why some alpine plants were found on isolated mountaintops far away from each other, and how he thought such distributions arose.

Did he see such patterns in America? Were the tundra plants far to the north of Boston the same kinds found in northern Europe and Asia? Some of Darwin and Gray's contemporaries believed that such distributions were the result of an enthusiastic creator who made new species—and often identical species—on each of those mountaintops. Species were created as often as needed to justify a scientist's failure to explain such patterns. Instead, Darwin hinted that perhaps these cold-hardy plants once enjoyed a much wider distribution. During the last ice age—a geological phenomenon that was only then becoming understood—the plants spread across the interior of the continents and then retreated to isolated patches when climate became warmer. Alpine plants migrated up the cooler mountains as climate warmed and their habitats disappeared. Each mountaintop with identical plants could be explained this way, without the need for hundreds of separate origins.

After reading the letters from Darwin outlining this hypothesis, and also lending his ear to a very interesting idea about how species originate (Gray was among the few confidants whom Darwin told about the theory of natural selection, and the only American who knew about it before its publication), Gray saw that a problem that had long vexed him made perfect sense. He had noticed, as had others before him, that there were uncanny similarities between plants in eastern Asia and eastern North America. In fact, he classified some species found in Japan in the same genus as plants found in America. But as the 1850s came to a close, his vast knowledge of the Northern Hemisphere floras made the pattern stand out even more. He became convinced that not only were several genera shared between the eastern United States and Asia, but some species were found in both places and *nowhere else*. Even in more widespread groups of plants found outside these regions—say, for example, maples and rhododendrons—interesting similarities were shared between the Japanese versions and those from the eastern United States. Gray's analysis of the distribution patterns confirmed his intuition—the floras of eastern North America and eastern Asia were more similar to each other than either was to other floras within its own continent.

Gray's explanation for this pattern relied on accepting the assumption that the world is very old, that very gradual changes occur incrementally, and that the history of life is quite ironically characterized by countless occurrences of death and extinction. All of these assumptions were shockingly new at the time, and none were considered foregone conclusions. Possibly the most controversial tenet of his hypothesis was that vast numbers of plants had gone extinct—in the nineteenth century the idea of a creator who made clunkers was theologically unsavory. Now we take the concept of extinction for granted, but at the time, many thought that species were made perfect.

Gray wrote that long ago an ancient deciduous forest once cloaked the entire Northern Hemisphere. It was a humid forest populated by diverse trees—including flowering and coniferous varieties—plus numerous lianas, shrubs, and herbaceous plants. The forest was not unlike those in some parts of the Southeast today. It stretched from the Panhandle of Florida across North America and continued unbroken across a land bridge between Alaska and Siberia, down into China, Korea, and Japan. From there it spread across Asia into Europe, never stopping even when it reached down into southern France and Spain. It kept going all the way around, meeting North America on the other side, across another land bridge. As Gray explained it, extreme climate change due to ice ages forced these forests into small refuges where the climate remained temperate. Not unlike those alpine plants migrating up mountains after the ice ages, the ancient deciduous forest survived only in the places where climate remained suitable for it. In the vast regions of the continental interior where the forest once held sway, thousands of plants died out. Many species went extinct. In only two regions did conditions remain suitable for their survival to this day: eastern Asia and eastern America. Published in 1859, Gray's hypothesis was one of the first Darwinian explanations for a biogeographic pattern published before *The Origin of Species*.

Shortly after publication of *The Origin of Species*, Gray became involved in two wars. The first was an intellectual war, and Gray was at the very center of it: the war between theist scientists who held on to their belief in God as the creator of species, and those who recognized the value of Darwin's theory. Gray was the earliest proponent of Darwinism in America and was personally responsible for the importation of the first American edition of the book. As an orthodox Christian, he attempted to bridge the philosophical chasm between the two sides. He thought of natural selection as a neutral scientific theory, while the devoutly religious denigrated it as atheism. As a world-renowned authority on plants, Gray would become one of Darwin's most important allies, and eventually—at least among scientists—their side won that war.

The very real American Civil War broke out within two years of the publication of *The Origin of Species*. Gray was in his fifties in 1861—too old to fight—but he contributed to the Union cause as best he could, raising cash to buy war bonds and joining a home defense regiment responsible for guarding the state arsenal in Cambridge. His network of botanical exploration was temporarily interrupted by the war. According Asa Gray's biographer, A. Hunter Dupree, one loyal Southern collector had turned his focus to "one subject, toward which my stomach urged me in times of scarcity . . . I mean the eatable mushrooms." But for the Union, transportation networks were still available, and it was only Gray's Southern collaborators who were cut off. He still had plenty of collectors out scouring the West. In this way, exploration of the most biodiverse region of our country was delayed—it was passed over for a time because of the Civil War. The focus of scientific progress, environmental awareness, and economic and technological development would instead turn west.

Besides his stature as perhaps the most important early American supporter of Darwinism, Gray's lasting contribution to science was his hypothesis about the past distributions of plants. The "Asa Gray disjunct hypothesis" has been modified over the last 150 years but remains the best explanation for the bizarre clumped distribution of plants in the Northern Hemisphere. We now know that steady climate deterioration over the last fifty million years—not necessarily the ice ages alone—was responsible for isolating the plant distributions.

The unfathomably vast distribution of Gray's ancient forest can be easily understood by considering an analogy. The current distribution of coniferous forests in the Northern Hemisphere offers a good comparison. The taiga—a similarly massive forest composed of spruces, firs, brown bears, and wolves—today stretches in a band nearly unbroken from Norway *east* to Nova Scotia. It trickles down the spines of mountains as far south as New Mexico and North Carolina. It is a fairly young forest, having just filled a zone previously occupied by a mile-thick pack of ice. The taiga, which during the ice age dipped to the south because of glaciers, spread across the interior of America, displacing the ancient deciduous forest far to the south. When the glaciers retreated to the Arctic, the taiga migrated up the colder slopes of mountains. There it remains, isolated atop mountain peaks in the Appalachians and Southern Rockies. Dry, cool regions in the interior filled with deserts and grasslands. The deciduous forest that once thrived across North America and Eurasia was replaced by spruce-fir forests, pinyon-juniper woodlands, steppes, prairies, and deserts, but it remains in the eastern United States and Asia.

Solid support for Gray's hypothesis comes from the fossil record, which Gray did not yet have access to at the time his theory was published. The ancient distribution of plants found now only in the eastern United States and Asia was once much wider—their fossil remains occur in places like Utah where climate no longer supports a rich deciduous forest. Some formerly widespread species of the ancient forest now occur only in Asia, which currently has the richest remaining remnant. Some plants are now restricted to pockets that trace the old forest's boundaries. The ginkgo—an incredibly unique cone-bearing plant with deciduous, broad leaves—once occurred throughout the Northern Hemisphere but now lives in the wild only on some isolated slopes in China. Fossils of sequoia and redwood prove they once towered over the whole Northern Hemisphere, but they are now restricted largely to California. The eastern United States has its own lone survivor of the ancient forest—the corkwood tree (*Leitneria*). It once occurred in Europe and Asia but is now found only in scattered pockets of the Southeast, including Georgia. These remnants occur where they do largely because of a gradual and ruthless process of deletion. Some of the magnificent plants of this ancient forest, which once thrived in forests across Laurasia, now survive nowhere: plants with wonderful names like *Mastixia, Macginitiea, Nordenskioldia, Limnobiophyllum*, and *Paleocarpinus* cannot be found in anyone's backyard; they cannot be seen by trekking to some remote mountain cove; and they can't be enjoyed at the Atlanta Botanical Garden. They didn't make it.

Fortunately, the eastern United States is rich with survivors of the ancient forest, and, according to the excellent floral checklist by Wendy Zomlefer and colleagues, thirty-eight species of Asa Gray disjuncts—plants found only in the eastern United States and eastern Asia—can be found on Kennesaw Mountain. Most of these plants have many more representatives in Asia. Additional plants found on Kennesaw belong to slightly more widely distributed groups that have additional pockets in places like the Pacific Northwest, southeastern Europe, and the Caspian region. An example of this kind of distribution is exhibited by Kennesaw's azaleas—two deciduous *Rhododendron* species with relatives in the eastern United States, Japan, Turkey, and California. Kennesaw has an excellent remnant of this ancient forest because of its protected status, moist, north-facing slopes, and relatively high elevation.

Some of these plants are familiar to most Southerners. The tulip tree, *Liriodendron tulipifera*, is common throughout the eastern United States. It is a codominant tree species among the oak-hickory forests of Kennesaw Mountain. It has a large and diagnostically straight trunk and the most distinctively shaped leaves of any American tree. Tulip trees are closely related to magnolias, another ancient plant group that shows Asa Gray's pattern. But unlike all other American magnolias, the tulip tree has lobed, devil-pointed leaves and yellow-green flowers with bright orange centers. It grows quickly after disturbance and needs full sun to sprout, which ordinarily would make it an early successional species. But this strange tree can live so long that it remains in the canopy of old-growth forests. Its soft, handsome wood is prized by carpenters. There is only one other tulip tree in the world, a smaller, much rarer species that is threatened by habitat destruction and survives on isolated mountain slopes in China.

Far less familiar but equally as fascinating is the state-protected bay star-vine, *Schisandra glabra*, which is reported from Kennesaw's moist ravines and other scattered locations in the Southeast. This vine is among the most primitive living flowering plants, occupying a branch at the very base of the flowering plant tree of life. It is a liana whose dark green leaves entwine around the trunks of understory trees. Its inconspicuous coral-red flowers bloom May–June, and each individual vine has separate male and female flowers. As with many primitive plants, the flowers produce small amounts of heat and odor through metabolic processes, which attract their pollinators—flies and beetles. The flowers are thought to deceptively represent a decaying organism and serve as a warm brooding chamber for the insects and their eggs. This strategy reminds us how the earliest flowers were pollinated during a time when bees and other specialized pollinators had not yet evolved—a time when dinosaurs roamed Georgia.

Bay star-vine shares North America with no other species of *Schisandra*, and its nearest relative is among the twenty-four species of star-vines found in eastern Asia. Fossil seeds of extinct star-vines are known from Oregon and Europe. Curiously, the Asian star-vines have developed novelties since they became separated from their American cousin about ten million years ago. The Asian species have yellowish-white flowers that contain both male and female parts. Two species have developed a tight relationship with gall midges, a kind of fly that feeds on the flower's pollen and broods its eggs on a spiderweb within a short flight of the vine. One of the bay star-vine's Asian relatives (*Schisandra chinensis*) is among the best-studied medicinal plants in Asia. Alexander Panossian and Georg Wikman summarized decades of Russian research claiming that plant's efficacy for treating a suspiciously extensive list of illnesses. Perhaps the American bay star-vine also contains great pharmacological promise.

Another Asa Gray disjunct found on Kennesaw Mountain has demonstrated medicinal value. Mayapple, *Podophyllum peltatum*, is a common herbaceous wildflower in rich hardwood forests throughout Georgia. It has an erect, jagged-toothed, paired umbrella of broad, rather large leaves. For these the Cherokee named it *u'niskwetu'gî*, meaning "it wears a hat." This plant is among the wildflowers that sprout and bloom after the tree canopy leafs out, so it must struggle to absorb dim light and sun flecks on the forest floor. The large white flower dangles between the leaves and is woefully underappreciated by woodland pollinators, probably because it does not offer any nectar. R. W. Rust and R. R. Roth found that solitary bees and bumblebees visit the flowers half-heartedly, on average once every thirty minutes. This leads to production of very few of the mayapple's fleshy yellow fruits, which were once used in the South for making a refreshing drink and a homegrown wine. The primary dispersers of the seeds are box turtles, which relish the yellow fruits and by eating them aid in the transport and germination of the seeds. The fruits hang down to the forest floor just low enough for the turtles to reach. The chanciness of mayapple's reproduction has led to the development of a backup tactic. Often mayapple can be observed growing in a round patch where there are few or no flowers. This patch is actually one large plant, and each leaf sprouts as a clone from an underground rhizome connected to all the other leaves. Plants that are losing in the game of reproduction will often resort to such extreme measures. For the Asian relative of mayapple, it's even worse.

The Asian mayapple is *Podophyllum hexandrum* of the Himalayas. It occurs in the alpine zone and is a spring ephemeral—one of the earliest-blooming flowers in the meadows where it grows—so it must attempt to gather enough sunlight to grow and reproduce during a narrow time frame. Pollination of its flowers is even less reliable than in mayapple, so it not only reproduces clonally but has evolved the capacity to fertilize itself. Incredibly, this does not seem to have resulted in inbreeding problems. But one can imagine that by clinging tenaciously to their old habits, these conservative dwellers of the ancient forest perhaps doom themselves to extinction. Maybe this is how the other plants that were once widespread residents of the ancient forest dropped one by one out of existence.

Mayapple has poisonous leaves that quickly become obvious to any farmer whose pasture abuts a patch of hardwood forest. Cows will leave the bright green new growth of mayapple alone while munching on every other herbaceous plant around it. The active ingredient is podophyllotoxin, which, according to Hank Becker, is a potent inhibitor of cellular division—an attribute that can arrest the spread of cancer cells. This poison has been used to the advantage of cancer patients worldwide as one of the key compounds in chemotherapy. Unfortunately, such chemicals can also inhibit fast-growing healthy tissues, which is why patients undergoing chemo have suppressed immunity and lose their hair. In a paper in *Economic Botany*, Rita Moraes and colleagues suggested that growing mayapple as a cash crop for biomedical research may be a profitable venture for rural Americans. Growing patches of mayapple would be more economically feasible than synthesizing podophyllotoxin artificially, and certainly more feasible then harvesting the much rarer Himalayan mayapple. Clearly, plants of Asa Gray's ancient forest are a virtual botanical drugstore.

Yet another example is the pharmacological bounty found within the mysterious juices of witch hazel, *Hamamelis virginiana*, an Asa Gray disjunct with close relatives in Japan and China. It occurs throughout the eastern United

States and grows in the understory of Kennesaw's forests. The bark of this woody shrub has a long tradition of uses among Chinese, Native American, and early American folk medicine. Its usages have persisted into the modern era—industrial distilleries process witch-hazel extracts in Connecticut and Indiana, and Susana Sánchez-Tena and her team determined that witch-hazel tannins have very specific action against colon cancer. Like many plants with an old folk tradition, witch hazel has a fairly sinister common name going back to at least the sixteenth century in England. There the name was used for a number of flexible plants useful for making bows, especially the Scotch, or *wyche* elm. The name derived from similar Anglo-Saxon words like *wic* or *wik*, meaning "to bend." Equally possible is that the name was derived from the use of its branches as a divining rod to find water—and/or witches. The colonists transferred the name to American plants of vaguely similar appearance, and *Hamamelis* is the shrub to which the name stuck, perhaps because it was the favored American plant used for divining. The plant's ecology adds yet another dash of mystery to its persona—strange, yellow-tasseled flowers inexplicably bloom during the cold days of fall after the leaves have dropped. These rarely visited flowers produce a tiny number of fruits an entire year later.

It is important to understand that all the potent chemicals in these plants are used to discourage parasites and herbivores from eating their tissues; the plants never intended them to treat cancer. The poisons that prevent insects from feeding also happen to have medicinal uses. Although some of these plants—such as mayapple—have certainly excelled in this area, other plants are in a constant struggle to stay one step ahead of those who would eat them, and they are continually developing stronger poisons to keep the vegetarians at bay. White-tailed deer are certainly not dissuaded by the superstitions or chemicals associated with witch hazel, and they browse on its leaves with relish.

The final Asa Gray disjunct I'll mention has come up with still more remarkable methods to prevent insects from eating it. The catalpa (*Catalpa bignonioides*) is a small tree usually found along sluggish watercourses, but it has been planted as an ornamental throughout the eastern United States far outside its natural distribution. It is likely that Kennesaw's catalpas are escapees from nearby homesteads. The reason catalpas populate front yards all over America is their tendency to attract moths whose caterpillars—known as catalpa worms—feed only on the leaves of catalpa. Having a catalpa in your front yard virtually ensures a constant supply of fat caterpillars useful as fish bait during the perfect fishing days of summer.

According to research by Evan Lampert and colleagues, the tree has two potent chemicals to combat the feasting catalpa worms—catalpol and catalposide—both of which have pharmacological activity. The worms indeed choose leaves with lower concentrations of the poisons, which helps explain why some trees have both branches with leaves and branches that have been stripped clean by caterpillars. The caterpillars tolerate a small amount of the toxins by concentrating them within their own tissues. They openly advertise their ill-gotten toxic tissue with contrasting black and yellow colors, warning coloration that probably helps protect them from predatory birds. But despite their sour taste, they still apparently make good fish bait, according to the tree field guide by George Petrides.

It is pretty clear that these chemical defenses often let the tree down, and the caterpillars have gained the upper hand in this arms race between plant and moth. Some trees are completely defoliated every summer after the emergence of the ravenous caterpillars. Somehow, the trees are still able to leaf out, flower, and fruit before being attacked again year after year. In the face of such intense pressure, the catalpa has recruited help.

Along the underside of leaves are small glands that secrete nectar. This nectar is not associated with flowers, so the glands are referred to as extrafloral nectaries. According to research by J. H. Ness, the nectary attracts some shady characters to this increasingly complex drama, including ladybugs, ants, and a parasitic wasp whose special skill is destroying catalpa caterpillars. The tiny female wasp searches far and wide for fat caterpillars, into which she inserts tiny eggs. These develop into nasty little grubs that slowly eat the caterpillar's insides. Eventually, before the caterpillar dies in agony, the wasps pupate. At this time the caterpillar is doomed, and covered with cylindrical white capsules. A caterpillar with a burden of these pupae looks almost comical, as if someone had placed three dozen Tic Tac candies on its back. But these Tic Tacs hatch into tiny wasps that then fly away to find their next victims. When they emerge, the caterpillar dies. The ants and ladybugs also help protect the plant by carrying off the eggs and younger caterpillars. By attracting these bodyguards, the tree is able to hang on to more of its leaves and produce more flowers and fruit. Incredibly, this edge may be due in part to the ability of the parasitic wasp to avoid the toxins originally produced by the tree to ward off herbivores, which become funneled into the caterpillar. The wasp grubs end up having lower levels of catalpol than the caterpillars, and Evan Lampert and colleagues have shown they suffer no ill effects at all from feasting on the caterpillars' toxic tissue.

The sneaky catalpa also has ways of defending its precious nectar supply. It produces numerous large, white, tube-shaped flowers fringed like doilies. Purple grooves lead bumblebees down the flower's yellow throat, where they drink nectar and smear pollen. Given the large amounts of energy the catalpa must commit to fending off caterpillars, as well as to satisfying its pollinators, you might expect it to be reluctant to let an insect feed from its flowers without assisting pollination. Such insects, referred to as nectar thieves, often attempt to consume flower nectar from the outside by piercing the tube. Some are so small they can move in and out of the open tube without touching any pollen or the stigma.

Curiously, ant thieves that drink the nectar of catalpa flowers quickly become disoriented and fall off the tree. Moths that drink from the flowers seesaw through the air like leaves falling in autumn. Meanwhile, the intended pollinators—large bees—are unaffected and feed freely. Catalpa has toxic leaves, recruits bodyguards, and secretes toxic nectar, giving this tree more tricks than a riverboat gambler.

I've selected a fairly random group of Asa Gray's disjuncts to highlight just a few of their fascinating natural histories. Many more incredible stories could be told about these plants and the adaptations of almost any other plant growing on Kennesaw Mountain, a subject to which we will turn in another chapter. But the ancient heritage these plants share makes them even more special. Besides all the other interesting facets of their lives, you can add that they are the surviving representatives of an ancient deciduous forest that once stretched unbroken across the Northern Hemisphere forty million years ago.

# 3

# Succession (Not to Be Confused with Secession)

More of Georgia is covered by forest today than at the time of the Civil War.

    —Georgian folk saying

THIS STATEMENT IS SIMULTANEOUSLY COMPLETELY true and entirely misleading. Georgia is now largely cloaked by forests, and at the time of the Civil War it was an agricultural region, very different from the biodiversity stronghold it was before the Civil War, and from the mixture of agriculture, suburban development, and forests it is now. After the war, development accelerated such that by the time Kennesaw Mountain National Battlefield Park was established, most of the land in Georgia had experienced intense forestry and cultivation. The parts of Georgia that aren't thick with pine plantations have become reforested through an entirely natural process. But before the Civil War, even more of Georgia was covered with forests, and these forests were full of giant trees. They looked much different than they do now. So although it is true that Georgia along with much of the eastern United States has experienced considerable forest regeneration, the virgin forests are now gone.

It is understandable to walk through a forest like the one on the north slope of Kennesaw Mountain and think that it is pristine and unchanging. The trees are so big, and the forest floor so prettily sprinkled with bright wildflowers that it appears ancient and immutable. Couple this with the short life spans of people relative to forests and you can easily have the mistaken impression that such old trees may have shaded General Johnston himself. But to truly know a forest you must engage in the thousands of minute dramas that take place there every day, and for this you need a keen attention to detail and a willingness to practically get on your hands and knees and crawl, scouring the leaf litter, taking notes, remembering interesting facts, and tracing the lines of connections. But these events happen year to year and day to day at a blinding pace compared to how slowly a forest changes over time. I think for most people this is a revelation. It certainly was for me. Nobody can live long enough to see an old field

Figure 4. A loblolly pine forest at the base of Kennesaw Mountain. This forest is a temporary plant community and will soon be replaced by hardwood trees by natural succession. Photo by Sean P. Graham.

change to an old-growth oak-hickory forest, but you can come pretty close.

When I was a kid I thought the forests of Georgia were primeval, without question. I imagined dinosaurs roamed forests like these. Once I noticed that a new development sprang up while I was gone on a family vacation to Houston. I was a little surprised and alarmed that they cut down a forest while I was gone, so it made an impression on me, even though this was around the time I first noticed music. It was when I first got a song stuck in my head: Hall and Oates's "Maneater." They never built anything after cutting it down—the vacant lot just sat there for years, so I guess nobody wanted to invest in putting another convenience store at that corner. As I grew up I went by that lot often, on my way to junior high at Pointe South, on my way to my first job, on my way to one doomed first date after another, on my way to college. As I grew up, the vacant lot grew up. At first, when I was in junior high, it was just a grassy old field, covered with the familiar tawny grass called broom sedge. Then isolated pines peppered the lot. By the time I was in college it was a full-blown pine jungle, and sweet gums had begun to chase the pines. In just twenty years the vacant lot had reverted to a pine forest, and it was on the way to becoming a hardwood forest. Then they cut it down again. Somebody decided we needed another convenience store at that corner after all.

I was seven years old when they first cut it. I remember this exactly because during our family vacation in Houston we watched the 1984 Olympics in Los Angeles. We saw smiling Mary Lou Retton win gold medals in-between thousands of "Where's the beef?" commercials. When we returned, I noticed the forest was gone. Driving by that old lot would always trigger fond memories of the vacation. It was only later that I realized I was keeping tabs on forest succession.

Succession is an ecological process of change and regeneration, which often occurs in a predictable, orderly progression. Succession is the ecological response to disturbance, which is common in the world. No matter how resilient or ancient, all the world's ecosystems are susceptible and can respond to disturbance, and natural disturbances are so frequent that entire ecosystems respond to them in predictable ways. Some disturbances occur frequently and are not terribly catastrophic, and the plants and animals that encounter them will quickly adapt to these disturbances in ingenious ways. Charles Wharton indicated that in the Coastal Plain of Georgia, frequent lighting-ignited fires burned the undergrowth of longleaf pine forests every three to five years for centuries. The longleaf pine forest came up with so many strategies for dealing with fire that it now cannot exist without fire. In the wetter Pacific Northwest, fire happens so infrequently that the big redwoods, sequoias, and Douglas firs have no solutions for it, so wildfires ravage those woods. Miles Hemstrom and Jerry Franklin estimated that catastrophic volcanic eruptions occur almost as frequently as fires in the temperate rain forests of the Pacific Northwest, and the plants in these forests have almost as many adaptations for surviving volcanoes as they do fires.

By contrast, the forests of the South are expert regenerators. At the time of the Civil War, the Piedmont region and the area surrounding Kennesaw Mountain were heavily agricultural. Many of the old-growth forests that were present when Europeans first arrived in Georgia were cut down and sold long before the Civil War. Enormous amounts of land experienced unprecedented topsoil erosion and withering exhaustion resulting from cotton agriculture. After the Civil War, the Southern economy was devastated, and every remaining bit of forest was sold, often to Northern speculators (carpetbaggers); every last stick of forest was plundered to try to make ends meet. After this, the Southern economy gradually recovered, but agriculture modernized and became centered in the Great Plains and California; in Georgia, it now continues only in regions where specialized products are still grown (Vidalia onions, peaches, and goobers, to name a few). Tree farms were eventually planted, but large sections of the South simply lay fallow, and forests regenerated.

Succession of the oak-hickory forests of the South is so predictable that the same series of stages will occur after disturbance every single time. This can be demonstrated in one of two ways: by keeping track of an old field after a forest is cleared (as I did with that vacant lot cleared in 1984) or by observing examples of regenerating land across the landscape and comparing the stages, like putting the sequences of a ripped-up book back in order from beginning to end. Both types of observations have led to a thorough understanding of forest succession in Georgia, and the forests of Georgia are living laboratories that helped ecologists develop the foundations for our understanding of this process. This is because the Piedmont forests of Georgia have all been cut at various times—and in some cases recut—and each time, the forest begins to regenerate from the same predictable starting point. This results in a mosaic of forests of different ages, and the curious thing is that they predictably end up looking the same way and always pass through the same stages. If you cut them down at any stage, they will start again from the beginning and wind up at the same end point.

If somebody had set up a time-lapse camera after the Battle of Kennesaw Mountain and loaded it with 150 years' worth of film in some old field near Marietta (assuming that nobody came along and knocked over the camera or built a 7-Eleven there), you'd be able to see the stages sprint by—the old field replaced by pines, the pines outpaced by hickories—like those movie sequences of grasses and flowers sprouting after snowmelt in the mountains.

The first stage after disturbance is the old field. It is important to note that if you cut down a mature hardwood forest, the acorns and hickory nuts that might be present on the ground do not immediately resprout into baby oaks and hickories. These seeds are not adapted to sprout in hot, bare mineral soil with abundant sunshine, so they don't. A hardwood forest doesn't spring back immediately. Instead, plants that love sunshine and don't mind nonnutritious soils colonize the disturbance. In the first year there will be only a few hardy annuals, mostly weeds and grasses like horseweed, crabgrass, goldenrods, and asters. By the next year new plants will have colonized, and perennial grasses will have already replaced the less competitive annuals. When the familiar broom sedge arrives, its yellow straw will carpet the old field for a few years. It is a rigorous competitor, going as far as to poison the soil around its roots to prevent other plants from growing near it. But this doesn't last long, and shrubs like blackberries and hawthorns soon grow in patches, and then the loblolly pine arrives. Within ten years broom sedge will be outcompeted and outshaded by loblolly pines, which grow so thick these forests should properly be referred to as jungles. These are my least favorite forests to walk through, with the possible exception of privet jungles. When young, they are a jumble of wrist-thick trunks that are impenetrable, even more so thanks to the tangles of briars and brambles that take up any space not occupied by a pine.

The pine jungle holds sway for decades as the individual pines unabashedly try to outgrow each other, leaving less rigorous or slower-growing pines to die for want of sunlight. Soon loblolly pine trunks can be two and a half feet thick at chest level, and their crowns eighty feet in the air. The jungle becomes less densely populated, but the forest is still a monoculture of pines. But look down on the forest floor. See any pines? There is a good example of a second-growth pine forest down on the trail near Cheatham Hill. The forest floor is covered with pine straw, and it is fairly shady down there. There are saplings of trees, but no pine saplings. Loblolly pine is an excellent competitor: it's fast growing, it's ubiquitous throughout Georgia, and it is therefore a pine of choice for timber companies. But it can't even sprout in its own shade.

Next, young hardwoods—which require shady, moist conditions to sprout—take over. They creep steadily toward the crown of pine boughs, first sweet gum and tulip tree, then white oak, red oak, and mockernut hickory. This stage can easily be observed along most interstate highways in Georgia, especially during autumn. You'll pass through endless expanses of young pine forests, but look carefully and you'll notice a layer of sweet gums—tagged by their brightly colored, changing leaves—growing halfway up toward the pine canopy. Loblolly pine doesn't live very long and is susceptible to all kinds of infestations by fungi, beetles, and their grubs, so the old pines soon die (they are really quite young by tree standards, only forty or fifty years old) and the hardwoods replace them. Oaks and hickories become dominant, and most of the forests of Kennesaw Mountain today contain these species.

When these trees become really big the forests start to look like the ancient forests of the South. Many hardwood forests in Georgia today are starting to look pretty mature, with oaks or hickories that are about two and a half feet wide at chest level. These forests have been regenerating since about the time of the Civil War, when the forest they replaced was most recently cut. Look at the hardwood forest floor of the Kennesaw Mountain Trail, which leaves from the visitors' center. This is covered with young oaks and hickories, which have no trouble sprouting in shady conditions. These too, for the most part, are doomed to die. But if an old oak dies, one of the lucky sprouts nearby will find its own place in the canopy. This is a forest that can self-perpetuate, and no new stage will replace it. This is the climax forest.

Some birds are characteristic of these stages of forest regeneration, and different species track the successional changes. Extensive old fields in the Georgia Piedmont have grassland species such as grasshopper sparrows, eastern meadowlarks, and bobwhite quail. The shrub stage sees the arrival of common backyard birds like northern mockingbirds, cardinals, and indigo buntings—which makes sense, since most suburban backyards look like this stage, with their small ornamental shrubs and grasses. When loblolly pines first invade, blue grosbeaks show up. Pine jungles don't support that many birds, but once hardwoods enter the forest, diversity peaks. Only a few additional species—such as Acadian flycatchers, Kentucky warblers, and hooded warblers—are added in the mature oak-hickory forest, while many of the other species found in pine-hardwood forests no longer seem to want to stick around. To the delight of foresters, ecologists Stuart Nicholson and Carl Monk found that second-growth pine-oak forests, not mature oak-hickory forests, have the highest diversity of breeding birds. So, this obviously means that cutting forests is good for birds, right?

The only difference between climax forests and old-growth forests is the size of the trees. Old-growth forests usually contain huge forest giants, and you really need to see one of these forests to believe it. Unfortunately, Georgia has very few old-growth forests left, although there are fine examples scattered all over the state of single old trees from these forests that were not cut down. There are gigantic tulip trees in North Georgia, and humongous cypresses in Chickasawhatchee Swamp. Mature second-growth forests have large numbers of older trees that are all about the same age because they all got their start during succession at the same time. Although they are mature, they are still not exemplars of what the ancient forest of the South was like. Instead, old-growth forests had large numbers of giant old trees, as well as a mixture of smaller trees of diverse sizes and ages, because when the big trees died, the canopy opened up, inviting smaller trees to vie with the crowded giants. It was a shifting mosaic of old and young trees.

A long time ago, Georgia contained a patchwork of maturing gaps in the old-growth canopy from when old giants finally crashed to the ground, and it included larger tracts of maturing forests as a result of larger-scale disturbances like tornadoes, hurricanes, fires, and clearing by Native Americans. Some of these forest openings were large enough to be considered grasslands and contained prairie species that are now restricted to tiny remnants scattered across the Southeast. This shifting mosaic stage probably supported maximum bird diversity, as high as that in today's maturing secondary forests or higher. It takes something like five hundred years for a forest to achieve this magnificent status—what is known as the shifting mosaic steady state. You'll have to wait a little longer to see forests like this around Kennesaw Mountain.

Another disturbance common to the Georgia Piedmont that influences forests near the mountain is flooding due to the beaver. This giant rodent deserves a top place among the hallowed environmental engineers of the animal kingdom, rivaling many animals that are considered important far beyond their size and abundance. For this, the beaver is considered a "keystone species."

The analogy is drawn from the keystone of a stone arch; you can remove any stone but the keystone from the arch and it will stand. Remove the keystone, and it collapses. Pennsylvania is the Keystone State because it provided the crucial centerpiece to maintain the flimsy union between the Northern and Southern states during the Revolutionary War. This union lasted eighty-five years before it collapsed. Ecologically, keystone species provide more services and connectivity among interacting species than others, and if you remove them, many other species will cease to exist or will suffer.

Beavers build dams from sticks, mud, and vegetation and divert water from creeks to fill basins with water. They do this because they like to eat the tender marsh vegetation that will eventually grow upstream of the dam (they don't eat fish). They make marshes where there was once a lowland forest or creek. These marshes can be acres in extent and provide habitat for hundreds of plant and animal species. In fact, the only natural standing-water habitat of the Georgia Piedmont is provided by beavers. Unfortunately, beavers rarely get the attention and respect they deserve as a keystone species because their activities sometimes put them at odds with humans. Instead, they are often considered pests. But beavers are second only to humans as habitat engineers in the eastern United States.

In the Georgia Piedmont, beavers use thousands of small streams to make their dams. Beavers have steadily recolonized Georgia from surviving pockets left over after the fur trade died. They are now common again and have begun building their marsh franchises everywhere. Beaver activity recently created a marsh from the far end of Cheatham Hill to Kolb Farm Trail, and this was one of the only places within the park where you could see marsh birds such as herons and egrets, along with the common yellowthroat in summer and the swamp sparrow in winter. But the beavers then abandoned this marsh, and forest plants have already taken over—succession strikes again. Beaver ponds, like forests on dry land, also undergo forest succession, although this has not yet been studied in detail in the South. But you can make out the stages of re-generating active and abandoned beaver ponds all over the Georgia Piedmont: when the beavers flood a forest, first there are open-water marshes with dead, drowned trees. These become marshes with bur-reed and arrow arum, then transition to marsh-shrub associations with alder and red maple, red maple monoculture forests, and finally red maple–water hickory–swamp chestnut oak forests. The species composition differs, but the climax is the same.

In any region there is usually a final stage of succession that can self-perpetuate as long as no additional disturbances come along, and these climax forests dominated the pre-European landscape of the Southeast. But some disturbances can arrest succession—they stop it in its tracks—leading to what is called a preclimax forest. The longleaf pine forests of the Georgia Coastal Plain are an excellent example of this: fire is so frequent that the pine stage is able to self-perpetuate. This is partly because longleaf pine is much more long lived than loblolly pine. I had the opportunity to work for a geographer who was reconstructing historical climate patterns by looking at tree cores and analyzing the rings of old trees. He hired me to help him find old cypresses and longleaf pines. We found an old longleaf pine along the Flint River near Pine Mountain that was something like five hundred years old. These forests defy the climax stage of the region because fires burn out the hardwoods trying to make a go for the canopy, but longleaf pine has a long evolutionary history with fire and can tolerate lots of it. Nowadays to keep these forests healthy we have to set fire to them on purpose, something called a prescribed burn.

Another example of arrested succession can be observed at Kennesaw Mountain. One of the stated missions of national battlefield parks is to maintain the sites in the same state they were in at the time of the battle, to capture the essence of that moment in time. Do not get me wrong—this is an excellent idea and I am in favor of it. But you must know that the National Park Service actively maintains the old fields around Kennesaw Mountain by mowing them. Mowing is a type of disturbance, and mowing every year keeps the broom sedge–perennial grass stage going in perpetuity. Without the mowing, loblolly pine would soon show up, and if the grassy fields of Kennesaw weren't actively maintained, they would all be hardwood forests by now.

The kind of succession outlined previously in this chapter—what ecologists refer to as "old field succession"—is common to most forests in the eastern United States. The results of forest succession can differ subtly depending on factors such as climate, soil type, and latitude, but overall this is the general pattern of deciduous forest disturbance and recovery. Old field succession takes place after disturbance in soils that have already grown forests. In this soil, there is plenty of organic material for colonizing plants to use, and the previous forest and the surrounding plants leave their mark in the form of a seed bank. The seed bank is made up of the thousands of unsprouted seeds that blow in with the wind, get dropped by animals, or drop down from nearby trees, and they interweave themselves into the upper soil layer. Because all plants produce many more fruits, cones, spores, and seeds than are necessary to replace themselves, there are always millions of seeds waiting for the opportunity to sprout. When you disturb a forest, the seed bank can influence the forest that eventually replaces it. Therefore, old field succession is not entirely unreliant on previous biological activity, and so it is referred to as secondary succession.

Primary succession takes place on undisturbed substrates that have never had any biological influence. It is succession starting from scratch. These kinds of surfaces are rare on earth, where plants and animals have had their way with the untouched surface of the planet for some 350 million years. In fact, the colonization of the earth's surface by plants and animals could be considered one gigantic, unending example of primary succession, with the climax shifting here and there with time, species composition, and latitude. But for ecologists, primary succession has a narrower meaning. Because of the never-ending reworking of the earth's crust by geological forces, new ecological real estate can and does become available.

Volcanoes are excellent examples of primary succession in action: after Mount St. Helens erupted in Washington State in 1980, John Baross and colleagues reported that all life within the blast zone was obliterated. The new volcanic soils and barren volcanic creeks became recolonized almost instantly, first by bacteria, then by algae, next by some pioneering plants, and finally by various animals. There is now enough forage near the blast zone to support mule deer and elk. Krakatoa, an Indonesian island volcano, erupted in 1883 and completely destroyed itself. A smoldering new island was born, and its recolonization by island-hopping ferns, spiders, palms, bats, figs, and pythons has been studied ever since, and summarized in an excellent book by Ian Thornton. But even plutons—the less exciting, closeted sisters of volcanoes, which cool in place under the earth's crust but never erupt—become sites of primary succession.

Recall that Kennesaw Mountain is an old pluton that burped into the deep crust of Georgia during the plate collision that formed the Appalachians. It was then crushed during subsequent collisions and the original gabbroic pluton became metamorphosed into a heavy metal-rich gneiss. The Georgia Piedmont region has numerous metamorphic and igneous rock outcroppings—domes, monadnocks, mountains, and flat-rock barrens—that are the result of similar happenings. Most of these outcroppings are made up of harder rock than the material they invaded, so the rock overlying them disintegrates at a faster pace under the humid, acidic weathering conditions of the Southeast. So the South, and especially the Georgia Piedmont, is generously dotted with granite or gneiss outcroppings, some as large as Kennesaw or Stone Mountain, and some as small as the metate-pocked granite chunk at Arrowhead in north Clayton County, now mostly hidden by apartments and shopping centers and grown over with Asian privet. It's helpful to think of these rocks as being similar to icebergs—you are looking at only the tip when you see them, and you can't see the rest of the outcropping below.

These outcrops weather so much more slowly than the surrounding soils that they can become exposed as giant bare rocks like Stone Mountain. The rock that is exposed offers a challenging environment for any plant that would colonize it. The rock and any thin layer of soil perched on it can have surface temperatures and dryness that would make some of the most extreme deserts blush. Bare rock and thin soils offer scant nutrients for plants. To make things worse, most of the plants nearby that might endeavor to colonize such outcroppings have adaptations for exactly the opposite extremes—deciduous forest trees, shrubs, and herbaceous plants are mesophytes adapted to a moderate amount of rainfall and rich organic soils, and they sprout in heavy shade. If these outcrops occurred in more arid environments, the plants would already have a head start for living on them. Instead, the rock outcroppings are desert islands in a sea of forests and are for the most part disconnected from each other by great distances.

Still, a collection of bizarre plants with unexpected novelties survive on these rock domes, and some are so specialized that they live nowhere else. Some of the most interesting of these little plants live on bare granite domes, and they are the vanguard of granite outcrop primary succession. Consider the outcrop snorkelwort, the most incredibly specialized plant I can think of. It is an *aquatic* outcrop plant, which may seem entirely contradictory, given the way I just described the outcrops. But some of the barren rock domes are pocked with oval depressions called solution pits, which form over millennia as rain fills pools. The slight acidity of natural rain steadily eats away a small basin. Imagine how long it must take for simple rainwater to dissolve a pit in solid rock! During the winter and spring, rains fill these tiny rock pools, and during the summer they are utterly, burningly dry. Eventually a small, flat basin about the size of a kiddie pool can form, and it collects a thin bottom of sandy mud. This must take an agonizingly long time. Out of this gritty mud grows the tiny outcrop snorkelwort, which sends up paired leaves that float on the surface, with a diminutive white flower between them. The snorkelwort survives the summer as seeds lying dormant in the shallow basin, which dries each summer and fills each winter. A secret patch of rock barrens within the park contains this rare species.

I visited this outcrop on a cold spring morning. It was at the very end of a very long Georgia winter—the winter of the great snowpocalypse when two inches of snow crippled Atlanta and made the city a national embarrassment. I went with Scott Ranger—a self-taught botanist, geologist, and local Kennesaw expert—and Tom Patrick, the senior botanist for the Georgia Department of Natural Resources (GDNR). I followed Scott from the visitors' center along US Highway 41 and ended up in the last place you'd expect to find a rare plant. We rode through nice old neighborhoods and stopped right on the side of the road as if we were locals parking out in front of a friend's house for a barbecue. There was no sign for a trailhead or any other indication that the park boundary was nearby. We waited for Tom to arrive in his big GDNR truck and then set out on a barely visible path into the woods. In five minutes the woods opened into a large, flat-rock outcrop—much larger and flatter than any of the outcrops I'd seen up on Kennesaw itself. Through the winter trees we could make out the outline of Kennesaw's horizon to the southeast. With the weather the rock was wet with puddles and trickling black seepage flow. Unfortunately, even though the calendar date was quite late, most of the outcrop plants were not yet in bloom. But we did see the early sprouts of rock-orpine (*Diamorpha*) and rabbit ears. Scott pointed out quillworts growing from the shallow, sand-bottomed puddles. I got down on my hands and knees to see them from their level. I photographed them and admired their primitive appearance.

We walked gingerly on the outcrop, which was heavily encrusted with lichens, mosses, and spikemosses, careful not to trample anything rare. This can be a difficult task indeed, given the number of species found on rock outcrops and nowhere else. We concentrated on tiptoeing on bare rock. Then we all noticed an oval black puddle directly ahead. Scott needn't have pointed it out to us; it was the only solution pit in the outcrop, and the only known solution pit within Kennesaw Mountain National Battlefield Park. This pit is deeper and darker than most pits I've seen in such places as Stone Mountain or Arabia Mountain east of Atlanta. Its basin is filled with leaf litter, which leaches tannins into the water and gives it an obsidian sheen. It is only about three feet long and two feet wide. Despite this, we noticed tiny green leaves balanced on the surface film of the pool, connected to a thin tendril and basal rosette of aquatic leaves a half foot below. It was snorkelwort.

Scott Ranger discovered this tiny population of snorkelwort some time ago, and it was quite a surprise, especially given that snorkelwort was not included in the a thorough inventory of rock outcrop plants at Kennesaw published in 1979 by Kent Leslie and Madeline Burbanck. Ranger and other botanists suspected the plants were introduced, especially because the amount of available habitat was small and no nearby populations of snorkelwort were known for miles. Ranger reported it to the Georgia DNR, and the snorkelwort is now the only known plant within the park that is federally protected as an endangered species. The botanist he contacted shared Ranger's suspicion that it was not a natural population, and rumors began circulating that a university professor—perhaps from nearby Kennesaw State University—had introduced the plant while practicing some kind of guerrilla conservation tactic. We talked about the plant's mysterious origin at the rock outcrop, and

Tom Patrick, seeming embarrassed, explained that it was in fact a GDNR botanist—the same one contacted by Scott Ranger—who had introduced snorkelwort to this tiny pool.

The botanist knew of a rock outcrop with the rare plant east of Atlanta that had been sold to a mining company. Before the company began blasting it to powder he sneaked in there and rescued some plants. He transported them to the one place he knew that would never become a hole in the ground and that definitely did not already contain the plant: a small solution pit on a little-known outcrop within Kennesaw Mountain National Battlefield Park. The plants took root and are now well established. In 1990 Ranger noticed them in flower. The population has fluctuated from year to year ever since, despite the splashing of neighborhood kids who play in the water. The genetic diversity of the plants from the destroyed rock outcrop lives on.

Shallower solution pits on Kennesaw Mountain contain no standing water and instead are simply the container for a ridiculously shallow and non-nutritious soil. These pits become colonized with rings of specialized zones of plants. The outer ring, with the shallowest soil—no more really than some grit blown in from who knows where—is colonized by the three-inch-tall rock-orpine, *Diamorpha smallii*, a ludicrous plant with bright red leaves and four-petaled flowers. This plant literally clings to bare rock, and only the humblest sprig of grit is secured by its roots. Eventually, generations of dying *Diamorpha*, accumulated grit, and windblown organic material can deepen the soil, which is colonized by annual grasses, additional herbaceous plants adapted to thin soils, and finally perennial grasses such as broom sedge, our friend from the old field mentioned in the discussion of secondary succession. This soil will acidify the bare rock outcrop just enough to begin the process of eating it away. The ringed zones of solution pits are actively eroding the rocks underneath, grinding them down into soil that will be useful to less-specialized plants. With some imagination you can picture a pit growing from a thin veneer of tiny annuals like *Diamorpha* and sandwort, marching outward, and then a patch of broom sedge and other perennials appearing and the vegetation steadily thickening in the middle. Eventually, as the outer rings continue, pines colonize the middle like a bull's-eye, until it becomes a pine forest. Over time, in the footage from the time-lapse camera loaded with 150 years' worth of film, the solution pit would appear to be expanding out from the central point and filling in with more and more complex plants, like a darkening bruise. Despite the different starting point for primary and secondary succession, the end point—oak-hickory climax forest—is the same.

Because Kennesaw Mountain is made of gneiss, and because the region's vegetation hasn't had as hard a time colonizing its rocky slope as it has on some granite domes, Kennesaw doesn't have as many examples of the fantastically specialized rock outcrop plants as places like Panola Mountain, Stone Mountain, or Arabia Mountain, which William Murdy and Eloise Brown Carter herald as exemplars of the habitat. But it has most of them, and owing to the rogue botanist, the park is now also home to one of the rarest and most special plants in the eastern United States.

Overall the mountain gives the impression of having at one time looked more like Stone Mountain, but in the case of Kennesaw perhaps the plants have had much more time to wear it down. The mountain has been more thoroughly crumbled yet still retains its domed shape. And there are some nice flat outcrops on Kennesaw, which have some of the rarest plants known from the mountain. These have the rock outcrop all-stars reported by Leslie and Burbanck, like rock-orpine, sandwort, cottony groundsel, Missouri rockcress, sunnybells, Confederate daisy, hairy spiderwort, open-ground draba, and rushfoil, and even succulents such as rock pink, prickly pear cactus, yucca, and Virginia agave. Many of the plants that thrive on rock outcrops are throwbacks to ancient times—strange, low-growing, primitive plants like ledge spikemoss and Piedmont quillwort—that still do quite well under conditions that mimic those grim and distant days when plants first colonized the land.

So what was it really like at Kennesaw Mountain at the time of the Civil War? Given what we know about forest succession, combined with historical accounts left by soldiers who spent a few tough weeks here in June 1864—including a few revealing photographs and drawings—we can get a surprisingly clear picture. According to period descriptions, maps, and photographs of the mountain, Kennesaw appears to have been more thinly forested than it is today. You can make out a band of pale rocky scree along the top of both Big and Little Kennesaw, and Samuel French, a Confederate general positioned on top, wrote that Kennesaw "rises abruptly from the plain, solitary and alone, to a height of perhaps 600 or 700 feet. Its west side is rocky and abrupt. Its eastern side can, in a few places, be gained on horseback, and the west of Little Kennesaw, being bald and destitute of timber, affords a commanding view of all the surrounding country as far as the eye can reach, except where the view is interrupted by the higher peak."

Some of the differences in the mountain's appearance then and now can certainly be attributed to the work of the Confederate army, whose seventy thousand men wreaked havoc on the forests in preparation for the battle. They cut down trees to build defenses and clear the way for observation and firing lanes. Even before this, the forests on and near Kennesaw Mountain were possibly logged, and there were farms and pastures present on the plain below. Even the Cherokee, who had only recently been driven out as a result of the Georgia gold rush of 1829, probably cut timber here for their own use and for sale. The forests were already regenerating from many historical starting points. It is also tempting to think that the bald appearance of the western slopes could have been due to their dry exposure and frequent lightning-ignited fires, which would have then burned unchecked. Frequent fire was a prominent ecological influence in Georgia in the past and sculpted forests in ways we're only now beginning to understand. Protected from the influence of fire, the cool, moist northern slope certainly could have been similar to what it is today.

Other differences can be gleaned from the reports of the soldiers, who—although not particularly interested in nature—left tantalizing hints. Many soldiers, including Sherman, mentioned the presence of the American chestnut in the area in their reports and correspondence (compiled in the Civil War *Official Records*, Vol. 38), a tree that is now functionally extinct because of an introduced fungal pathogen. It can still be found on Kennesaw, resprouting from its very old taproots, only to be struck down again by the blight. The presence of American chestnut and the name Pigeon Hill strongly suggest that at one time Kennesaw Mountain was an important feeding and roosting area for the now-extinct passenger pigeon.

The area was already a patchwork of open fields in cultivation and uncut woods. Perhaps some of these woods were spared the ax and may have been in old-growth condition as late as 1864. Most of the forests on the flats surrounding the mountain were oak-hickory forests, like many of the forests near Kennesaw today—with white, red, southern red, and post oak, as well as mockernut and pignut hickory, with a dash of sweet gum, tulip tree, and red maple. The forests of this type remaining today are not old growth but have instead just recently reached the climax phase. They were probably cut around the time of the battle and have regenerated from what were then old fields in 1864. Soldiers complaining of thick woods with tangles of briars indicate that some land had already been cleared within decades of 1864 and was regenerating into formidable second-growth thickets armed with pine and blackberry bushes. These regenerating forests favored the defenders. Brigade commander Giles A. Smith reported (see *Official Records*) that the ground was "so densely covered with underbrush as to compel the men to crawl almost on their hands and knees through the tangled vines." Regenerating forests in the South could be impenetrable jungles of vines and thorny shrubs, as they can be today. Unless they were cleared since then, these thickets are now mature oak-hickory forests as well.

The forests on the mountain itself differed slightly from those on the flat areas surrounding it, and today a characteristic tree of the higher elevations and rockier terrain on Kennesaw is chestnut oak. The forests along the northern slopes of Kennesaw have chestnut oak and northern red oak as dominants and can be considered chestnut oak–red oak forests (chestnut oak gets its name from its leaf shape, which is similar to that of the American chestnut). American chestnut often co-occurred with red oak and/or chestnut oak. In its place, trees characteristic of forest disturbance now grow: red maple, sourwood, and loblolly pine. The presence of the chestnut oak and American chestnut indicate that in the past Kennesaw Mountain had at least a small stand of chestnut oak–chestnut forest; these trees were once common in the Appalachians but were otherwise rather uncommon in the Georgia Piedmont.

Photographs of the mountain at the time of the battle (for example, in Earl Hess's and Albert Castel's histories) reveal a much more open, rocky exposure on the slopes and provide a clue that fire may have once influenced the mountain's forests much more than today. The same can be said of many rocky ridges of the Georgia Piedmont, such as Pine Mountain near Columbus, and the Talladega Uplands near Cartersville. Those ridges even have longleaf pine, a tree that requires fire for its very existence, but this tree has not been reported from Kennesaw. So perhaps fire was less frequent here. Rocky ridges were probably more lightning prone than lower elevations nearby, and lightning-ignited fires probably burned the ridges occasionally. These fires would have burned better on the hotter, drier, and more exposed south- and southwest-facing slopes of the mountains, and the comparatively wetter north-facing slopes probably did not burn often, if at all. The rock outcrop communities probably thrived when fire maintained openings near outcrops. Frequent fires would have maintained a more open, parklike forest on the slopes and would have encouraged growth of grassy meadows between the trees.

In 1864 Kennesaw Mountain may have had more extreme contrasts among its forest types, with open, grassy woods on its southwest slope and rich, moist woods on the north slope. The flats surrounding the mountain would have been made up of a kaleidoscope of beaver marshes and a shifting mosaic of old-growth oak-hickory forests and farms. Today, because of the fire suppression practiced throughout the South, the forests on the mountain have now achieved what is probably an unnatural uniformity, and the park is hemmed in on all sides by housing developments, parking lots, and shopping malls. But one thing is certain: in 1864 near Kennesaw Mountain, Georgia, there were more forests, more kinds of forests, and fewer convenience stores.

# 4

# How the Forest Works

A s COMPLEX AS IT IS, the forest covering Kennesaw Mountain is remarkably easy to understand. A few players contribute disproportionately to
the cycle of energy and nutrients through the forest. The diversity of the forest
subdivides these goods and services in a thousand ways, but such complex-
ity can blind the observer to its simplicity. It is always important to remember
that none of these interacting organisms have the health of the ecosystem in
mind while they are going about their business. They are out for themselves,
but by performing the tasks that benefit their own survival and reproduction,

Figure 5. The leaf litter of deciduous forests is teeming with life; this is the "brown world"
food web. Photo by Sean P. Graham.

it is as though they were organs and the forest a superorganism. Some say the whole planet is like that.

## THE GREEN WORLD

The most important thing to any ecosystem is energy, which ultimately comes from the sun. It cannot be overstated how important plants are in this regard. Plants perform life's single greatest achievement—the conversion of sunlight and an otherwise common gas into the organic molecules most life on earth depends on. Photosynthesis is the process that supports all forest ecosystems. In fact it is the process that supports nearly all ecosystems on earth. Given its importance, one can understand why ancient peoples worshipped the sun and wonder whether perhaps they were onto something. Now that we know how important photosynthesis is to life on our planet, perhaps it is time to reconsider our own outlook. There are ecosystems that do not require photosynthesis, but they are hellish, sulfurous environments deep under the ocean occupied by bizarre creatures—nothing like the inviting forests of Kennesaw Mountain.

Photosynthesis is a remarkably complex process carried out by the oaks and hickories of Kennesaw's forest canopy, by the ferns in moist pockets near streams, by forest floor wildflowers during the brief sprouting period, and by the low-growing and modest quillworts living in the shallow sheet flow of rock outcrops. Humans, with all our technological potential, cannot replicate the process undertaken by these graceful plants in a laboratory. At first glance the reaction seems easy: sunlight + carbon dioxide + water = a simple sugar and oxygen. But this equation belies the dozens of enzymes and complex structures plants use to catalyze the reaction. You can replicate the reaction in the lab . . . if you have a plant.

Plants use their leaves like solar panels, breathe in carbon dioxide through tiny pores in their leaves, and manufacture tons of simple sugars, which can be further processed into all the complex molecules required for living things. The reaction releases oxygen, which humans and most other organisms breathe and is used in turn to combust those same sugars for all bodily functions. Plants also breathe oxygen, and they too use oxygen to burn calories for growth and body functions. They devote any surplus to developing flowers and fruit. Compared to plants, which can manufacture their own food, animals are half-rate organisms dependent on others for their needs. Animals ultimately require plants—either directly or indirectly—for all the energy, proteins, and nucleic acids they use to grow, move, and reproduce.

Many of the carbohydrates produced by plants are quickly packed away into complex storage molecules that are so stout that very few plant eaters can make use of them. Kennesaw's trees are the main producers of the energy available in the forest, which they masterfully use to grow new leaves each year, package new rings of growth, or devote toward the year's flowers and seeds. Trees are jealous hoarders of their products, a fact that anyone can observe each fall. By the time plants drop their leaves in autumn, most are still very much intact.

Kennesaw's forests are not home to leaf-eating mammals like monkeys, sloths, or koalas. Their leaves are so well protected by unpalatable chemicals that hardly any creature can feed on them. The primary herbivores in Kennesaw's forests are not mammals or birds. The humble inchworm does most of the grazing. Scores of moth caterpillar species, most in the family Geometridae (the inchworm moths), are the most important consumers of canopy leaves and form the basis of a short but important grazing food chain in the forest canopy, known as the green world food web. The specialized digestive tracts of these caterpillars allow them to munch on the well-guarded leaves and convert the plants to animal tissue. The caterpillars—which number in the millions—can then support thousands of predatory insects, along with a few kinds of breeding birds and their predators. They are also relished by the diverse flocks of migrating songbirds that move through Kennesaw's forests during spring and fall. The migrants carry all that hard-won energy off and demonstrate the interconnectivity of all earth ecosystems. We will discuss caterpillars in greater detail in chapter 9, and the birds that feed on them in chapters 10–12.

## THE BROWN WORLD

Before the leaves are dropped each autumn, the miserly trees drain them of most sugars. Still, tons of unused energy is wasted each year in the form of leaves that have not had a bite taken from them. These settle into a layer of leaf litter on the forest floor. Then fungi join the show. Fungi and animals are similar in their dependency on organic compounds produced by plants. But unlike animals, fungi usually have the decency to wait until another organism is dead before they consume it. Unlike animals, fungi instead secrete enzymes and feed by absorption. Fungi are the lords of decomposition, and they are the second most important organisms for the function of forests. All of that wasted carbon (as well as vital nutrients) is recycled by the activities of fungi, which infiltrate every square inch of the forest floor. When you see a mushroom, you are observing only the brief reproductive structure representing the whole fungus. The growing and feeding part is underground, infused in rotting logs, or living in close association with plant roots. Fungi are strange—genetic material can freely move among different cells through pores, and some individuals exchange genetic material among their cells for years—*years!*—before actual sex occurs. They occur as swarms of thin, wispy cellular structures called hyphae, which together form a pervasive body called a mycelium. We will forgive fungi for their eccentricity, however, and instead appreciate their contribution to nutrient recycling in our forests.

Because most of the canopy's energy ends up on the forest floor, the most important food chain ends up being down there, giving forests an upside-down energy flow. This food chain, begun by the conversion of plant material into fungal biomass available to animals, is called the decomposer, or brown world food web. This food web supports more animal life than all those leaves in the canopy, which may at first seem counterintuitive. But imagine how much energy is provided by the caterpillars that chew a few thousand holes in the leaves of the canopy, compared to the tons of leaves that are fully recycled and eventually turned into soil and biomass by fungi.

This food web supports a diverse cast of creepy crawlies, starting with trillions of soil bacteria and fungal hyphae, followed by the billions of microscopic invertebrates that feed on them. These include tiny roundworms, mites, and protists, which in turn are grazed on by swarms of insects like springtails. Snails and harvestmen (whisker-legged arachnids often called "daddy longlegs") are larger consumers of fungal tissue. Pulling back a thin layer of leaf litter or rolling a rotten log will reveal dozens of small arthropods, and at certain times of year these are so abundant the forest floor is quite infested with them. Wolf spiders, tiger beetles, and small salamanders are among the many "leopards" of this microcosmic forest floor Serengeti. The relative importance of the brown world is revealed by the number of salamanders it can support compared to the number of birds the canopy can support. Salamanders can outnumber and outweigh perching birds in these forests, a fact explored in more detail in chapter 6. These small vertebrates and arthropods in turn support the hundreds of small mammals, birds, and snakes that nowadays serve as top predators on Kennesaw Mountain.

Fungi provide another critical function in the forest. Many plants develop intimate connections with these organisms, in some cases welcoming fungal hyphae to live inside the cell walls of their roots. These mycorrhizal (meaning "fungus-root") associations are among the finest examples of ecological mutualisms—interactions that provide benefits to both partners. Since the interaction is between two kinds of organisms in rather cozy proximity, it is considered symbiotic. The fungal partner of the association contributes its excellent ability to absorb nutrients because, try as they may, plant roots are not as good at spreading across acres of forest to find all the minerals and vital molecules needed for the whole plant. By contrast, fungi are pros at absorption.

For their part, plants provide the fungi with spare energy in the form of sugars produced by photosynthesis. When first discovered, mycorrhizal associations between plant roots and fungi were thought to represent interesting novelties—many orchids, for example, have very specific fungal partners they can't live without. As more and more examples were discovered, it became increasingly clear that these associations are more the rule than the exception. Marc-Andre Selosse and colleagues report that 80–90 percent of plants probably take part in mycorrhizal associations with fungi. In some cases the plants recruit fungal partners only when they need them, or when they have the energy to spare. In other cases the relationship is so intimate it is difficult to distinguish what part of the organism is plant and what part is fungus. In recent years it has become clear that not only are most plants associated with fungal hyphae, but in many cases multiple plants and multiple fungi are associated in promiscuous mycorrhizal networks. Plants have even been shown to exchange material across the forest floor via fungal middlemen. The full extent and impact of this amazing interchange will take decades of research to understand, but what is clear is that mycorrhizal associations provide a crucial recycling link between living and decomposing plants by recovering nutrients lost to leaf fall and death.

## A NUTTY WORLD

Another important food chain is supported by canopy trees, and it also has a mutualistic benefit for others. Reproduction can be a risky proposition for canopy trees, and they sometimes need the help of animals to reproduce at their maximum capacity. In order to ensure this, Kennesaw's trees must satisfy hundreds of hungry animals so that at least a few of their offspring survive. Oaks and hickories produce millions of nuts each year in hopes that a few will be left alone to sprout, preferably as far from the parent tree as possible and in a nice spot for germination.

In order to disperse, oaks and hickories deal with constant harassment by a squad of hungry animals that relish their seeds and do not help them. They must contend with bucktoothed rodents able to gnaw through the hardest of husks, intelligent blue jays able to select the most delicious acorns, and wild turkeys with gizzards able to pulverize rock-hard nuts. It used to be even worse for the trees. Once there were also flocks of millions of passenger pigeons that would blacken the sky and descend upon a forest, vacuuming up the year's reproductive effort. Bears could gulp down pounds of nuts in a sitting. Both of these animals influenced Kennesaw Mountain's forests in the past, but passenger pigeons are now extinct, and black bears no longer occur in the area. Now the nut brigade is led primarily by gray squirrels and eastern chipmunks, the latter of which are extremely abundant at Kennesaw Mountain. Every spring their whistling and skittering on the forest floor distracts unfocused birders from their intended quarry.

Oaks and hickories have developed several strategies for simultaneously satisfying the rodent hordes and also ensuring nut dispersal to a high-quality germination site. Fossils of ancient versions of modern nut-producing trees show they once relied on wind dispersal—as maples and ashes still do. During the maximum extent of the ancient deciduous forest, their seeds became larger. The bigger nuts of today drop like bricks from the trees, straight down below their parents where they are doomed to compete with the much larger tree. This contradiction is explained by two key benefits to having larger seeds. First, they contain a huge reserve of energy useful for getting a head start in the shady, competitive forest floor environment. And second, they are often moved around, and in some cases cached, by rodents and birds. This in turn presents the tree with a new difficulty: how to get nuts moved around, but not eaten, by potential dispersers.

Many nuts are not very tasty, laced as they are with tannins—the same bitter chemicals that also protect leaves. This makes them unpalatable, or at least not as tasty, to certain animals, insects, and parasites that consume the nuts without dispersing them. The nuts have also become increasingly solid or difficult to remove from husks over generations, which the animals had to overcome with strategies of their own. Another novel strategy is to delay reproduction for a few years and then litter the forest floor with more nuts than any population of squirrels could ever deal with. This mast crop strategy works remarkably well, and most oaks and hickories have two- to three-year mast delays. This ensures that at least some nuts are stored in a cache by rodents and forgotten. By swamping the nut feeders all at once, the trees ensure that many of their seeds are available to sprout on the forest floor. And by allowing species with hoarding tendencies to collect them, oak acorns and hickory nuts are spread far and wide away from the parent tree and then literally planted in the ground—as if by a gardener—by the rodents. Although the strategy requires a lot of energy to ensure it works, the nut dispersal method clearly works better than wind dispersal, as evidenced by the dominance of nut-producing trees in the eastern deciduous forests.

I calculated the number of nuts provided by three of the most important canopy trees growing on Kennesaw Mountain. In similar forests, the average density of red, white, and chestnut oaks is about 430, 150, and 500 trees per km$^2$, respectively. The forest on Big Kennesaw, Little Kennesaw, and Pigeon Hill covers about 5 km$^2$ (the area fills about five squares of a US Geological Survey [USGS] topo map, each of which is a single square kilometer, or 1.9

square miles). According to a census of deciduous forest trees by Catherine Keever, this means that Kennesaw's forest has about 2,150 red oaks, 750 white oaks, and 2,500 chestnut oaks. When I stand on the summit of Little Kennesaw during winter, looking north toward Big Kennesaw, that seems about right to me. According to data collected by Anita Rose and her team, on average, the individual trees of each species produce thousands of acorns annually (red oaks: 1,463.3 per tree, chestnut oaks: 246.3 per tree, white oaks: 1,884 per tree). Thus, the total number of acorns produced is incredible: Kennesaw's red oaks can produce 3,148,245 acorns per year. Chestnut oaks produce 615,750 per year. White oaks, despite being relatively uncommon, produce 1,413,000 acorns per year. Each species has acorns that vary slightly in size and weight. Red oak acorns weigh a little less than a tenth of an ounce (2.12 g), those of chestnut oaks about half that (1.21 g), and those of white oaks still less, on average (0.83 g). When you add them up, the result is an astounding total weight of acorn production: red oaks produce 6.7 tons of acorns, chestnut oaks contribute a little less than a ton, and white oaks produce 1.2 tons—a total of 8.6 tons of acorns produced per year, on average, by just three oak species on Kennesaw Mountain. Based on Allen Lewis's determinations of the energy content of individual acorns, this results in 23,889,358,047 calories available to the inhabitants of Kennesaw's forest. That's almost 24 *billion* calories.

Such a volume of nuts becomes even more remarkable when we consider that one of the most important trees in the eastern United States is no longer present on Kennesaw Mountain. In 1864, several troops, including Sherman, commented on the presence of American chestnuts on Kennesaw. They are still there, although they no longer contribute much to the forest ecosystem. Once they were a major contender. One of the reasons eastern deciduous forests are home to such a diversity of animals that feed on nuts is because chestnuts were once the most generous tree. Instead of delaying reproduction for several years like oaks, chestnuts produced a massive, nutritious mast every single year. These nuts were virtually unprotected except for a spiny bur that surrounded them, which could easily be pried open by enterprising squirrels and patient blue jays. Chestnuts could be eaten right off the ground even by people, but as you might suspect, they were more often roasted. The hordes of nut feeders could depend on the tree. The huge flocks of passenger pigeons could count on it. Native Americans pounded the nuts into flour and survived the winters with it.

This trusty contribution each year influenced the decisions made by the hordes of nut hoarders. Squirrels would feed freely on chestnuts as much as they could—along with blue jays, deer, bears, pigeons, deer mice, and turkeys—until they were all gone. While feeding on chestnuts, they would then stash away the next best thing for winter storage—the relatively tasty acorns of the white oak. The acorns of red oaks, chestnut oaks (no relation to American chestnut), and hickories were shunned and eaten only under extreme circumstances. By doing this, squirrels influenced the dynamics of forest change. Forgetful squirrels rarely returned to eat every acorn in their caches, which meant that white oak was once the best disperser—aided as it was by squirrels that smuggled its seeds far from the parent tree and planted them in some nice place for germination. At the time of the Civil War and for thousands of years before, large areas of forests were composed of white oak, American chestnut, and red oak, which struggled for dominance in the canopy. Thanks to the shrewdness of white oak and the generosity of American chestnut, white oak was winning the game.

Enter the chestnut blight, a filthy fungal pathogen that arrived in America just after the turn of the twentieth century. Not all fungi are humble decomposers that wait for their food to die. Some fungi are among the scariest pathogens because they seem to spread rapidly and sometimes destroy populations, even whole species, with astonishing rapidity. The chestnut blight had maintained a well-behaved and pleasant relationship with the Chinese chestnut in Asia, but when some of these trees were brought to the United States as ornamentals, the fungus jumped ship. American chestnut had not enjoyed a long evolutionary relationship with the blight and was therefore defenseless against it. The stately and important American chestnut was wiped out in a matter of decades in one of the most tragic episodes in our environmental history. The fungus infiltrated the tree's fluid transport tissues, strangling the plant. Airborne spores spread the infection rapidly. In perhaps the saddest part of the tale, the victims are actually still alive to this day. The conservative trees stored so much starch in their taproots that they can send up new sprouts each year. These grow high enough to develop bark before the blight—which is always there, waiting—reappears. As reported by Gabriel Popkin, the US Department of Agriculture and others are actively attempting to bring back the chestnut using a variety of measures, including genetically modifying the trees to increase their resistance to the blight. But for now, their absence is still conspicuous on the mountain. Before they can flower and provide their ancient contribution to the forest, the new saplings are struck down. Some of these heart-wrenching reminders of this once-grand tree can be found on Kennesaw Mountain.

Incredibly—especially considering the staggering number of acorns produced by Kennesaw's trees—total mast production in eastern forests has decreased by 80 percent since the elimination of chestnut. Without the yearly mast of delicious chestnuts, the squirrels had to adjust. They began feeding heavily on white oaks, which do not provide as predictable a crop as chestnuts do. Populations of nut feeders probably plummeted. It's probably for the best that passenger pigeons were on their way out before the chestnut blight, because the great flocks of these birds would have struggled to survive off oaks alone. Squirrels began to use red oaks as a backup winter food. This led to a decline of white oak saplings sprouting from squirrel caches, and instead red oaks began increasing. If you observe the saplings growing from the forest floor along any of Kennesaw's trails, you can see the results of this dramatic shift caused by the extinction of one important tree species. Most saplings are red and chestnut oaks, whose acorns were once shunned by rodents. White oaks are present in the canopy but are rare as saplings. Over time, the forest structure will change.

There are of course a dozen other minor food chains supported by such outputs as fruiting shrubs, trees that produce smaller seeds, flowers and their pollinators, meadow grasses, and freshwater algae, but compared to the grazing, decomposer, and mast food webs—the green, brown, and nutty worlds—they are relatively insignificant. It is always worth admiring how the complex webs and interactions discussed here—the flocks of migrating warblers and thrushes feeding on millions of inchworms, the hundreds of salamanders feeding on swarms of springtails, and the rich harvest of nuts satisfying the resident chipmunks—are all made possible because of the world's most important biological process, which begins in the forest canopy and is provided by shimmering summer leaves.

# 5
# Plant Adaptations

O N A STROLL ALONG A trail in the middle of summer on Kennesaw Mountain, it is remarkable how much dimmer the light is under the trees, compared to the hot rays experienced in an old field or a parking lot. But it is not complete shade. The light filters through the thousands of leaves of the forest into a dim ethereal light. Thin shafts shine down like laser beams through tiny gaps between the leaves. Remarkably, the plants at your feet can make use of this light.

Physical influences have sculpted the plants on Kennesaw Mountain, and by far the most important one is available light. This somewhat unfairly reduces the importance of soil and moisture, but we are speaking here about a deciduous forest that receives a similar and sufficient amount of rainfall from year to year, such that—within the relatively small area within the boundaries of Kennesaw National Battlefield Park—there is not that much variation. Plants do show adaptations to different moisture regimes here, and some dry,

Figure 6. A mafic glade on Kennesaw Mountain. These open habitats develop because of the presence of rare heavy metals and low amounts of more nutritious minerals in the soil. Photo by Brandon Westerman.

desertlike habitats occur in some spots. Kennesaw's rock outcrops present unique challenges to plants, including thin, dry soils with little moisture, as well as soils with nearly toxic levels of strange minerals that are unusual for the region. These make up a small but interesting percentage of the landscape and will be considered at the end of this chapter. There is no great range of life zones represented on this mountain—no gradient from grassland at the base through various forest types up to alpine tundra, as you might observe on a real mountain in Colorado. There is only one major plant community, and it is the exact one you'd expect given the average rainfall near Atlanta: oak-hickory forest. This forest type shows its share of interesting plant adaptations, but in many ways the plants reflect the ease with which plants grow in such nice conditions.

For example, the leaves of nearly all the plants are similar to each other in thickness, which is not very thick at all. Plants with thin, medium-sized leaves are referred to as "mesophytes" in botanical terms, with an average type of leaf not adapted to any particularly difficult environment. Plants adapted to drier places have leaves that are much thicker and often much smaller, and they have several other adaptations for reducing water loss. Fully aquatic plants have several adaptations of their own. But the plants of Kennesaw, living as they do in a region of moderate climate and moisture, are fairly average.

By far the most obvious and important adaptation shared by most plants on Kennesaw is deciduousness. This adaptation should not be taken for granted, although it is very easy for easterners to do so. In order to fully appreciate its strangeness you have to travel outside our deciduous forests to see how other plants do things. You could travel to the high latitudes in Canada and see a forest dominated by conifers that remain green—albeit a dark blue green—year-round. You could travel to the misty, mossy Pacific Northwest and see towering evergreen conifers living in wetter climates that receive much more rainfall than Georgia. Go to the Desert Southwest and see cacti in full greenery in winter. In California's heavily populated coastal region, evergreen oaks and shrubs dominate the landscape. Perhaps visit Australia, where the climate can be similar to Georgia's, yet eucalyptus forests remain green—albeit a very strange gray green—year-round. Then imagine how peculiar the forests flanking Kennesaw must seem to an outsider not familiar with deciduous plants. How dead the place must look in winter, with its thousands of trees bare, and a thick layer of summer leaves lying dead on the forest floor, creating sounds like waves when you walk through them. We are reminded every year about our forest's deciduous nature when chestnut oaks turn brown red on Kennesaw, and tulip trees bear banana-yellow leaves before they fall off. The color display on Kennesaw is rarely as magnificent as the conflagrations seen annually in northeastern forests, but it is hard to miss. But why do they do it?

Deciduous flowering plants developed over sixty-five million years ago in strange forests at very high latitudes. Nothing like these forests still exists, because places that far north are no longer warm enough to support such forests. But at that time the world's climate was much warmer, and flowering plants and even dinosaurs occurred in regions as far north as present-day Alaska. Although it was fairly warm up there, there was still the problem of long periods of seasonal darkness. At some latitudes winter days were brief or nonexistent for weeks. When the light petered out, plants dropped their leaves and remained dormant. During the Cretaceous summer, there were times when the sun shone warm and bright for months on end with barely a sunset.

According to Jack Wolfe, these plants gained an advantage after a key moment in the history of life on earth—a time when dropping leaves and dormancy would have given them an unprecedented evolutionary edge. This was at the end of the Cretaceous period, when dinosaurs and many other animals and plants became extinct after a giant asteroid impacted the earth. As the familiar story goes, this explosion threw up so much atmospheric dust that photosynthesis was interrupted for some significant period, and most large life forms at the top of complex ecosystems died out. Deciduous plants would survive to inherit a large portion of the Northern Hemisphere.

These plants diversified greatly over the next several million years and had a keen advantage as climate steadily became more unpredictable and seasonal. When full temperate zone conditions developed—warm, wet summers and cold, wet winters—these plants developed to their maximum extent, spreading across the entire Northern Hemisphere, as described in chapter 2. But "temperate zone" is a misnomer. There is nothing temperate about it; nothing moderate. Climate is quite extreme in the temperate zone. Temperatures range from below freezing in winter to above 100°F in summer. The average between these extremes, if it stayed that way, would be very comfortable and moderate. But it is temperate only in an ethnocentric sense and is called that only because most of western civilization is parked here. The temperature is far more variable in Georgia than in the tropics. Summer highs can be far more brutal in Georgia than in Panama, and of course the winters here can be unpredictably cold. The variation between winter lows—when Arctic systems can dip down far to the south for a week or two of bitter cold—and summer highs—when drought conditions can kill venerable old trees—is extreme.

Even when this variation is not so extreme, the winter presents a quandary for plants. During two or three months of the year in Georgia, the sun shines from low angles for only a short part of the twenty-four-hour day.

Temperatures drop low enough to form ice crystals in plant cells, which can rupture and kill them. Some plants, such as conifers, have developed ways to continue life processes through the winter, but deciduous plants have instead opted out and simply give up each fall. They go dormant during winter, when the available sunlight is unimpressive and the chance of freeze damage is high. In this way they share the same strategy as animals that hibernate. When conditions are harsh and there is very little return for your efforts to find food, it makes sense to wait until better times. Plants withdraw the green pigment in their cells (chlorophyll), which absorbs certain wavelengths of visible light during photosynthesis. Suddenly other color pigments in the leaves—which absorb different wavelengths (xanthophylls and carotenoids)—become visible. The fall colors are then apparent.

Plants shore up their energy and store it in roots and other safe tissues before they finally jettison their leaves. It is a drastic measure that must be compensated by such efficient light gathering during the growing season that they can pay for the next year's crop of leaves in advance. Apparently, it works. And this dramatic event influences the lives of other plants and animals throughout the forest.

We will now turn to other interesting adaptations of Kennesaw's plants, remembering always the major contribution of deciduousness to those that are less obvious. And it is worth considering that, for plants, this bold display of color is not some whimsical moment, no colorful advertisement—no poetic gesture. Despite how beautiful the fall color change is and the vast amount of admiration people have doted on this phenomenon, the plants are preparing for hard times and, sadly, must waste a year's worth of leaves to do so.

## GETTING LIGHT

Light is the most precious resource of the deciduous forest, and it is the resource that plants must fight each other for. It is the resource that results in the most readily observable adaptations of forest plants. It is easiest to see how light is divided among the plant kingdom in Kennesaw's forests by considering first those plants that receive most of it. The clear winners in this competition are the large forest trees that can replace themselves in the canopy: at Kennesaw, the oaks, hickories, and tulip trees, for the most part. These trees can reach heights of over one hundred feet and crowd their oval crowns into a rather thick canopy. The canopy cuts off light to the rest of the plants below them. Given that 90 percent of the light is blocked by these trees, one might expect that there would be no other plants in the forest.

But a quick glance shows this is not the case. There are certainly more plants, and they grow in rather neat layers below the canopy. You can make out two more layers of plants: an understory tree-shrub layer, and a layer of herbaceous plants (small wildflowers and ferns) plus numerous saplings on the forest floor—the offspring of the canopy trees. This orderly arrangement of vegetative layers is referred to as forest stratification and has to do with how plants align themselves to absorb sunlight. The plants in the lower layers must somehow make do with the 10 percent of the light that penetrates the canopy layer. This light either filters through an infinity of oak or hickory leaves and is therefore greatly reduced in its usefulness for photosynthesis, or it shines through tiny gaps in the canopy under full power as sun flecks. The plants below the canopy use these two sources about equally, and both are worth your admiration: consider that half the light used by forest wild-flowers is that magical green aura coming down through the canopy leaves. The rest comes from shafts of pure light slipping through spaces between branches—through empty jigsaw spaces between trees. These range from a fleeting beam of narrow light that can last ten seconds to full set lighting that lasts an hour in the morning.

The shrub–small tree layer, also known as the subcanopy, is most easily observed in spring, around April when the canopy is beginning to leaf out on the saddle between Big and Little Kennesaw. At this time some of the showy plants are flowering, and they cannot be missed by even the least interested city boy. Redbud, with its tiny pink (not red) pea flowers, the large and showy blossoms of the beloved dogwood, and the pink honeysuckle blooms of pinxter-flower dot this layer with color. The flowers reveal that the small trees and shrubs living in the shadow of the canopy are in fact arranged neatly in a layer. If you used a long scaffold and tape measure you'd find that the tops of these trees were at about the same height, within a few feet or so. Unlike the canopy trees, which have oval crowns, these subcanopy trees have flat tops. Also unlike the canopy trees, which have their leaves arranged at angles to the rising and setting of a seasonal sun, these subcanopy trees have thin leaves arranged rather flatly, like the upright palms of hands. The explanation for this observation lies in the complicated trigonometry of sun flecks shining through the canopy gaps.

John Terborgh, a Princeton University forest ecologist, determined that if you consider all the light shining through all the thousands of tiny gaps in the canopy averaged over a day, summed over a year, and consider them shining as beams from all possible angles while simultaneously considering the sun's position along the zenith, you can determine the best place for a subcanopy to be in order to receive the most light. In simpler terms, imagine two big gaps between two trees in the canopy, and sunlight beaming down through these gaps across one day. If you needed to catch light for a solar panel, there would be a place below the canopy where you could set it up and absorb the most light. It would be where the two beams intersected for the longest amount of time—where two diagonal beams crossed. Then think instead about the kaleidoscopic reality of sun flecks coming and going during the day, throughout the year. It becomes much more complicated—like an annual disco ball of sun rays penetrating down ethereally. Given how complicated the real story is, we will trust the Ivy League ecologist's calculations, especially when it is revealed that his equations predict to within a few feet where the subcanopy tree crowns actually grow, given the height of the canopy above them.

Now consider the forest floor. These plants must make do with the leftover light not used by the canopy as well as the subcanopy. This is a difficult proposition indeed, but the herbaceous plants have adopted a few ingenious strategies. The first strategy is simply to avoid the problem. Many woodland wildflowers do not attempt to compete with trees for light and instead take advantage of the short time in the spring when it is warm enough and sunny enough to grow while the trees still have no leaves. When the trees eventually leaf out and the shade arrives, they again go dormant. These are the spring ephemerals—rue anemone, chickweed, violets, foamflower, Catesby's trillium, trout lily, perfoliate bellwort, and bloodroot—which are able to gather enough sun during these brisk few weeks of spring to grow and reproduce for an entire year. Many of these plants can continue growth at near- or below-freezing temperatures, so even a freak late ice storm is not a problem for them. A bigger risk is that unpredictably bad or cold weather will interrupt and chill down their pollinators. Reproduction is most chancy for these plants, because they rely on warm weather to bring out solitary bees and other insects for maximum cross-fertilization. Spring ephemerals hug the ground where it is warmest and attempt to attract the early wave of flies and bees with showy white flowers. When this fails, many reproduce asexually by sending up sprouts from old roots and rhizomes.

A selection of evergreen species use another strategy. These "wintergreens" can undergo a small amount of photosynthesis during warm days in winter and rely on sun flecks and weak, filtered sunlight for the rest of the growing season. These include small plants like little brown jug, wintergreen, partridgeberry, cranefly orchid, and Christmas fern, which are often the only greenery on the forest floor in winter. They can have small, waxy leaves often quite different from one another in shape. Partridgeberry has tiny oval leaves arranged on stems running along the forest floor. Wintergreen has thin, prickly leaves. Cranefly orchid has strange, crinkly, warty leaves with a felt-green color on top. Underneath, inexplicably, the leaves are purple red. This orchid is one of the easiest plants to find growing on the forest floor during winter, but when it flowers over the summer it has no leaves at all.

Finally, some brave herbaceous plants take the "summer green" approach and must compete directly with the one-hundred-foot giants as well as the trigonometric precision of subcanopy trees above them for the very last drop of light filtering down. Like the subcanopy trees, they rely on a small amount of filtered light, but about half of their photosynthetic gains are met by absorbing light from sun flecks that manage to shine through the canopy and subcanopy. These plants can take full advantage of these rare opportunities because of their leaf architecture—they often have thin, umbrella-like leaves—as well as their modified leaf functions. They are much better at taking advantage of brief bursts of light than canopy trees or herbaceous plants more at home in open, sunny habitats. They maintain photosynthetic readiness—a high state of light-alertness—and require fewer precious moments to initiate activity. Fleeting shafts of light are exploited fully. Examples of plants using the summer green strategy include mayapple, several ferns, and some woodland representatives of plants more at home in meadows—the woodland asters and goldenrods that bloom during summer under Kennesaw's forest canopy.

## POLLINATION

Although many plants have developed ingenious strategies for reproducing without pollination, and some can even get away with pollinating themselves, most plants require pollen from another individual plant—cross-pollination—in order to successfully reproduce. Given that plants cannot simply move themselves and copulate with another individual plant, they must instead rely on more indirect methods of sex. The plants living within the three stratified forest layers have each adopted different pollination strategies, probably in part because of their distance above the ground and the availability of certain kinds of pollinators.

The canopy trees, the crowns of which are up to one hundred feet above the ground, can take advantage of gravity and wind to spread pollen, especially in the breezy conditions of a Georgia spring. Oaks and hickories are wind pollinated, and cross-pollination is frequent. They display long tentacle-like flowers on the ends of branches before they sprout leaves, and these flowers broadcast millions of pollen grains upon the breeze. Pollen from the mountains of Alabama might be carried on a strong gust all the way to Kennesaw, and certainly a white oak on top of the mountain could breed with a tree somewhere east of Atlanta, perhaps beyond Stone Mountain. Oaks in particular show strong evidence that this mating system works very well to effect long-distance pollination—so well that oak species hybridize with each other rampantly, as noted by field guide author George Petrides.

The trees of the subcanopy, as we have noted, often have large flowers that decorate their flat tops in spring. At this level of the forest, breezes are not as effective for transporting pollen—air is more stable thanks to the wind-breaking crowns and trunks of canopy trees. Dogwood, redbud, pinxter-flower, and buckeye rely instead on some of the largest and most reliable insect pollinators like bumblebees and butterflies.

Spring ephemerals are the first to bloom in the forest because they are in a race with the canopy for light. This gives them fewer options for pollination, and they generally cannot depend on the larger, more reliable pollinators like bumblebees because it takes warmer conditions to heat up a large bee. Instead, these small flowers are visited by native solitary bees—brilliant blue, green, or yellow gems—as well as flies, bee flies, hoverflies, and other small insects. Since they hug the ground, some of these flowers are even pollinated by ants. Some herbaceous plants—whether they grow early on the forest floor or bloom during summer along forest edges—show definite preferences for certain kinds of pollinators, which has led to the development of numerous adaptations for enhancing their appeal to these flower visitors. A flower's shape, color, and scent often reflect the kinds of visitors it attracts. For example, flowers that rely heavily on bumblebees for pollination are often large and white, and their petals form a tube that only a strong bee can tunnel into. Certain major pollinator groups have influenced distinctive "pollination syndromes" in plants, and Kennesaw Mountain has excellent examples of these. An astonishing case is revealed in chapter 9.

## DISPERSAL

Assuming that cross-pollination is successful, the inability to move around presents the offspring of plants with a major problem. It is axiomatic among ecologists that the worst lot for a young plant is to start out life growing under its parent. There a young plant will have to compete for light, moisture, and nutrients with an individual very similar to itself that has a considerable head start in life. It is rarely successful, and scores of unlucky plants are cursed to die young because they can't find their way to good growing sites. Because of this key problem, plants have developed ways to escape the shadow of their parents. Some of these methods are most miraculous, and it sometimes stretches credulity that plants would need to go to such extreme measures to ensure their dispersal. But leaving home is only one motivation. After the basic requirement to leave the vicinity of the parent, plants with the ability to make their way to better germination spots might be favored. These might be sites with no competition from a member of their own species, or even a nice open place with superior soil quality and no plants growing at all. Any method that increases a plant's chances of finding such a spot might be expected to turn up as an adaptation. The plants of Kennesaw show an incredible diversity of dispersal adaptations. The architecture of the forest—dictated by forest stratification and light availability—again plays a role.

The canopy trees exploit the luxury of relying on gravity and wind. Many canopy trees have developed light seeds with thin, membranous wings whose aerodynamics allow them to spin like little propellers down and away from the parent tree. Depending on chance and luck, these little whirling seeds can travel quite far. Maples, ashes, pines, tulip trees, catalpas, trumpet creepers, and crossvines have winged seeds that can fly passively away from the parent plant like thousands of tiny children's toys. But the dominant trees in the canopy forgo this easy solution to dispersal and have instead adopted the nut.

Oaks, hickories, and American beech (and formerly, the American chestnut) have large, heavy, highly nutritious nuts that career like grand pianos straight down to the forest floor. They might bounce and roll by luck out from under the parent tree—those that are borne at the tips of branches have a better chance of rolling away—but for the most part this tactic seems to contradict the need to disperse. Instead these heavy fruits attract various animals that feed on them, which at first also seems very counterproductive. But these trees produce so many nuts at once that animals like squirrels, chipmunks, blue jays, and turkeys cannot possibly eat them all. And in fact, because there are so many nuts, the animals are often compelled to temporarily store them in small caches—underground chambers in the forest floor—which turn out to be excellent places for germination. They are often buried quite far from a parent plant, and they are safely stashed away from insects that would also feed on them. As long as the animal that placed it there doesn't come back and eat it, the nut will have a wonderful chance to sprout. Since nuts are so large and heavy, they also have much more stored energy and have a much better head start than your average wind-dispersed seed.

Nut-bearing trees have tight relationships with their dispersers but have to constantly maintain a balance between several counteracting forces: the benefits of movement by seed dispersal versus the dangers of seed predators; the benefits of having tasty nuts versus the costs of being tasty to fungal and insect parasites; the benefits of having light seeds that are easily dispersed by wind versus heavy seeds that can provide a good head start for sprouting in a shady forest environment. Nuts represent a compromise between these outcomes. Nuts are so important as a food crop for animals of the eastern

deciduous forests that they influence forest function and the very composition of the forest—which trees are present over time—as we saw in the last
chapter.

The next forest layer can also utilize gravity and wind, but being closer to
the ground, fewer of these plants rely on this method. Redbud has winged
fruits that spiral in the air, and wild azaleas like pinxter-flower have tiny
winged seeds that are able to glide away from the parent tree. But many of the
subcanopy trees and shrubs have small fruits that are attractive to fruit-eating
birds like thrushes, catbirds, mockingbirds, and waxwings. Dogwood, serviceberry, spicebush, and hollies have red fruits easily located by these birds,
and they provide them with a tasty meal. Red is a particularly apt color for attracting birds because—as we will see again in a later chapter—birds can see
red very well, and other animals cannot. This way, the plants can attract birds
while simultaneously disguising the fruits against a swarm of animals that
are more likely to eat them without dispersing the seeds—animals like rodents and insects.

Since birds eat the fruits whole, they typically pass through the guts of their
intended dispersers with the seeds intact. Some seeds are specially treated by
the guts of their dispersers, and some in fact require chemical or mechani-
cal preparation by the stomach and intestines of their dispersers before they
sprout. Many plants produce sugary fruits that are quickly snapped up by
swarms of birds. These fruits frequently go unnoticed by all but the most at-
tentive naturalists, for they are not present for long. Who has tasted the delicious fruits of a Kennesaw serviceberry, which appear briefly in June before
rapidly disappearing down the throats of brown thrashers and catbirds?

Birds can disperse the seeds far, especially during migration. Many of these
plants time their fruiting to correspond with the waves of migratory fruit-
eating birds—especially migrating thrushes—that pass by Kennesaw's summit during late September and October. Some plants that are dispersed by
birds may have arrived on Kennesaw by this route, especially plants that are
found here far away from their nearest known population. Perhaps this is how
prickly ash—a rare tree in Georgia found in abundance far to the north—arrived on Kennesaw Mountain. Others, like deciduous and evergreen hollies,
produce low-quality fruits that add a dash of red to the winter landscape of
Kennesaw. These rely on the nomadic flocks of waxwings and bluebirds that
search during winter for every last red berry of summer.

Plants on the forest floor also have fruits that are eaten by birds, but perhaps because there are fewer ground-foraging birds in the Georgia Piedmont
region, there are fewer of these plants. Or maybe I've put the cart before the
horse here, and the reason there are not many fruit-eating birds underfoot is

that there are no plants bearing fruits under Kennesaw's canopy. Many forests farther north have herbaceous plants that bear bird-dispersed fruits, but Kennesaw has very few of these plants. Those that are present may have arrived via the poop of migrating birds, and it is possible that they are not effective at dispersal because few breeding birds here eat their fruits.

Gravity and wind are not useful close to the ground, so most herbaceous plants on Kennesaw's forest floor rely on other methods of dispersal. Some of these are quite unexpected. Many forest floor herbaceous plants are dispersed by ants. Thousands of ants belonging to dozens of species scour Kennesaw's forest floor for food, and these plants are favored by the ants because they provide a small packet of protein and fat that the ants can feed to their youngsters in underground chambers. The tiny seeds of these herbs are unpalatable, but they come attached to highly nutritious "elaiosomes." As summarized by Dennis Whigham, ants crawl purposefully up and down the stems of bloodroot, perfoliate bellwort, violets, trilliums, fire-pink, and hepatica gathering the seeds, carrying them as far as six feet away before disappearing down tunnels underground. These turn out to be excellent sites for germination. The ants feed on the elaiosomes and discard the seeds. Besides ants, Catesby's trillium—a charming three-leafed wildflower with exquisite pink-petaled flowers—has even recruited yellow jackets as a dispersal agent. These colonial wasps are voracious protein eaters, going as far as scavenging meat from carcasses to support their hives. They too pick up seeds with rich elaiosomes and, according to Jennifer Zettler and colleagues, fly with them as far as twenty yards away from the parent plant. Yellow jacket hives are underground as well, so the seeds find their way to fine germination sites this way.

A few understory plants have adopted the shotgun, or ballistic, method of dispersal. Witch hazel, the strange subcanopy tree first mentioned in chapter 2, has small fruits dispersed explosively by a spring mechanism. It is said that one can sit quietly on an autumn day and hear the snapping sounds as the little seeds are shot through the forest. Wild geraniums are a summer green wildflower with spring-loaded fruit. It consists of a woody capsule that eventually dries to the point that it splits along five seams, each edge rapidly curling back on itself. The seeds are shaped like coiled arrows, complete with fletching, and, according to Nancy Stamp and Jeffrey Lucas, they are shot as far as twelve feet away from the plant by the propulsive mechanism of the snapping fruit. Jewelweed grows in wet places along creeks and seepages, and its bright orange, jug-shaped flowers become fleshy green packages filled with hundreds of small brown seeds resembling fat little caterpillars. As a fruit matures, it becomes stout—almost like the texture of plastic—and begins to twist upon itself. A passerby can trigger it to split open and unfurl like a model airplane propeller. Stamp and Lucas report that this fires the seeds as far as nine feet from the plant. For this it is also sometimes called "touch-me-not." It is not the only plant that requires a passerby for dispersal.

Any hiker who returns from Kennesaw and checks their pants and socks will quickly discover another clever dispersal mechanism favored by woodland herbs. Several plants have seeds within sticky, spiny, prickly fruits that cling to clothes; hikers make a fine substitute for the fur of mammals, which is the usual target for these hitchhikers. Many plants that are at home in disturbed habitats are dispersed this way, and for this reason they are often most common in openings near forest trails. These plants include beggar-ticks, tick trefoils, and harvest lice, the most outgoing of Kennesaw's plants—plants that are so friendly they'd like to come home with you. Beggar-ticks belong to a sunflower-like plant (*Bidens*) with dark seeds covered in downy, microscopic hooks. Half the seed's length is made up of two or three evil-looking spines that burrow into the fur of rabbits—or your socks. Kennesaw's six species of tick trefoils (*Desmodium*) are actually pea plants, but the individual pea pods have become loose, sticky seed packages. Hikers are often covered by the individual sticky seeds—shaped like tiny guitar picks—but occasionally a whole row will stick to you. Then they look more like pea pods. They easily break off and are carried by the legs of deer—or your pants. Finally, there are the agrimonies, or harvest lice (*Agrimonia*), which lurk within easy reach of most forest trails, their tiny, hairy green spheres waiting for a ride. Upon close examination, the harvest lice have small seeds covered with tiny barbs shaped like the hooks of Velcro. And they work much the same way as Velcro on the bellies of squirrels—and your shirtsleeves. Harvest lice are in the rose family, closely related to blackberries and strawberries. But they have forgone producing tasty fruits and instead rely on the relatively cheaper method of hitching rides.

A final disperser worth considering is a reptile. The charismatic box turtle—the yellow-spangled walking half-shell—patrols the forests of Kennesaw looking for juicy treats from March to October. Box turtles get their name from their unprecedented ability to withdraw their head, neck, and limbs into their shell and completely close it behind them. The hinged lower shell allows them to close up so tightly that no part of them is visible to a would-be predator—not one little piece of flesh for a mink or some other villain to nibble. Box turtles have excellent color vision and are particularly well suited to disperse the seeds of low-growing herbaceous plants. Like birds, box turtles have only a beak and therefore usually swallow the large fleshy parts of fruits and leave the seeds intact. Many box turtle plants have medium-sized red or yellow fruits that dangle low to the ground within reach of the turtle. We already mentioned the mayapple, whose fleshy yellow fruits are favored by the turtle. In fact, the germination of mayapple seeds is enhanced by passing through the gut of the turtle. Other plants of Kennesaw's forests with fruits carried away by box turtles include jack-in-the-pulpit and perhaps the turtle's all-time favorite—wild strawberry.

## SOILS AND MOISTURE

Soil chemistry and moisture can be extremely important for plants, and certain habitats present plants with incredibly challenging environments. But the Georgia Piedmont provides plants with a fairly even and desirable moisture regime (according to the USGS, usually about fifty-five inches of rain spread evenly through the year), and soils are on the whole rather nutritious. Despite this, because of its unique geology, Kennesaw Mountain exhibits an interesting mosaic of habitats for plants, many of which are considerably more trying for plants than those at other locations in the monotonous Piedmont region.

First there are the bare rock outcrop barrens and glades in certain areas of the park, such as near the summit of Pigeon Hill. As described in chapter 1, the mountain is made up of a monolith of metamorphosed gneiss, which erodes more slowly than other rocks in the Georgia Piedmont. Within this huge rock, folded and faulted sections have eroded more slowly than others, in some cases exposing bare rock that is more resistant to erosion than others. These barrens have shallow soils exposed to abundant sunshine, so they present environments not unlike deserts for plants. This readily explains the presence of the prickly pear cactus, Virginia agave, and yuccas that you might find growing from cracks in rock outcrops, which may come as a surprise to hikers expecting the typical hardwood forests of the region. These plants and other, less conspicuous species are known as succulents because of their thick, fleshy, and rather waxy tissues. Succulence, an adaptation for storing and conserving water, is most commonly exhibited by desert plants of the Southwest but can be found in some plants growing on rock outcrops in the much wetter South.

Succulents have yet another functional adaptation for living in extremely hot and dry conditions. They have a shrewd physiological mechanism that allows them to segregate when they undergo two crucial parts of photosynthesis—the breathing in of carbon dioxide, and the actual light-dependent reactions that require chlorophyll. Most plants do all of this at once during the daytime, which requires them to open small pores in their leaves to allow the entry of carbon dioxide. This can lead to too much evaporation of crucial water during the heat of the day. Instead, many succulents open these pores at night when humidity is higher and temperatures lower, so less water evaporates. They temporarily store the carbon dioxide in their cells as an organic acid. The next day, they shut the pores and finish the process of photosynthesis by using sunlight to convert the stored acid into sugars. This is called crassulacean acid metabolism (CAM), and the plants that use it are referred to as CAM plants.

You may also notice that near these rock outcrops coniferous trees are slightly more abundant, and hardwoods seem to differ in composition, stature, and leaf texture. Conifers like pines often do better in thinner, drier soils than hardwoods. Eastern red cedar, loblolly pine, and often shortleaf pine are dominants in the canopy surrounding rock outcrops on Kennesaw. The hardwoods at these sites appear short and gnarled because of their much slower growth rates and the generally harder life in these much drier conditions. Hardwoods of rock outcrops are well adapted to drier and thinner soils, and on Kennesaw Mountain blackjack and post oaks are the usual occupants of these habitats. You might notice that these two oaks have much thicker and glossier leaves than other species. They have more of a waxy layer on the leaves to prevent water loss, giving them this thicker appearance. Oaks in even drier habitats of the southwestern United States have even thicker and much smaller leaves, exhibiting the so-called sclerophyll growth habit. No trees or shrubs on Kennesaw are quite challenged enough to show a truly sclerophyllous growth habit.

On the other side of the modest spectrum of soil moisture within the park is a suite of plants that prefer exceedingly rich and moist soils, which ecologists refer to as mesic soils. Mesic soils are very moist—but not wet—and are thick, rich, dark, and very nutritious because they are packed with organic nutrients from generations of decomposing plants, fungi, and animals. The thick humus develops most luxuriously in very old forests, usually in protected coves with north-facing slopes that receive less sunshine. There the soil develops a texture almost like that of freshly baked brownies and looks delicious enough to eat. This soil condition supports a maximum diversity of wildflowers, ferns, and other herbaceous plants, achieving its most flamboyant development in the cove hardwood forests of the Southern Appalachians. There, in places like the Great Smoky Mountains, hundreds of small, delicate herbs coexist in a riotous profusion. These forests are nearly as diverse as rain forests and receive only perhaps a dozen inches of rainfall per year less than the amount required to be considered just that.

In Georgia, conditions are slightly drier, and cove hardwood forests occur in only a few places—usually in very moist soils on north-facing slopes in the mountains. But the wildflowers that dwell within such forests can make their way farther south if conditions permit, and within the much drier and less nutritious forests of the Georgia Piedmont there are on rare occasion tiny pockets that offer suitable conditions for plants usually found much farther north. On Kennesaw, these plants of "northern affinity" include such herbaceous species as monkshood, angel hair fern, goat's beard, black cohosh, and pink lady's slipper and are found only in rich, north-facing ravines in the park. More-typical wildflowers are also more common in these same habitats.

A final soil factor strongly influences the types of plants that grow on Kennesaw Mountain. Whether the soils are dry or moist, their chemistry can determine what plants can grow on them or how well they grow there. Since the underlying geology of the Georgia Piedmont is similar across most of the state, the forests have a somewhat uniform plant community. But some interesting anomalies occur, one of which is Kennesaw Mountain. The mountain's origin as a slow-cooling magma intrusion from deep within the earth gives it an entirely different soil composition than that of most sites within the Piedmont. Magma from deep within the crust is often composed of rarer, heavier minerals like aluminum, iron, magnetite, and magnesium, and geologists give these rocks the curious moniker "mafic." Mafic is a combination of the words "magnesium" and "ferrous," the latter of which refers to iron. Lighter rocks, with more silica, are referred to as felsic and are more typical in our region.

Mafic rocks and soils have chemical properties very different from those of more typical soils, and sometimes their chemistry can be so intense that they are essentially toxic. Most plants cannot deal with them. Such soils—ultramafic soils—give rise to what are known as serpentine barrens, which can be entirely treeless meadows of strange plants found nowhere else. Ultramafic soils can have high concentrations of truly daunting heavy metals like nickel, cobalt, chromium, and serpentine, and low levels of nutritious minerals like nitrogen, potassium, and phosphorus. The concentrations of the heavy metals can make what few minerals are actually present in the soil more difficult for plants to take up—minerals such as calcium that plants require for growth. The key factor appears to be the relative availability of calcium to magnesium; soils with a low calcium-to-magnesium ratio make it very difficult for plants to absorb calcium from the ground. And without calcium, most organisms, including humans, cannot survive.

Mafic outcrops in the Southeast do not give rise to fully serpentine soils, but some, including certain areas on Kennesaw Mountain, support low-diversity mafic "glades" that are home to a few hardy plants that manage to do well on these soils. These plants are very rare in Georgia, and only a few glades provide appropriate habitat for them, including soils with a low calcium-to-magnesium ratio. The precise ways such plants overcome this dreaded ratio are not known. They do it either by selectively absorbing calcium over magnesium (which is difficult for plants), or by absorbing toxic levels of magnesium and storing it in their leaves. Possibly these plants use some savvy combination of these strategies. Special plants become so well adapted to these conditions that they can no longer compete in more favorable soils. They become mafic outcrop specialists and actually require high levels of magnesium that would kill their close relatives.

In such soils trees typically grow in well-separated and stunted patches, allowing increased light penetration. The soils can be thin and rocky, and mafic rocks can form rock outcrops that present plants with a double whammy: not only are the soils nonnutritious and slightly toxic but there are also the hot, dry conditions to deal with. A grassy understory develops, and some of the rarest plants on the mountain grow among these habitats. Missouri rockcress, a small native member of the mustard family usually more at home in rocky prairies of the Midwest, finds a lonely outpost on Pigeon Hill. Open-ground draba, another, even less conspicuous mustard, can be found by sharp-eyed plant hunters hiding under eastern red cedars in the same vicinity. This is a very special plant indeed. It loves and even requires mafic soils, making it one of the finest indicators of this habitat. It was named from specimens collected here in 1901, making this the only plant whose "type locality" is Kennesaw Mountain. The park includes dozens more plants that are strongly associated with mafic soils, such as purple coneflower, hoary puccoon, and crested coralroot, as well as others that are more common on such soils but can also survive elsewhere.

Light, moisture and nutrients, fertilization, and dispersal are the key requirements for plants in the deciduous forests of Kennesaw Mountain, and the plants have clever adaptations to maximize their chances to successfully achieve each one. But no plant lives its life in a vacuum and is able to develop individual strategies that best fit its needs. Instead, the actions of some plants influence the responses of others. The use of one animal for pollination may reduce its availability to another plant. The broad adaptations of these plants are therefore best viewed as a series of balancing acts between conflicting needs. The forest floor plants would be very different if the canopy trees grew differently. Seed dispersal would be very different if fruit-eating birds were not available. Even the humble box turtle has a role to play. The varying influences of rocks, soil moisture, and soil nutrients result in a quilted distribution of plants on the mountain. The millions of interactions between all the plants, animals, and fungi of Kennesaw Mountain are imposingly complicated and interwoven into a web too intricate to be understood in total by any brain or computer program. And, as we will find next, these interactions often involve unlikely tiny creatures hidden away in the forest floor, whose individual impact is modest but whose summed influence on the forest has been enormous for millions of years.

# 6

# Webster's Salamander

EVERY WINTER ON KENNESAW MOUNTAIN for the past four million years or so, a feverish mating ritual—in this case, literally a dance—has been carried out by tiny, slimy inhabitants of its ancient forest. These creatures rely so much on moisture and cool temperatures that they prefer to breed from January through March and cannot even be found above the surface from April through September. Males and females occupy the wet space under nearly every small log, stick, and loose rock of the mountain, and on rainy nights, males emerge to look for females. A male will tap his snout on the ground, sensing chemicals left from the female's slick, wet skin using the fleshy nubs hanging down from his lips. When he locates her, he approaches and nudges her, wiggles his tail, and arches his back. He has a perfectly circular gland on his chin and slaps her with it. It contains a pheromone that will influence her decision to mate—like an aphrodisiac for amphibians.

If she accepts his advances, she straddles his tail and they walk together on the forest floor, the male leading her with his tail between her legs. After a

Figure 7. Webster's salamander. This unassuming creature reveals the fascinating ancient history of the South. Photo by Noah K. Fields.

period that has been hardwired into their small brains for untold generations, the male will stop and, wiggling his tail, deposit a small gelatinous packet of sperm on the ground. If the dance is completed without a flaw, she will proceed forward and hunch over to pick it up with her cloacal lips. This is considered internal fertilization, even though the sperm is deposited on a surface. She then stores the sperm in passages within her body for several months until she lays her eggs. These are not laid where you might expect—they are not laid in a pond, or near any water whatsoever. Instead, they are laid in a cluster deep underground. The eggs do not hatch into tadpoles or larvae but develop directly into juvenile salamanders that at hatching look like tiny replicas of their parents. Such is the mating routine of the Webster's salamander, one of Kennesaw Mountain's most fascinating inhabitants.

Every southerner should know about and have a sense of pride in salamanders. Salamanders are more diverse in the southeastern United States than anywhere else in the world. The reason is that almost every kind of salamander belongs to the lungless salamander family, and the Southeast is loaded with these as well as many other salamanders from many other families. A full two-thirds of all salamander species—439 out of 654 species, according to Amphibiaweb—belong to this unique and ancient group, which has its diversity centered in the South and probably arose here. They are distributed mostly in North America, nearly anywhere it is wet enough for forests, and they have diversified impressively into tropical rain forests as far south as South America. They are significant members of the vertebrate fauna of deciduous forests. In a New Hampshire forest, Thomas Burton and Eugene Likens found that individuals of a single species of lungless salamander— the redback salamander, *Plethodon cinereus* (a relative of Webster's salamander)—outweighed perching birds and small mammals in terms of biomass. There are literally tons of redback salamanders in this forest type, hidden away below the forest floor, unseen. These have an enormous influence on the "brown world" food web on the forest floor: they feed on the millions of tiny invertebrates that in turn feed on decomposers. This impacts the kinds of fungi that churn up the leaf litter of deciduous forests.

It's hard to say exactly why there are so many of these salamanders in the South, but the temperate climate with lots of rainfall seems to favor the kind of moist, cool habitats lungless salamanders love. However, a small number of isolated species of lungless salamanders were long known to occupy caves in a small region of Mediterranean Europe, suggesting an ancient biogeographic connection. The Mediterranean lungless salamanders are most similar to a small group of crevice-dwelling salamanders in California, indicating that they once spread west through Asia and not east through Europe.

Such a connection is entirely plausible given the ancient distribution of plants in the Northern Hemisphere, and the fact that a land bridge between Asia and North America has been available a few times in ancient history (a more recent land connection enabled Native Americans to populate the Western Hemisphere some twenty thousand years ago). The distribution of some genera of plants, and some animals, proves that an extensive and diverse temperate forest once stretched unbroken from Eurasia to North America, as we learned in chapter 2. Examples of plants that show this distribution are of course numerous, but some animals, such as hellbenders and alligators, also have their sole representatives in the eastern United States and China. For some reason, China has many more representatives of the ancient plant groups (for example, China has hundreds of species of rhododendrons and azaleas, and the United States has only about twenty), while in North America it was the salamanders that diversified and survived. In Asia they did not. Or at least that's what everyone thought.

The leading expert in the biology of salamanders—David Wake of Berkeley—once predicted half-jokingly in his classes that a lungless salamander would eventually be found in Asia. He thought that one was just waiting to be discovered somewhere in the former USSR. There really had to be one; the bizarre distribution of lungless salamanders meant that at one time in the ancient past, salamanders were once more widely distributed throughout the Northern Hemisphere, and surely somewhere in Asia a relict population had to still be around.

Once, one of Wake's graduate students played the ultimate practical joke: he sent him a crummy specimen of a California crevice salamander—the American species most similar to the European ones—complete with fake Soviet diplomatic papers, from a supposed location in Kazakhstan. Wake once told me he recognized the individual specimen and immediately detected the ruse. But some say the cat wasn't let out of the bag until he had written a draft of the formal description of the species as the world's first Asian lungless salamander, which was intended for the most prestigious scientific journal in the world: *Nature*. Supposedly, Wake was actually crushed.

These salamanders do seem to turn up, almost magically, in the most unexpected places. On a hillside in southern Alabama in 1959, a snail biologist was looking for—well, snails—when he found a large and unusual-looking salamander. He gave the specimen to Richard Highton, the leading expert on salamanders of the genus *Plethodon*—the group Webster's salamander belongs to. Highton described the snail biologist's salamander as an entirely new *genus* of salamander, *Phaeognathus hubrichti*, after its discoverer, Leslie Hubricht, and it turned out to be one of the largest lungless salamanders in the world. How such a large salamander could be overlooked for so long became clear to those who sought additional specimens, which went uncollected for years. *Phaeognathus hubrichti*, the Red Hills salamander, is a burrower and rarely leaves the small holes it peers out of. The chances of Hubricht finding one outside its burrow at all were astronomically low, and this species could easily have been overlooked for several more decades. This remarkable salamander lives in mesic ravines in the Red Hills of southern Alabama, and nowhere else. It is a federally endangered species.

This discovery was trumped in 2004 by a schoolteacher. Mr. Karsen learned how to look for and identify lungless salamanders from a college biology course. One day he took his class out to poke around the woods near his school. He searched the way most American herpetologists do, by flipping over rocks and logs. He was surprised to find a small terrestrial salamander, complete with the hallmark field feature that readily distinguishes lungless salamanders from all others: a groove between the nostril and lip. He immediately knew this was a sensational find because, as we have just learned, lungless salamanders had long been known only from North America, the tropical forests of Central and northern South America, and a small region in Mediterranean Europe.

But Mr. Karsen was an English teacher, and the school was in South Korea.

Mr. Karsen sent some specimens to salamander expert David Wake, who overcame his initial skepticism and described the salamander as *Karsenia* after the teacher. The last time *Karsenia koreana* shared a biogeographic connection with its American relatives, dinosaurs were still around. Finding the first lungless salamander in Asia was the biogeographic equivalent of discovering a new species of tiger in Virginia. The paper ("Discovery of the First Asian Lungless Salamander") appeared in the prestigious journal *Nature*.

These salamanders were sensational finds so different from other species that they were quickly recognized as such after their discovery. Both required a brand-new genus to be recognized, and both are still the sole members of their genus. They appear to be ancient remnants, early offshoots of the salamander family tree that managed to survive in small outposts along the ancient range of the lungless salamanders, which once included the Eocene forest. The Korean lungless salamander bridged a substantial gap—sixteen thousand miles—in the world distribution of lungless salamanders, leaving two much smaller gaps (now only eight thousand miles) to fill.

Another reason lungless salamanders are so numerous in the United States, or at least the reason the number of species keeps going up, is that scientists have been carving new species out of old ones. They separate unique populations from what we used to think was a single, widespread species.

Sometimes these new species are not really that different physically from the species they were split from. In fact, sometimes they're impossible to distinguish. The number of lungless salamanders known to science has jumped significantly in the past thirty years, and not just from folks discovering obviously new species in far-flung localities like Korea or Alabama.

Many new species have been recognized and described not from their unique physical features, but from their unique genes. One of the first of these "cryptic species" that was described based on molecular information alone—these are species that are genetically unique, but quite similar to their close relatives physically—was Webster's salamander, *Plethodon websteri*, our salamander from Kennesaw Mountain. This salamander is only about two inches long, including the tail, and usually has a zigzagging orange, red, or yellow stripe down its back. They are fairly skinny as salamanders go, and the belly is made up of gray flecks with a wash of orange. The story of how this salamander was discovered is similar to that of many other salamanders belonging to its genus: the first person to notice its distinctiveness wasn't an expert on salamanders, and the describer of the species was Dick Highton.

Highton wasn't necessarily interested in naming new salamander species when he began work on *Plethodon*, although in the end he certainly didn't shy away from doing this. He is nearly single-handedly responsible for doubling the number of known lungless salamanders in the eastern United States in the past thirty years. Originally Highton was interested in how salamander proteins varied geographically, but during his collection trips he would collect any *Plethodon* species he encountered. He eventually accumulated one of the largest collections of salamanders in North America, made up of dozens of individuals from hundreds of populations.

In 1972 Highton received a letter from Preston Webster, a promising young molecular biologist who was also interested in redback salamanders. Webster had discovered some interesting chromosomal patterns in some redback salamanders he had found near Harvard, where he was working on his PhD on an entirely different topic. Webster was doing cutting-edge research using a brand-new technique, and his former adviser proudly asserted that Webster "learned it faster than anyone else in the lab."

Webster could identify different forms of the same genes that lead to protein formation—so-called allozymes—using the most sophisticated technique of that time: starch gel electrophoresis. After a poor salamander was homogenized with a kind of blender, a slurry of salamander proteins could be inserted into a gooey gel, and after an electric current was passed through it, the proteins were dragged along the gel according to their size and formed distinct bands that could be compared and analyzed. Webster wasn't a complete "lab nerd" or "gel jock," though. These are disparaging names field biologists give to molecular biologists who spend too much time in the lab and wouldn't know how to recognize their study animals even if they found them. Instead, Highton told me that "Webster was a good collector." They went on a collection trip together from May 15 to 17, 1974. They collected hundreds of individuals of several species in the Southern Appalachians.

Highton hired Webster to work in the lab on his massive collection of salamanders, and to teach his other grad students the new technique. Webster used the opportunity to continue working on the genetic puzzles he was interested in, which involved linkage disequilibrium (I will spare the reader an explanation of what this is). But when Webster began analyzing the series of zigzag salamanders that Highton collected throughout the South, he was stunned by what he found.

Zigzag salamanders (formerly *Plethodon dorsalis*) are named for the wavy orange-red stripe on their backs (similar to the Webster's salamander), and at that time they were understood to occur in a large area centered on the Cumberland Plateau, with small, isolated populations in the Ozarks and the South. The isolated southern populations Highton had sampled, including a series collected from Kennesaw Mountain in 1974, had completely different proteins than those collected from the populations centered near Kentucky. In fact, the proteins of these populations were as different from each other as the proteins of tigers are from lions. However, *within* the northern and southern populations, the proteins were similar to each other—the hallmark of an interbreeding population.

After his rotation in Highton's lab, Webster took a faculty job at the University of Montana. In 1975 he was on his way back from watching bald eagles feeding on spawning salmon with a couple of other faculty members when he fell asleep at the wheel. He and another passenger were killed. Preston Webster was only twenty-eight years old.

Highton later received all the allozyme data Webster had been working on from Preston's girlfriend in Montana. When Highton looked over his work he found that none of the data he was generating would have helped with Webster's study. Sadly, the entire time he was working in Highton's lab, Webster's own project was failing, although he never mentioned this to Highton. Webster may never have known that he had stumbled onto some very important work. Webster had discovered a new species of salamander, but not by turning over a rock. Instead, he had inadvertently discovered it by grinding it up and analyzing its proteins. Highton described the southern populations of zigzag salamanders as *Plethodon websteri* in 1979, in his friend's honor.

These salamanders presented a remarkable problem: two identical salamanders, once considered the same species, occurred in the same region and could be told apart only by using electrophorcsis. The selling point for skeptics was that Highton was eventually able to show that both species do look different when they occur in the same place. Small *Plethodon* species show an interesting range of variation in how frequently they exhibit a stripe; some populations are stripeless, others all have stripes, and still others can be mixed. The reason for this is still not well understood. But in one location in Alabama, zigzag salamanders and Webster's salamanders occur together, and at this site, each individual is either striped or not. In the one place where both species co-occur, they are distinct. I have heard old-school herpetologists deride Webster's salamander as "*Plethodon blenderi*" and refer to a cryptic species as a "Highton species." Many are still reluctant to believe in a species they can't see. But when the two types occur together they are different, and you can tell them apart. This is the hallmark of two similar, co-occurring species. When found apart, two similar species can show some overlap in physical features. When found together, usually because of competition for similar resources, they will become more different to reduce competition.

The reason this salamander remained physically similar to its relatives is the tendency of lungless salamanders to remain physically conservative while diverging quite a lot genetically. This is called evolutionary stasis. Berkeley's David Wake pointed out how similar the Asian lungless salamander *Karsenia* is to eastern US *Plethodon* species. Despite being isolated on the Korean Peninsula since the time when dinosaurs terrorized the earth, they haven't changed much.

The real evolutionary innovations of these salamanders would be obvious if we could see salamanders through their eyes or, as it were, through their noses. According to Lynne Houck and Stevan J. Arnold, the courtship sequence of all lungless salamanders (such as the naughty description from the beginning of the chapter) appears to be remarkably similar, and all species include similar features, such as the tail-straddle walk, during courtship. The courtship rituals of lungless salamanders involve the stereotyped dances I've described, as well as sophisticated pheromone drugging by males and possibly countermeasures developed by females to keep a level playing field. These pheromones are conducted to the brain via the distinctive nasolabial groove that defines the lungless salamander family. If we knew the full extent of the battle between the sexes in lungless salamanders, their distinctiveness might become as obvious as the differences between painted and indigo buntings.

In almost every kind of *Plethodon* he sampled, Highton found genetic differences, and finding new cryptic species "happened over and over." Using allozymes and electrophoresis, Highton began describing unique salamander populations all over the United States as new species, most notably carving thirteen species out of what used to be only one kind of slimy salamander. In this case there was no corroborating evidence of morphological character displacement between the populations, and the protein data were to speak for themselves. There are now seven recognized slimy salamanders in Georgia. The one that occurs on Kennesaw Mountain retained its original name, *Plethodon glutinosus*. There are now four species carved from what was once a single zigzag salamander, one of which is the Webster's salamander. The culmination of all of this was the description of a new ravine salamander—in this case one split off a previous split—into the new salamander species *Plethodon electromorphus*, named in honor of the technique that enabled Highton to recognize it.

This trend isn't peculiar to salamanders. Taxonomists in every subdiscipline of zoology have used cutting-edge genetic data to discover and name cryptic species, and field guides have struggled to keep pace. With birds it seems most of the subspecies recognized by earlier scientists were indeed local variants, or worse, simply the ends of geographic extremes in morphological measurements used by overzealous museum scientists to name new forms. Many of the new bird species named in the past thirty years were not simply erected from what was previously a subspecies; we now recognize the eastern towhee, a common resident in forest edges of the park that is different from the spotted towhee found out West, which was once considered the same species. Previously, there were four named subspecies of eastern towhees and some half dozen western ones, none of which are genetically distinct, so only two new species were needed to resolve this mess of names. All of this splitting and lumping of species contributes to the consternation of lay naturalists who have to make sense of it all, but what we have gained is a realistic and evolutionary basis for the taxonomy, which is truly worthwhile.

In an attempt to further explain his splitting spree, Highton wrote an influential paper ("Speciation in Eastern North American Salamanders of the Genus *Plethodon*") about the evolution of *Plethodon* in the eastern United States. His explanation for the diversity of these salamanders harked back to the ancient history of the eastern United States: as dwellers of deciduous forests, each previously widespread representative of the major groups of *Plethodon* diversified as the forests fragmented during the arid conditions of the Pliocene (two to four million years ago). Further diversification occurred during the last ice ages (twenty thousand to two million years ago). Highton indicated that Webster's salamander was the most ancient representative of its species group and possibly last shared an ancestor with other salamanders four million years ago. Subsequent genetic research has supported his hunch.

Considering this and the current distribution of Webster's salamander, it appears that this species of small *Plethodon* is indeed quite ancient. The Webster's salamander has one of the most bizarre distributions of any salamander. It is found in isolated pockets: one in South Carolina, one in Louisiana, a few in Mississippi, one in southern Alabama, and a large core region in eastern Alabama and western Georgia. But this core area is not really as big as it seems; thorough searches in western Georgia reveal that these salamanders are found in only three isolated pockets in Georgia as well: Taylor's Ridge in northwestern Georgia, the Pine Mountain ridges near Calloway Gardens, and Kennesaw Mountain.

Presumably, Webster's salamander once occurred throughout the South, but something forced it to retreat into these relictual pockets. Similar distributions have been found in *Plethodon* salamanders of the West, but in this case the explanation is easy: they occur in forests that became isolated on mountaintops during ancient climate changes. As the climate became hotter and drier after an ice age, wet coniferous forests retreated up the mountain peaks, and salamanders along with many other species became isolated with them on these mountaintops. This is how two lungless salamander species ended up in New Mexico; they are isolated in cool evergreen forests of the Jemez and Sacramento Mountains, separated from their nearest relatives by hundreds of miles of uninhabitable desert.

But with Webster's salamander, there is really no rhyme or reason, no distinctive habitat common to their homes that can't be found elsewhere. The eastern deciduous forests are supposed to be a big, uniform ecosystem and don't show the well-defined life zones you see out West. Available books will tell you Webster's salamanders are found in moist ravines. But I've found them atop rocky knobs in dry forests with longleaf pine and yucca. Many will say they need lots of loose rock, but I've found them in the sandy loess hills of Mississippi. Forests seem to be a prerequisite, but they have even turned up in old fields adjacent to perfectly suitable slope forests in southern Alabama. Given this apparent lack of scruples, why isn't the Webster's salamander found everywhere? Why isn't it found in forests between Kennesaw Mountain and Taylor's Ridge? For that matter, why isn't it found throughout the Southeast?

Part of the reason may be its relative, the southern redback salamander. The southern redback appears to replace Webster's salamander in western Georgia and literally surrounds it on Kennesaw Mountain. Carlos Camp's studies of small *Plethodon* species show they are highly territorial, fighting and biting their neighbors over their modest retreats. Where two similarly sized species occur together, the more aggressive species soon becomes dominant and can replace the timid one. Competition between Webster's salamander and the southern redback has never been studied, but Camp showed that males of both species will duke it out with each other. These aggressive encounters include impressive body slams and disrespectful threatening tail wiggles. Perhaps when the two species co-occur, as they do near Kennesaw Mountain, things sometimes get nasty.

The mostly nonoverlapping ranges of the southern redback and Webster's salamander suggest that these species may hate each other, and this may explain the bizarre distributional patterns of both species. In fact, this may be an ongoing war that is far from resolved. At Kennesaw, Webster's salamanders occupy the high ground, and southern redbacks encircle them at the bottom of the mountain like so many federal troops. At Pine Mountain near Columbus, this pattern is reversed; southern redbacks are for the most part restricted to the ridge's highest point, Dowdell's Knob, and otherwise this region is a stronghold for *websteri*. Southern redbacks inexplicably honor the Georgia-Alabama border and are exceedingly rare in Alabama's *websteri*-rich Piedmont region. They have turned up in only one small area in Alabama, encircling Coldwater Mountain near Anniston, which is loaded with Webster's salamanders. It's as if these two salamanders are involved in a salamander civil war, defending strategic heights for regional dominance like the blue and the gray.

This may be true in part, but by itself competitive exclusion cannot explain the rest of the bizarre distribution of both species, especially their far-flung outposts in places as far away as Louisiana and South Carolina. Both species also appear to be contending with the historical climatic forces that Highton proposed, which typify the distributional patterns of many lungless salamanders.

Outposts occupied by Webster's salamanders also happen to be sites well known for harboring relict plant species. In Louisiana, Webster's salamanders are found in the Tunica Hills, an area known for a number of rare plants found nowhere else in that state, species usually found much farther north, in the Southern Appalachians. In South Carolina, the salamander is found at the Steven's Creek Heritage Preserve, known for dozens of rare plants and numerous plants usually found in the mountains. Southern Alabama's *websteri* site is in the Red Hills, known for disjunct populations of plants usually found much farther north, and of course the bizarre Red Hills salamander. Kennesaw too has some of these plants with more northern affinities—plants more at home in the Blue Ridge Mountains of North Georgia—such as maidenhair fern, doll's eyes, black bugbane, goat's beard, foamflower, and bay star-vine.

   While at first glance the Webster's salamander does not seem to be picky about where it lives, closer scrutiny reveals that it may be hanging on in tiny remnants of the most ancient forests of the Southeast, areas that have been spared intensive logging as well as much of the steady drying and cooling of the past four million years. Like other ancient lungless salamanders that are stranded in much more obvious colonies, Webster's salamanders appear to be ancient relicts of a wetter and cooler time. The eastern deciduous forest—at first glance so uniform—may in reality have more texture and history than we can easily perceive, and this little salamander may be able to teach us this history.

   Kennesaw Mountain, which protrudes just high enough from the Piedmont hills, acquiring just enough moisture from low clouds and having rock crevices just deep enough to serve as retreats during the hot, drought-prone summers, is one of the ancient garrisons of Webster's salamander.

# 7

# Copperheads

Northern "Copperheads" caused all kinds of problems for the war effort, and the name was not supposed to be flattering. The most notorious Copperhead, or antiwar Democrat, was Ohio congressman Clement Vallandigham, who openly defied a decree that outlawed speaking out against the war—by speaking out against the decree. He was sentenced to live out the rest of the war in prison for this minor offense, but Lincoln commuted his sentence and instead exiled him to the South. The South didn't want Vallandigham either, so he found his way to Canada, where he ran in absentia for governor of Ohio. He lost. During the election year of 1864—when Sherman made his way down to Atlanta and made his frontal attack at Kennesaw Mountain—Vallandigham vied for the presidential nomination on the Democratic ticket. Instead the Democrats nominated former Union general George B. McClellan, who lost the election, in part because of Sherman's success at the doors of Atlanta during the summer and fall of 1864. After the war, Vallandigham was unable to regain his congressional seat, so the old Copperhead returned to

Figure 8. The copperhead is among the most common snakes in the Atlanta area. Photo by Noah K. Fields.

his former cold-blooded occupation—practicing law. He shot himself by accident while demonstrating how his client's alleged victim could have accidentally shot himself while getting up and drawing his handgun. He died from this self-inflicted wound, but the demonstration worked; his client was later exonerated.

Meanwhile, copperheads—their venomous namesake—have remained one of the most common snakes in the eastern United States, living out their lives deep inside human-infested territory throughout the South. Copperheads are also among the most populous snakes in the Atlanta area as well as within the Kennesaw Mountain National Battlefield Park. If you've hiked the trails on Kennesaw, you've most likely walked within a few feet of one and never knew it. And that's exactly the way the secretive copperheads want it.

Copperheads are experts at avoiding detection and have some of the best camouflage of any North American animal. The copperhead's skin pattern—a pretty series of gray, pink, brown, and orange bands that are narrow at the spine and wider toward the sides—gives it the appropriate nickname "ol' saddlebags." Copperheads blend in seamlessly among the fallen leaves of a deciduous forest, and when they are partially buried within the leaf litter, lying perfectly still, they are virtually invisible. During the day they lie in the leaf litter, often in thick second-growth forests, and wait for prey to come to them. Like ninjas, they avoid detection by their enemies and their victims by lying still and blending in.

When a hapless creature ambles within striking distance, the copperhead perceives its presence using a sophisticated blend of senses: thermo-visual imagery, and a sort of taste-smell using its tongue. Copperheads are pit vipers, so called by virtue of the pit that can easily be observed between the eye and the nostril of the snake. A thin membrane enriched with capillaries and sensory neurons is suspended within the pit. The neurons can determine tiny differences in temperature between the capillary bed and the outside air. The unique structure and orientation of the pit organ enables pit vipers to sense the presence of something that is slightly warmer (or colder) than the environment, and the nerves serving the pit send this information to the same area of the brain where visual information is processed. There, cues from the eyes and facial pit are processed together, producing an overlapping image, exactly like the alien from the Schwarzenegger movie *Predator*.

All snakes and some lizards also have a thinly forked tongue that is used for "smelling." People have two ways to sense chemicals: we can smell airborne particles with our noses, or we can taste surface substances with our tongues. Since humans are heavily visually oriented, our abilities to use both of these sensory organs are rather limited compared to many other animals.

Compared to those of snakes, our chemoreceptive capabilities are a joke. By contrast, copperheads use their forked tongue like a reptilian bloodhound to track their prey and keep tabs on each other. Since the tongue is forked, the snake is able to sense tiny chemical differences from each side of the tongue. In this way, a copperhead can tell in which direction a meal or a mate went. The tongue is also used to set up ambush sites. A copperhead will flick its tongue about, tasting the air and the ground, smelling scent trails left by tiny critters. When the copperhead finds a path frequented by these animals—which is otherwise entirely invisible to the human eye or nose—it slowly coils next to it and deploys its characteristic S-shaped ambush coil perpendicular to the trail. Then it waits. It can wait for weeks for a meal to come within reach because its metabolism requires a fraction of the calories of a similarly sized mammal or bird. It burns no calories to maintain a constant body temperature and instead allows its core temperature to passively mirror that of the outside air.

When the prey comes within striking distance, in a split second the snake straightens the S shape of its neck, opens its mouth wide, and the paired fangs in the front of its mouth flash erect. The snake usually bites the prey behind the shoulder, preferentially injecting venom into the chest cavity.

After a copperhead strikes its prey, it lets go and lets the venom do its work. That's what the venom is for. It's not really to defend the snake, although the snake will certainly use it for that secondary purpose if it is attacked. Venom is primarily the way a snake subjugates its prey and begins the process of digestion. By the time the snake finds its victim, it has been tenderized by the potent cocktail of enzymes in the venom.

The copperhead is a sniper. It lies in wait, and as prey passes, with lightning speed it strikes and injects venom. The victim then hops or runs away, often several yards, before the venom finishes it off. The copperhead uses its tongue to find the victim; evidence suggests that pit vipers can tell the difference between an envenomated mouse and one that hasn't been bitten. The venom contains some sort of tracer that allows it to tag and later find its prey.

Despite their bad reputation (which I have not, until now, done anything to repair), copperheads are rather docile and are reluctant to give away their strategic ambush positions. If you walk past one, it is liable to sit still and let you walk by. You could probably step on one and it wouldn't bite, and even if it did, you'd probably be OK since it is a fairly small snake with fairly small fangs. It is unlikely that it would be able to bite you through a pair of hiking shoes. In any event, copperheads have the least potent venom of any North American pit viper. Although copperheads are responsible for the highest number of snake bites annually in the United States (mostly because they are found in some of the most heavily populated regions of the country), they are responsible for very few deaths. And like every pit viper I've ever met, when approached, nine out of ten copperheads try to get away from you rather than stand their ground.

However, when I have approached and cornered copperheads on roads at night, I have found some to be determined fighters. It is most easy to find copperheads at night, and the best way to do so is to drive around on low-traffic roads with your high beams on. Then you will discover how common copperheads are. Copperheads move at night, perhaps from one ambush spot to another, perhaps in pursuit of mates, or perhaps to come onto a warm road surface for a while. At this time they betray their presence, and this is probably when Atlanta-area copperheads are most often killed. Not too long ago I saw a road-killed copperhead on Clifton Road within the city limits of Atlanta.

At night copperheads will sometimes stand their ground and viciously attack and strike the tongs I use to move them off the road. One struck multiple times with enough enthusiasm to practically lift itself off the pavement. With each strike it moved an inch toward me. But these were defensive measures. If you experience grumpy copperheads like this, you're most likely asking for it. So don't ask for it. If you find a copperhead, leave it alone, and it will leave you alone.

Along with their camouflage, cryptic behavior, and a general reluctance to fight, copperheads have a few more ingenious tricks that have allowed them to remain common in the suburban landscapes of the eastern United States. They have rather variable diets and will eat nearly anything they find living on the forest floor, from small mammals and lizards to caterpillars. This dangerously venomous snake seems to be surprisingly fond of the latter, and I once found a couple of dozen fat sphinx moth caterpillars in the belly of a copperhead. These were certainly not killed during ambush, indicating that—sometimes at least—copperheads will actively seek out and consume certain prey. Snakes with more restricted dietary requirements, or those whose dietary requirements cannot be met within a developed landscape, cannot persist so easily.

Copperheads also have small home ranges and can make do in fragmented second-growth forests. Since copperheads are immobile most of the time, they don't need that much space to live out their lives. Snakes that move around a lot need more space and are quickly eliminated in heavily fragmented landscapes, mostly by cars when they are moving from one patch of woods to another. It could be that copperheads surviving in urban and suburban landscapes move even less than their counterparts out in the boonies, but determining this would require a detailed study. It's just as likely that copperheads have smaller home ranges than other snakes, and that's why they are among the most successful city snakes.

A few other snakes have managed to persist in the metro Atlanta area, and some do even better than the copperhead. Dekay's brown snakes (which are harmless) are probably the most common city snake in Atlanta and need only a backyard garden or vacant lot to make do. This is mostly because they are so small—large adult females are only about a foot long and as skinny as my pinky finger—and they eat worms and slugs. Likewise, garter snakes, which will eat almost anything, can hold on in neighborhoods as long as there is plenty of vegetation. Rat snakes can even make it as long as there are trees around (they like to climb trees to eat birds and their eggs), and they turn up in some of the older neighborhoods in Atlanta near Grant Park. All of these snakes and a fair few more are also found within Kennesaw Mountain National Battlefield Park. But most of the other venomous species found throughout Georgia are conspicuously absent from the metro Atlanta area. Cottonmouths are found in some Southside swamps that most people would never dare venture into. Timber rattlesnakes—a very large, dangerous, and conspicuous species—require special protected areas where they can avoid the wrath of people. They've been wiped out by 150 years of continual occupation by snake haters in the metro Atlanta region.

With all of their solitary hunting—scattered throughout the forest floor, hiding—you may be tempted to assume that copperheads have a rather dull social life. In fact, that's fair. Compared to most birds, anyway, the social lives of copperheads are pretty uneventful. Even compared to lizards—which can have colorful badges and male posturing, and social systems not too dissimilar to those of birds—snakes in general are social misfits. They're loners. But when it comes to finding mates, courtship, and mating, copperheads are exciting to watch, and their strangeness adds a dash of mystery—if you can find some to watch.

Because of their reclusive nature, snake behavior is one of the most difficult things to study. There can be hundreds of snakes in a patch of woods, and you'll never see them. This is partly because they're so hard to see, and partly because they spend almost all their time hiding in some crevice, tunnel, or burrow. When you do find them, or when you find a place where you can find many individual snakes at a time, they usually see you before you see them. And they don't like to be seen. Unlike birds and lizards, which can be observed carrying on normal behaviors from a distance, snakes freak out and try to escape the moment they're found. Or they can remain motionless for weeks, waiting for prey to come by, boring their observer to tears, doing nothing interesting at all.

One way to overcome this is to catch a bunch of snakes and bring them into captivity. But now you've got new problems. Laboratory observations are very difficult because snakes do not like to be in captivity. If they see you watching them, they don't behave normally. Laboratory observers have to resort to extreme measures to hide themselves from the unblinking eyes of their wary snake subjects. Most of what we know about snake behavior has been derived from the steady accumulation of chance observations in the field, and a couple of very meticulous studies using habituated, captive snakes. Some of the most fascinating studies involving the love lives of snakes were conducted with copperheads by my former graduate adviser at Georgia State University, Gordon Schuett. But first, some background.

Chance observations of snakes by early naturalists led to the misconception that many snakes, especially pit vipers, take part in courtship "dances," in which males and females wrap their necks and upper bodies around each other lovingly before mating. This misconception underscores yet another drawback to studying snake behavior: males and females of most species are difficult to tell apart. Male and female snakes are usually not different in color pattern like most birds are. A lot of snakes differ substantially in size between the sexes, but when two snakes are intertwined and jerkily moving around each other, it's hard to tell who is who and what the hell is going on. So, we will forgive the early naturalists who assumed that such snakes were mating and instead note that, as more detailed reports trickled in (summarized by David Duvall and colleagues), it became apparent that the snakes taking part in these sexy dances were both males.

Detailed observations (summarized in a book by Howard Gloyd and Roger Conant) have shown that mating males and female copperheads are instead confined to the ground. A female is usually found with an accompanying male after she sheds her skin, as if she has just undressed. The freshness of her new skin is flush with a musky perfume that is irresistible to the male and indicates her willingness to mate. The male alertly flicks his tongue and snout-rubs the female along her back, nudging her tenderly while passionately jerking his head. The female usually remains motionless. Courtship can last hours, and the female sometimes tries to avoid males by slithering away. When she is willing to accept him, she arches her tail up in the air and offers her cloaca.

So, if that's what lovemaking is like in snakes, what's the deal with the dancing males? Once it was realized that the dances were undertaken by males and not mating couples, it was assumed that this must be some sort of contest to gain access to females. The "dances" became categorized as aggressive encounters and are now referred to as male-male combat. Several observations of a female third party in the vicinity of dancing males indicated that two males must be fighting over a female. But all of this was mere speculation until Schuett devised his series of experiments with copperheads. He staged male combat in captivity, took careful notes of the results, and knew which snake was which by virtue of the big numbers he wrote on their backs with a marker. He took blood samples periodically so he could measure hormones in the snakes' blood. And after males fought, he allowed the winner and loser of the fight access to a receptive female.

The results were incredible. First of all, a clear winner usually emerges from combat, and this winner is almost always the bigger of the two snakes. When the two snakes first come into contact, they briefly raise their necks off the ground and face off, snout to snout, as if to size each other up. After coiling their necks around each other, the bigger snake usually gains an advantage in elevation and pushes the other snake down to the ground. This is called "topping," but what this really is—almost—is arm wrestling, given that snakes don't have arms. Once the smaller male is toppled a few times, he seems to realize that he has lost and tries to get away. The winner then chases him away from the scene. The hormone results showed that the loser has high levels of a stress hormone compared to the winner, and this hormone remains elevated for hours. During this period of high stress, loser males will lose all subsequent fights, even if pitted against a smaller male.

When males are introduced to a female after a fight, something very strange happens. She raises her head up and squares off with the male, just as in the beginning of the combat sequence between males. If a male has just lost a fight with another male, he frantically slithers away after she challenges him. If the male is a winner, he confidently accepts her challenge and assumes the same raised-neck posture. She then lowers her head back down submissively, and he begins courtship.

This winner-loser effect has been documented in other kinds of animals, including humans. Have you ever noticed how bad you feel after losing a ball game? Studies have shown that winners have different hormone levels than losers after human contests, too.

Schuett concluded that the drastic winner-loser effect experienced by copperheads is exploited by females to determine male quality. It is hard to say exactly what is going on here, but when a losing male approaches a female, he may not know quite what he's dealing with yet. It is possible that at such a range he doesn't yet know she's a girl. I certainly wouldn't be able to tell. So, if she threatens a male who has just lost a fight, he may be fooled into thinking she's a male getting ready to fight. By doing this she may be able to tell that he's a loser and chase him off. A winner will behave differently, so she can tell he's among the bigger, more successful males and mate with him.

When venomous snakes fight over females, they have potent weaponry at their disposal that could potentially escalate their combat activities. But it is as though long ago some sort of evolutionary truce was forged between male venomous snakes. Using venom during ritualistic combat must be taboo, because males that bit each other during combat would have long ago taken themselves out of the breeding pool. According to Rick Shine, biting is not usually observed during combat bouts between venomous species. But some habits die hard.

Recall that our understanding of snake behavior relies on a steady accumulation of chance observations, along with some select, meticulous lab studies. I am not a very good experimental biologist, and so I'm very impressed with Gordon Schuett's patient lab work. Instead, I am way better at getting out in the field and stumbling onto chance observations. Giff Beaton—a crack naturalist, bird expert, and Kennesaw Mountain frequenter (you will make his acquaintance in later chapters)—is even better at this than I am. On September 27, 2007, Giff and some other hikers found a pair of copperheads near the summit of Big Kennesaw. In his field notes that day, he observed, "Coolest of all, saw two copperheads near the summit stairs. They had been reported as 'mating' (when I asked Ray he said they had been intertwined for a few minutes but that's all he could say) but when we got there they had separated. One had several recently bloodied wounds on its head, the other was uninjured."

Giff's companion on the mountain was Ray Kauffman, an avid hiker, a nature lover, and, as we shall soon see, a low-down copperhead sympathizer. He didn't see the fight either, but he heard from others who saw it that it lasted for something like forty-five minutes, and that "the snakes were intertwining and rising up and pushing each other." After talking with me about it years later, by some miracle Ray bumped into one of his old hiking buddies within a few days. Ray pressed him for details, and a witness who saw the fight with his own eyeballs said that the "two snakes had lifted about one-third of their bodies upward and were intertwined. They writhed in that position and occasionally dropped down and then went back up again." When Ray arrived, they had crawled away from each other into the grass patch behind the parking area near the summit of Big Kennesaw. Ray stood by for another thirty minutes. He told me he did this "because I didn't want anyone to bother them" and because "they seemed completely exhausted."

Thus, two remarkably rare occurrences took place on that crisp September afternoon. One, a pair of copperheads engaged in combat that escalated to biting. Two, and most improbably, somebody watched over them afterward to ensure their safety.

Most likely, two males of similar size fought an epic contest on Kennesaw Mountain that day, and it was witnessed by some lucky park visitors. Because they were of equal size, the fight continued for close to an hour and no clear winner emerged, so one of the males (I would like to guess it was the male on the verge of losing the fight) resorted to a cheap shot. From the photographs it is pretty clear that one of the copperheads was bitten by the other during this fight. Copperheads are not immune to their own venom. I know of at least one case where a copperhead bit another on the head and it resulted in death for the victim. It is possible that the loser of this fight (which may in fact have been the legitimate winner!) ended up more than just stressed out.

This sort of escalation might be expected in animals with such poor social and political skills as copperheads. In vertebrates with more frequent social interactions, these sorts of exchanges tend to be more refined and stereotyped. But, perhaps because of their reclusiveness, copperheads must trade highly organized social interactions for stealth. It seems to be working. The copperhead's camouflage and covert activities have made it one of the most adaptable snakes in the South, allowing it to continue its subversive campaign on Kennesaw Mountain.

# 8

# Unlikely Links in a Web of Interactions

IT IS HARDLY NECESSARY TO mention that everyone loves hummingbirds, and for good reason: they are beautiful, and they are utterly remarkable. Despite their tiny size, the list of hummingbird superlatives is long and places them among the upper echelon of the greatest vertebrates. They are the only vertebrates that can fly backward. They have the highest metabolic rate of any vertebrate, which they use to maintain their athletic flying, and as a direct result they have to consume more calories per body weight than any other vertebrate. Christopher Clark discovered that, adjusted for size, they're faster than peregrine falcons and Lockheed Martin's F-22 Raptor. The species that zips around Kennesaw Mountain also undertakes one of the longest and most energetically demanding migrations—adjusted for body size—of any vertebrate. Thanks to their greatness and innate charisma, most folks know a surprising amount about the natural history of whatever hummingbird species happens to live nearby. Most folks know they feed on flowers, and what kind of flowers

Figure 9. Ruby-throated hummingbird pollinating fire-pink. Photo by Giff Beaton.

they enjoy. They set up specific feeders to lure them and maintain fancy gardens to sweeten the proposition. Some folks set up *only* hummingbird feeders and could care less about sparrows, cardinals, and the inevitable hassle of gray squirrels. Not many other birds are so beloved.

During the late summer and fall, hummingbirds move through metro Atlanta, tanking up on the nectar of abundant plants like cardinal flower (*Lobelia cardinalis*) and trumpet creeper (*Campsis radicans*) and following their bloom times south to the edge of the Gulf Coast. Here, they stay a few weeks sipping as much nectar as possible, buzzing around Biloxi, Mobile, and Pensacola feeders, becoming as fat as a hummingbird can get. I've never seen such crowds of hummingbirds as I saw on Dauphin Island, Alabama, in late September. Since they require so much energy, they're not entirely reluctant to waste a little trying to monopolize feeders or flowers, and they stingily defend small territories around the most modest gardens, sometimes attempting to chase away much larger birds of other species. According to Lynn Carpenter and colleagues, hummingbirds gain about a tenth of an ounce (2 g) while fattening up for migration, the equivalent of an adult human doubling their body weight in two weeks. They then start forth over the waves, their tiny beaks turned toward the Yucatán Peninsula.

For a long time it was thought that ruby-throats did not undertake direct flights across the Gulf and instead curved south along the coast from Texas to Mexico. It was thought that there was no way a bird so small with such big requirements for food could fly for so long without feeding. But careful calculations by Robert Lasiewski revealed they can deposit just enough fat to pull it off. The flight can take eighteen hours, and by the next day they've landed in Mexico, where they feverishly begin feeding again to refuel. By scaling up the number of calories necessary to undertake this migration to human terms, we can arrive at the estimated number of McDonald's cheeseburgers you'd need to eat to do it yourself. For a human—22,500 times bigger than a hummer—you'd need 387,022,791 calories to make the crossing, assuming you could fly like a hummingbird. You'd need to eat 1,290,076 cheeseburgers.

Ruby-throats spend the winter in Mexico or the extreme south of Florida, where there are flowers and nectar year-round. Other hummingbird species are becoming more and more common as winter residents of Georgia, mostly thanks to the availability of nectar feeders left out over winter by hummingbird enthusiasts. The rufous hummingbird, which breeds high in the Rockies and Pacific Northwest as far north as Alaska, has become an uncommon but regular visitor to the South in winter. It has yet to be seen within Kennesaw Mountain National Battlefield Park, but keep your eyes peeled on your next winter visit.

If you've ever taken the time to observe hummingbirds feeding, you might have noticed they seem to like certain flowers, often red ones. Their preference for red flowers is so extreme that sometimes they'll fly close to investigate your head if you're wearing a red ball cap or bandanna. For a long time scientists thought maybe they had an innate, hard-wired preference for red, and this makes sense—many hummingbirds have bright red gorgets, chins, or foreheads, so obviously they can see the color red, and maybe they have some kind of instinctual obsession with the color. But experiments by Frank Bené determined that as long as vessels contain the kind of nectar that hummers like, the birds quickly learn to feed from containers of any color. In fact, you can make individual hummers switch color preferences if you lure them to feed from fake flowers with other colors. It turns out their apparent preference for red is learned. And the wonderful thing is, it's the flowers that taught them.

From antiquity, early naturalists noticed how flowers and their pollinators seemed to show complementary features, like a lock and key. Flowers develop features that mirror the behavior and features displayed by their visitors, because the flowers are advertising their presence to entice certain species. And since groups of pollinators often have their own distinctive sensory or behavioral proclivities, the flowers eventually gear themselves to them. This results in what is known as a pollination syndrome—a suite of features used by plants to lure certain pollinators—and each syndrome reflects the features of a discrete, influential pollinator group. Big nocturnal moths are important pollinators in some regions, and in these places you can find white flowers that open at night and have a heavy, sweet smell and copious quantities of concentrated nectar. This is known by the fancy term "sphingophily"—the hawkmoth flower syndrome. Certain plants are equipped for visits from massive, barging bumblebees and have pale white or blue flowers shaped like half-open tubes that bees can force open. Often these flowers have streaks inside them, like landing lights that indicate where the bee is supposed to go, because bees are receptive to such instructions. Inside, they get powdered with pollen. The large penstemons (*Penstemon laevigatus*) that line the road on the lower slopes of Kennesaw Mountain are good examples of this syndrome.

Ornithophilous flowers (popularly known as "bird flowers") are narrow, closed red tubes that dangle and have little or no scent and copious, dilute nectar. Dozens of American species have features consistent with this syndrome, but most occur in the western United States where there are more hummingbirds. A remarkable feature of pollination syndromes is that flowers in entirely unrelated groups become molded by their pollinators through coevolution; there are red flowers preferred by hummingbirds that at first glance appear quite similar but belong to some sixteen unrelated families throughout the Western Hemisphere. A careful evolutionary analysis (by Paul Wilson and colleagues) of bird flowers in a single genus in the Desert Southwest showed how these flowers developed from plants originally adapted for bee or moth attraction, so this adaptation can come about multiple times independently within the same group. The American tropics are filled with numerous bird flowers that show incredible contraptions for luring hummingbirds and dashing their foreheads with pollen. In other parts of the world where there are no hummingbirds, other birds take over the pollination duties. Instead, red flowers feed sunbirds in Africa and honeyeaters in Australia.

The Southeast has only a few species of bird flowers because there is only one breeding hummingbird, a fact that is very strange to me considering the bounty of plants in the South and the nice warm climate. This curious observation, along with the fact that the center of hummingbird diversity is in South America, implies that hummingbirds must have gotten to North America only recently, and the eastern United States even later. Still, at least five entirely unrelated species display the bird flower syndrome on Kennesaw Mountain alone.

When hummingbirds take nectar it is good for the flowers, too, so much so that flowers will devote a lot of their own energy to produce generous tanks of dilute, sugar-rich nectar. By doing this and by developing certain other adaptations, the plants themselves are showing a kind of preference, a preference for hummingbirds. They want the birds to come in, hover for a second, take some nectar, and get their faces covered with pollen. When the bird flies on to find another plant of the same species, the bird will effect cross-pollination when it dips its bill into the next flower. Cross-pollination is extremely important for many plants—perhaps most plants—and without it many species fail to reproduce, or reproduce much, much less. Frankly, the plants need the birds for sex.

Many plants don't show very obvious preferences for the kinds of animals they rely on for this reproductive transaction. They are promiscuous, producing a mixed bag of nectar or pollen for all comers to feed from. These are the asters and goldenrods of Kennesaw Mountain. Their flowers are wide open, with plenty of space for all kinds of bugs to land on them. When you examine them up close you'll see a crowd of strange insects shoving their way all over plant's reproductive parts: beetles gnawing on anthers; bugs inserting their sucking mouthparts into nectar spurs; flies, bees, bee flies, sawflies, hornets, wasps, ants, butterflies, and dozens of other kinds of insects piling over corollas. It's a mess, and it's a wonder that pollination ever occurs. But it makes sense; although it's messy (and probably costly, since many of the insects are just going to stay right there and feast on the flowers, stealing nectar, pollen, and ovaries without providing cross-pollination), with this many visitors, eventually one of them is going to move to another plant and provide cross-pollination.

During early spring on Kennesaw, waves of generalist pollinators vie for the pollen and nectar of the ephemeral wildflowers, which are each generalists themselves, allowing solitary bees, flies, bee flies, bumblebees, carpenter bees, and early butterflies of all sorts to visit them. These wildflowers impose little order on this floral orgy, and waves of hepaticas, rue anemones, Catesby's trillium, chickweeds, and trout lilies share many of the same pollinators. They have developed a few key adaptations to ensure that this disorderly procession results in their pollination. Most are white, and some give off ultraviolet reflectance, since the insects that visit them can see well in that edge of the color spectrum, even if human beings cannot. Some of the earliest bloomers, like hepatica and bloodroot, can't count on visits because it's still quite cold when they bloom, so they have the capacity to self-pollinate. They receive so few visits that they don't even produce nectar, just pollen and showy flowers that might lure some early bee into coming for a visit. Most early spring species have prolonged bloom times, and single flowers can stay receptive for over a week in case the weather is bad or nobody shows up. The diverse pollinators themselves—though messy and wasteful, spilling pollen among different species—ensure that somebody will come along eventually and transfer the pollen.

Other plants develop specializations for certain kinds of pollinators to guarantee more efficient pollination. This is risky, because if you become too specialized and your partner doesn't show up, reproduction fails and you're doomed. But at some point generalized networks of pollinators may start to exclude some species that don't get their share of pollination, and more specialized interactions develop. This is how pollination syndromes begin: when more specialized pollinators become available, formerly generalist flowers begin to develop adaptations that make them less available to the more common pollinators, and they become invaluable to the specialists. When they do this the plants gain very efficient and dependable pollination, and pollinators gain a food source they don't have to share. The plants remove themselves from the sloppy buffet of generalist pollination, and in fact they may begin to hide themselves from the other pollinators. The pollinators surreptitiously visit their special flowers, while more generalized pollinators are stymied.

Many of the adaptations of bird flowers are less about what a humming-bird likes than what the other visitors don't like. Hummingbirds can see in the red part of the visible spectrum, but they have to learn to prefer that color. Bees, butterflies, and other insects can't see red at all. In effect, these flowers are hiding and becoming camouflaged from those other pollinators, because red is the only color birds can see that insects can't. Other features are similar: the long nectar tube ensures that only birds with long beaks and long tongues can get to the nectar and still tap the stamens. The dangling flowers are inex-plicable to a bee that has been spoiled by the upright landing pads offered by most flowers. Hummingbirds have no problem with such a contraption and hover nimbly, turning their body and head to stab the flowers from below. Bird flowers don't usually have perfume, since most birds have a poor sense of smell. All of these features exclude bees and many other insects—which can be inefficient at transferring pollen and are often nectar thieves—while si-multaneously allowing hummingbirds complete access.

It is worth stopping here to mention that pollination is very much worth studying because it is one of the most important ecological interactions on the planet, if not the most important. It drives the generation of an unbeliev-able profusion of animal and plant diversity and assists the reproduction of thousands of plant species. And these pollinators are in trouble. Around the world, populations of pollinators of every stripe are in decline, the most fa-mous being honeybees, which have recently been added to the long list of animals whose populations are crashing for mysterious reasons. This cannot be ignored. It has direct implications for your standard of living, since a very large proportion of the food you eat relies on animal pollination. Those who don't think pollination is important should be forced to spend the rest of their lives eating nothing but corn, wheat, and the few other grains that are wind pollinated. No more strawberries for you. No more mangoes, avocados, po-tatoes, tomatoes, bell peppers, jalapeños, guavas, pumpkins, or beans. All of these fruits and vegetables, and many animal products as well, are produced through the reproductive assistance of billions of anonymous animals, duti-fully pollinating the plants for us free of charge. If we had to start doing the pollinating ourselves it would cost billions, and the cost of an onion would probably shoot to about $300.

Now that we've established that pollination is important, let's get back to the topic at hand: the nature of pollination networks. Ecologists studying plants have shown that in many cases plants have apparently never read an introduc-tory biology textbook and are not following the plan. Bird flowers allow trans-gressions by bees, and bee flowers apparently do not mind the occasional visit by hummingbirds. In fact, you couldn't ask for a more flexible pollinator than the ruby-throated hummingbird, which will fly among red flowers while darting in and out of white bee-flowered penstemons, butterfly-loving phloxes, sphingophilous spider lilies, and many others. So in many cases plants assumed to have very selective pollinator preferences are in fact not very choosy. And there are fewer examples of intense specialization that correspond directly with syndromes. However, one of these can be found on display each April on Kennesaw Mountain.

The plant is the gorgeous fire-pink, *Silene virginica*, which is a deep scarlet and not even remotely pink and grows on the slopes just down from the summit of Kennesaw Mountain. A good place to look for it is on the small section of trail along the saddle between Big and Little Kennesaw Mountain, just uphill from where the park road crosses it. This plant shows all the features consistent with the bird syndrome: bright red flowers, tilted corollas closed into narrow tubes (each of which hangs down), lots of dilute nectar, and no scent. Charles Fenster and Michele Dudash studied the interactions between fire-pink and ruby-throated hummingbirds and confirmed—by a series of ingenious field experiments—that fire-pink does indeed need hummingbirds, even if the birds don't absolutely need them in return. By enclosing some plants in cages that excluded all visitors, they found that seed production in fire-pink was massively reduced. By enclosing other plants in cages that would allow bees to enter (but not birds), they found the same thing. Only plants that received visits from the birds were effectively pollinated, resulting in reproductive success. In this particular case, the syndrome concept works beautifully.

It turns out that interacting communities of plants and their pollinators are neither completely generalized nor totally specialized. Instead, they are simultaneously both. Studies of entire networks of interacting species by Jordi Bascompte and colleagues have shown that they definitely have structure; they are not completely random sets of interacting species. However, this structure implies that neither completely generalized interactions nor one-to-one specialization dominates, but rather that there are nested subsets of interactions. There are usually generalists, it is true, and these generalists tend to interact with each other. So, you have large clouds of interactions between things like honeybees and daisies, spring wildflowers and solitary bees, and each of these generalist species interacts with more and more specialized species that have narrower and narrower feeding preferences. Within the clouds of generalists, there are specialist pollinators that select the generalist plants. There are also specialized plants that receive visits from generalist pollinators. Diagrams illustrating these interactions end up looking just like those network clouds representing your Facebook friends, and Jens Olesen and colleagues actually used social network analysis software to categorize networks of plants and pollinators. So, the specialized fire-pink developed since it is within the nested subset of plants that ruby-throats will visit. One-to-one interactions between two species that are both specialists are rare but do occur. The syndromes still apply, although they are now recognized to be much more complex and flexible. These nested subsets of interactions associated with very distinctive pollinators appear to coevolve and influence flower morphology in predictable ways, resulting in syndromes.

Another plant that has tubular red flowers and is frequently visited by ruby-throats in spring is the red buckeye, *Aesculus pavia*, a shrub or small tree found in floodplains and along moist slopes of rivers south of Atlanta, from Florida throughout the Coastal Plain from North Carolina to Texas, and up the Mississippi embayment to Illinois. Red buckeye flowers have no scent and a lot of dilute sucrose-rich nectar, similar to most bird flowers. The flowers are well timed to the arrival of hummingbirds; the flowers always appear a week or so before the birds do. The birds definitely visit the flowers, and so do bees, although for some reason both do so fairly infrequently; ecologist Robert Bertin observed only one visit every five hours or so. However, the birds moving along during migration feed most frequently on the flowers and almost certainly transfer pollen between plants.

On Kennesaw Mountain, there are no red buckeyes, but instead the forest subcanopy contains a close relative, the painted buckeye, *Aesculus sylvatica*. This species is found in upland habitats in the Piedmont from Virginia to Alabama. Elsewhere, this species has larger, more open flowers than red buckeye, and they are white, which is more consistent with bumblebee pollination. Claude DePamphilis and Robert Wyatt confirmed that they are visited by both bees and hummingbirds, but mostly by bees. They have a much lower volume of more concentrated nectar than red buckeye, consistent with bee pollination.

Something strange has happened to the buckeyes on Kennesaw. Here and elsewhere in the Georgia Piedmont their flowers are a kind of yellowish pink—colored like strawberry and banana yogurt—and they have different nectar characteristics than either red or painted buckeye. It turns out they are hybrids between the two. Genetic studies by David Thomas and colleagues confirmed their hybrid origin and showed that they are the result of pollen from red buckeye finding its way to painted buckeye. The curious thing is where these hybrids live: there are no hybrids within the range of red buckeye, and they are instead found entirely within the range of the more northerly distributed painted buckeye. This means that the pollen is being transferred from the south to the north. In fact, there are some three-way hybrids between red, painted, and yellow buckeye (*Aesculus flava*) in North Georgia. To get these, pollen from a red × painted buckeye hybrid had to be carried from the Piedmont and transferred to a yellow buckeye, a common tree of the Appalachians. In some cases the pollen must have been transferred scores of miles from the nearest population of red buckeye to have contaminated a population of painted buckeye. There is only one animal that could have done this.

The ruby-throated hummingbird, along with all of its other wonderful talents, has left its mark on two of the beautiful wildflowers of the mountain, by reliable pollination and unintentional hybridization. But the bird doesn't really seem to need these plants all that much, even though during the few weeks fire-pink is in bloom, ruby-throats will certainly seek it out. Another spring bird flower—red columbine (*Aquilegia canadensis*)—also occurs on the mountain and blooms around the same time as fire-pink. However, by the time fire-pink and red columbine are blooming, ruby-throats have been in the Kennesaw area for weeks. In fact, when ruby-throated hummingbirds begin to arrive in Georgia, there is hardly a bird flower to be found, with the single exception of the red buckeye. The woods are still bare and the ephemeral wildflowers are in bloom on the forest floor, offering their extravaganza for bee flies but scant food for a hungry hummingbird that requires copious sweet nectar. The red buckeye doesn't exactly seem up to the task either, since it is visited only once every five hours. It's not like the late summer and fall, when the ruby-throats are heading south to Mexico and enjoying hundreds of thousands of blossoms of common species like trumpet creeper and jewelweed. Unlike on their southward trip, when they aggressively tank up on the nectar of abundant flowers so they can fly across the Gulf to flowery Mexico, on their northward flight the ruby-throats arrive from the same trip when there is hardly a flower in sight. How do these little birds survive?

All of these interactions—the seemingly exquisite timing of blooming, the syndromes, the supermarkets of spring wildflowers and their bee consumers, the coevolutionary dances between plants and pollinators—may have left you with the impression that all of this occurs as part of some kind of natural plan, a beautiful, purposeful, and breathtaking cycle of life. Nothing could be further from the truth. Remember, none of these species are really *trying* to help one another. They are only helping themselves. The ruby-throated hummingbird has no idea it is transferring pollen from one fire-pink to another and ensuring pollination, or that more fire-pinks will be around next year to feed on. It will likely be dead the next year, and there is no guarantee its offspring will arrive either. It is only drinking nectar. The fire-pink, for its part, definitely has no idea a hummingbird is supposed to visit it, although in a way it knows it has been pollinated, since after pollination the flowers shrivel and the seeds become set. It just wants that pollen gone. It just wants sex, and for this it needs the bird's help.

A good example of this aimless and random mutualistic anarchy is the inadvertent hybridization the ruby-throated hummingbird has caused between the two buckeye species. In this case, the hummingbird may have harmed one of the parental species—the painted buckeye—by contaminating its offspring with the DNA of another species. But the hybrids have larger quantities of nectar than painted buckeye does, so if the hybrids maintain themselves genetically—and it appears they might—this might eventually help the hummer by making the painted buckeye more like the red buckeye over generations.

Another example of how loose and opportunistic these interactions can be involves the answer to the riddle of where the hummingbird gets its nectar during its early spring arrival. It's not even a flower.

Yellow-bellied sapsuckers have a common name that is an embarrassing mouthful for a birder who might have to sheepishly explain to a nonbirder what kind of woodpecker they are looking at. If this happens to you, just say it is a woodpecker. It's a plump bird about the size of a robin, and it's the only woodpecker in the vicinity of Kennesaw with yellow on its body, so it's pretty easy to recognize. Yellow-bellied sapsuckers are so named because they use their bills to peck and drill perfectly round holes into trees, which then fill with sap. You can find trees with their characteristic drillings all over Kennesaw Mountain, and sapsuckers are occasionally seen hopping about on the mountain's trees from November to March drilling their wells, lapping up sap, and feeding on the insects that become trapped in the sap. They evacuate the Georgia Piedmont in late March, heading north to continue their drilling on northern trees, right around the time sap starts flowing again up north. An impressive list of other species also feed from their wells, either on the sap or the insects trapped there. The list includes flying squirrels, bats, chipmunks, porcupines, woodpeckers (red-bellied, red-headed, hairy, and downy), great crested flycatchers, eastern phoebes, nuthatches, robins, vireos, twelve species of warblers, and the ruby-throated hummingbird.

When ruby-throated hummingbirds arrive in spring, they feed from the sapsucker wells, which are dripping with abundant, dilute, sugary sap, and thousands of trapped insects. This provides the hungry migrating hummingbirds all the energy and protein they need. In fact, studies in Michigan by Edward and Allie Southwick showed that hummingbirds feed from sapsucker wells more frequently than the sapsuckers themselves. Hummingbirds in Michigan are completely reliant on sapsucker wells for food and always nest near a tree with good, flowing wells. Nearly the entire summer range of the ruby-throated hummingbird is contained within the boundaries of the combined winter and summer range of the yellow-bellied sapsucker, suggesting that hummers can't even expand outside their current range without the help of this other bird. The fire-pink and red buckeye are certainly appreciated, but without the sapsucker, it is unlikely the ruby-throated hummingbird would ever have colonized the eastern United States. Its trans-Gulf spring migration would certainly not be possible without the sapsucker wells. Without the sapsucker, there would probably be no hummers and no fire-pinks, and all buckeyes would be yellow or white. These observations—the scarcity of bird flowers and hummingbirds in the East, and the recent hybridization of buckeyes—all seem to point to the recent arrival of the hummingbirds in North America, which was made possible thanks to the sapsucker. It's no tightly organized web of life, just species interacting in unexpected and self-serving ways.

It is interesting to note that when hummingbirds arrive in March at Kennesaw Mountain, yellow-bellied sapsuckers have already moved north. And when sapsuckers arrive on the mountain during autumn, ruby-throats are just leaving and heading south to the Gulf Coast. The hummingbirds arriving on Kennesaw Mountain have no idea who made these wells for them, and where the two birds coexist, hummingbirds are ungrateful enough to try to chase sapsuckers away from their own wells. The sapsuckers have no idea that when they leave Georgia, hummingbirds will rush in to feed from their wells. Even though the ruby-throats probably owe their entire existence to this woodpecker, the two birds have probably never been seen on the same day on Kennesaw Mountain. They just miss each other.

# 9

# Little Green Eating Machines

I F I WERE TO TELL you that millions of hideous, supple green worms—each with an uncanny resemblance to a Martian—emerge from the ground every spring to devour plants in the forests of the Atlanta area, you might be tempted with some justification to drive to the nearest Walmart to purchase insecticides and wage war against them. If I told you these worms often have fearsome spines and hairs and come equipped with six sets of clawed legs and several additional rubbery feet used to climb far into the forest canopy to feast on fresh leafy growth, you might never leave your house. Surely you'd shudder in disgust if I told you they feed with a pair of jagged black plates that smash down upon their green food with such relish that on quiet mornings you can sit still and all the background white noise stirring in the leaves is their thousands of munching mandibles. It is still more horrifying that these hordes have an insatiable appetite and are known to consume plants so rapidly and efficiently that they can grow to one thousand times their body size at hatching before they undergo a miraculous transformation.

Upon transformation they pull off perhaps their greatest trick, a trick that the devil himself would envy. These damaging monstrosities change into one of the most beloved of all animals, animals so well admired that even the most apprehensive country grandmother will take a moment to note their beauty. They metamorphose into perhaps the *only* group of insects that average people with no interest in nature enjoy. And yet they begin their development, and in fact spend most of their life, as disgusting, destructive enemies that can cause great damage to plants. Few animals are admired as far out of proportion to their ecological reality as butterflies.

Some would try to lay the blame for the destruction of caterpillars at the six stilted feet of moths. They might argue that moths are the real offenders, and butterflies are colorful, harmless day fliers with less destructive caterpillars—or at least as adults they are so beautiful they offset the destructive power of their caterpillars. But this is clearly an ignorant and dead-wrong justification. Attempting to divorce the butterflies from the moths is an exercise in futility and chauvinism. Essentially, butterflies are just a highly successful and noteworthy group of day-flying moths. And they're not even alone. Day-flying moths have developed more than once, such that there are clearly

Figure 10. The coral hairstreak is rarely observed in Georgia but is commonly found atop Kennesaw Mountain. Photo by Giff Beaton.

identifiable "moths" with brilliant colors that fly during the day in addition to the highly successful butterflies. Butterflies make up a natural group that emerged from within the moth lineage, and both are considered part of the excessively large and important insect order Lepidoptera. Any attempt to consider butterflies anything else would be like trying to convince somebody that baseball day games are much better than night games. There may be some differences between day games and night games. But it's the same game. This becomes all the more clear when you consider the larvae of moths and butterflies: caterpillars of both are virtually indistinguishable in habits, appetite, and sheer herbivorous force. They also both have the membranous wings covered in fine scales that give the order its name. The only way to be entirely sure that you are seeing a butterfly and not a moth is to note the fine structure of the antennae—butterflies have enlarged clubs at the end, whereas the rest of the Lepidoptera often have fine, brush-like projections.

Yet compare the literature associated with the two kinds. Butterflies have long been vaunted by poets, who rarely avoid the opportunity to liken them to flying flowers. Consider Robert Frost, whose "Blue-Butterfly Day" describes these insects as "flowers that fly and all but sing." By contrast, moths have been described in far more sinister language. Edgar Allan Poe's "The Sphinx" is a humorously close-up description of a "living monster of hideous conformation," wherein the protagonist mistakes a nearby sphinx moth for a yonder giant flying monster. Surely Poe's death's-head moth was in Thomas Harris's mind when he wrote the Buffalo Bill character in *Silence of the Lambs*.

I don't want to give you the impression that I despise butterflies; like anybody else, I'm quite fond of them. I simply want to draw attention to how unfair it is that, since they transform into something pretty (and in fact useful), they somehow get a pass. I also like other insects, and about equally. I like pretty beetles, bees, robber flies, and bugs. I like just about all creatures but cockroaches. But these other insects—partly because they are perhaps inherently less attractive than butterflies, and partly because butterflies receive more hype—are often reviled and feared by Southerners without cause. I certainly don't see any good reason to consider moths less valuable than butterflies because they fly at night and have muted colors. In fact, you can't find a much more admirable invertebrate than a hawkmoth. They are very special insects: they can fly as fast as hummingbirds and with equal maneuverability; their metabolism is so advanced they are warm to the touch; they are among the largest insects; they can have recoilable, foot-long tongues; and they can see color at night. Although vertebrates are often considered far superior to insects, very few can claim such a list of superlatives.

I also want to draw attention to the true importance and reality of both butterflies and moths. As adults, these flying insects are almost wholly preoccupied with sex, and the essential purpose for this stage in their life cycle is to find mates and lay eggs. At this point they can be important as pollinators, since most species seek out flowers and nectar to fuel their flights, which are otherwise motivated entirely by procreation.

Kennesaw Mountain is a good place to observe this fact in action. Many of Kennesaw's birders take advantage of this situation and change over from birding in the morning to butterfly watching in the afternoon. One April morning I was at the summit of Big Kennesaw, which was then swarming with large congregations of tiger and zebra swallowtails, red-spotted purples, and morning cloaks. They swirled around in colorful swarms, darting quickly along the trails and among the cannon displays. They deftly stayed one wing beat ahead of being battered by the winds and occasionally formed living, rotating funnels of yellow, white, and black wings.

The explanation for such behavior is that many species of larger and long-lived butterflies use an ingenious strategy for finding mates. Most butterflies are short lived and the females mate only once. Males of such species would do best to locate virgin females, and their best option is to find them emerging from their chrysalises close to the larvae's preferred host plant. Many species therefore mate near the host plant. But other species are longer lived and mate multiple times, taking part in behavior called "hilltopping" in order to find each other. Along prominent ridges where males can see long distances, they are able to patrol for females. Sometimes these hilltops become crowded with multiple species in an outrageous display of carnal exuberance. Kennesaw Mountain, being the most prominent topographic feature for miles and miles, can attract an almost embarrassingly large number of butterflies seeking reproductive gratification.

Some species take sex so seriously that the adult stage does not feed at all. An example is the luna moth, a hauntingly beautiful green-and-pink species that can be found in oak-hickory forests throughout Georgia. This species and others like it store enough fat while feeding as caterpillars that as adults they have no mouthparts and therefore do not feed at all. They flit around for a little over a week, mate, and then die. Butterflies and moths spend most of their lives as caterpillars, and it is in this stage that their ecological effects are most apparent. When you see a butterfly or moth, remember that you are seeing only a fleeting representation of what this insect really is. In the same way a mushroom is simply a brief reproductive structure representing a giant, wispy underground fungus, these flying insects are a distraction from what they are in essence.

Despite their small size, caterpillars are the chief herbivores of many forest ecosystems, and this is especially true in the forests of the eastern United States, including on Kennesaw Mountain. Caterpillars are the dominant herbivore of the "green world" food web. You have no doubt already noted that there are no monkeys, sloths, koalas, pandas, kudus, or gazelles frequenting the forest canopy and browsing on the fresh green foliage of our native trees. The most abundant herbivorous mammals are squirrels, mice, and chipmunks, which do not feed on leafy foliage. In fact, they can't. Instead, they feed on much more nutritious seeds and nuts, and to some extent the trees are fine with that. The white-tailed deer is an accomplished browser, but it feeds far more selectively on herbaceous and shrubby growth and of course cannot feed in the trees. The reason mammals do not browse on the growth of trees is largely because plants are very good at preventing herbivores from feeding on their tissue. Plants deploy ingenious defenses that prevent many animals from feeding on them. They larder their leaves with toxic chemicals, growth inhibitors, and indigestible compounds. They grow thorns, bristles, and stiff and sometimes stinging hairs that prohibit feeding. Grasses reinforce their tissues with silica—tiny shards of glass, essentially—that wear down the teeth of most plant eaters. The animal that is best at circumventing these defenses is the ravenous caterpillar.

Caterpillars have developed counterdefenses for every defense developed by plants. The sophistication of the ongoing arms race between plants and caterpillars is exemplified by the black swallowtail butterfly, a species found throughout Georgia, whose striking tiger-striped caterpillar feeds on plants in the carrot family such as Queen Anne's lace, which is a common weed in the old fields of Kennesaw Mountain. These plants produce potent toxins known as furanocoumarins, which are rare in other plants and highly toxic to herbivores like insects and mammals. But the black swallowtail caterpillar can munch on these plants with impunity. According to entomologist Michael B. Cohen and his team, it does so by virtue of a gene that produces an enzyme with a daunting name: cytochrome P450 monooxygenase. Despite the terrifying tongue twister this name presents, all the enzyme does is add an oxygen molecule to just the right place within a complex molecule of furanocoumarin, rendering it helplessly inert. By virtue of this gene, these butterflies alone can feed on plants within this toxic group.

This is but one precise example of the adaptations caterpillars have developed in response to plant defenses. Most butterflies and moths have been observed feeding on very specific plant groups and have very specific host plants, revealing that one of the main drivers for the generation of butterfly species has been this struggle between the plants and their enemies. As caterpillar populations began developing solutions for the challenges posed by specific plant groups, they began to change and specialize, diverging from simpler ancestors. There are well over one hundred thousand species of Lepidoptera, so this has been an incredibly important factor in the development of the biodiversity of the planet.

The intimate tie between butterflies and their host plants is the key for enjoyment of these insects; without a detailed knowledge of the feeding preferences of the larvae, an aspiring butterfly watcher will always be a novice. Rarer butterflies must be sought near their very particular host plants and cannot be expected to simply show up in your butterfly garden. The same can be said of most birds; if you ever really need to see a certain species, you must leave the comfortable confines of the weekly field trip hosted by your local birding club and learn a little bit about the habitat requirements of your bird. You might have to learn how to identify a plant or two that may serve as indicator species for the habitat type the bird prefers. This approach is better in general for enjoyment of nature, and it is especially true for butterflies.

Perhaps because they are among the more abundant trees in the eastern deciduous forests, offering tons of potential food to herbivores, oaks and hickories support a large number of caterpillars. And the numbers are truly astounding. In a paper in *Ecological Entomology*, Keith Summerville and his colleagues sampled moths in five different eastern forest patches for a total of about four weeks during the summer of 2000. They captured over 28,000 individual moths representing 636 species. Summerville and Thomas Crist sampled another set of nine forests and captured over 40,000 individual moths of 800 species. In yet another study, Summerville and colleagues sampled just 24 individual trees within a single forest and recorded over 500 individual caterpillars from 64 species. Clearly, what the caterpillars lack in size, they make up for in numbers and appetite. In this way they are much like Edgar Allan Poe's sphinx moth: although tiny, when viewed through the lens of their effect on the forest, they are monstrous.

It's a wonder that trees have leaves at all, given the hordes of tiny herbivores dining on their greenery. But according to Jill Landsber and Cliff Ohmart, on average only about 9 percent of tree foliage is destroyed each year from the browsing of caterpillars and other insect herbivores in most forests throughout the world. Most of this browsing takes place in the early spring when the leaves are just sprouting and most vulnerable. After a few weeks the plants can defend their leaves more capably and the munching stops, for the most part. Even with all of the caterpillars' ingenious strategies for avoiding the bristles, poisons, and bitter chemicals plants use to dissuade them, they are usually unable to completely devour all the leaves available. This is partly due to the capacity of plants to defend themselves. But there are also many factors that limit the populations of caterpillars.

Like most animals, caterpillars can increase in numbers only so much before resources start to run out. And the kinds of resources available will determine to some extent how large populations get. In some habitats trees and other plants grow under more stressful conditions, so they are less able to defend themselves. In such conditions caterpillars thrive. Some plants can increase levels of defensive compounds in response to tissue damage—so-called inducible defenses. If herbivores spend too much time munching on one plant, it will eventually become unpalatable for future generations. But these defenses are costly for plants, so levels of defensive compounds and herbivory can fluctuate up and down in a cycle.

Also like most kinds of animals, caterpillars are plagued by all kinds of enemies: bacteria, viruses, parasites, and predators. Of these, the most important enemies for caterpillars are the parasites, or more specifically, the parasitoids. A parasitoid is a special and intensely sinister type of parasite that lives inside or upon its host and devours it slowly before eventually killing it. We met one of these nasty little beasts in chapter 2: the tiny wasp that destroys catalpa worms. There are many more where it came from. Another good example is the ichneumon wasp—a slender, sleek, and often glossy wasp with a very long "stinger" held in position behind the abdomen in a hoop. This is not really a stinger, but rather an egg-laying device more appropriately known as an ovipositor. Female ichneumons patrol the forest looking for caterpillars, and when they find one they use their long ovipositor to inject an egg into their prey like some malicious hypodermic needle. The egg develops inside while the caterpillar is still alive and then the wasp maggot bursts forth from its body, at last putting the caterpillar out of its misery. It goes without saying that this nasty little insect was the inspiration for the life cycle of the creature from the *Alien* movies. Since caterpillars are so abundant, soft skinned, and diverse, hundreds of parasitoids have evolved to exploit them. And it's probably just as well, even though we might permit a tinge of sympathy for the way they are killed. As populations of certain caterpillars rise, their parasitoids can reach plague proportions and bring their numbers under control.

Even with all the parasitoids, germs, and plant defenses that conspire to keep caterpillars from devouring every last leaf in the forest, occasionally some caterpillar species have outbreaks and cause considerable damage to forests. One of these outbreak species—the gypsy moth—is not native to the United States and is therefore a particularly unwanted pest that can defoliate oak forests. Other species are native to the United States and can still reach seemingly unnatural numbers in some forest environments. Perhaps the most famous of these is the spruce budworm, the larva of a moth that feeds on spruces and firs in coniferous forests of the northern United States and Canada. When these forests have budworm outbreaks, migrating insectivorous birds have terrific years: Robert MacArthur noted that they feast on the thousands of extra caterpillars and raise more young than usual. The population cycle of the budworm supports population ups and downs of birds.

These caterpillars are so abundant that they are the primary food source for several wood warblers each summer, and Robert Marquis and Christopher Whelan (among many others) showed that wood warblers, as their major predator, help to control caterpillar numbers. Some of these wood warblers migrate through the Atlanta area each spring and fall and use Kennesaw Mountain as a stopover each year. A famous study by Robert MacArthur examined the way these warblers fed on the caterpillars in a spruce-fir forest in Canada. According to tested ecological principles, it was thought in the early 1900s that two similar species competing for the same exact resource could not last forever; one of the species would be just a hair better at obtaining resources, and it would eventually outcompete and replace the other. But at his study sites in Maine, MacArthur observed not two but five species of warblers feeding in one place all summer long. All five species were very similar in size and bill shape. According to the established theory, this should not happen. So MacArthur made careful observations of their feeding patterns and found to his and everyone else's astonishment that the warblers appeared to be divvying up the caterpillars by feeding in separate zones of each tree: black-throated green and Blackburnian warblers fed mostly on caterpillars out on the upper branches, bay-breasted warblers fed mostly in the central part of the crown, Cape May warblers fed mostly on the tip of the crown, and myrtle warblers fed mostly on caterpillars on the lower branches near the ground. Thereafter these warblers became known in textbooks as "MacArthur's warblers," and I always think about their ecological stature with fondness when I see one of these birds. All five can be seen during migration on Kennesaw Mountain.

In fact, many migrating songbirds rely quite heavily on caterpillars as prey, especially during spring migration when caterpillars are most abundant. At this time you will likely not see any of these five species feeding in any restricted part of the Kennesaw Mountain forest canopy; instead they seem to feed voraciously anywhere they can get their beaks on a fat caterpillar. And many other bird species get in on the game. If you take the time to watch these birds as they move rapidly through the forest (rather than simply identifying them and returning to look for new species), you will notice them devouring caterpillars. Sometimes theses caterpillars are way larger than you would think a bird could handle; big green kinds nearly as wide as the bird's own head. Other times they batter to death extremely furry and spiny species—to me they seem quite unappetizing—before choking them down with relish. Each year the migrating wood warblers exploit the superabundance of these wiggling green vermin that feast on the newly green leaves.

We will now turn our attention away from these little green eating machines, perhaps with a newfound respect for their inordinately large contribution to forest ecosystems and a renewed understanding that the dainty butterflies skipping about your backyard aren't quite what they seem.

Because now that I have introduced them, we will turn our focus to what has become Kennesaw Mountain's most famous inhabitants—its birds.

# 10

# Mixed Foraging Flocks

ONE OF THE FIRST THINGS a starting birder notices is that you can spend long hours not finding any birds, and then all of a sudden, the forest seems alive with them. One minute you're walking up the Kennesaw Mountain Road with a group of other birders, breathing warm breath into the crisp April chill of your hands, chitchatting with people about what new arrivals have been spotted lately. An explosive squeak in the leaf litter is revealed to be nothing more than a chipmunk. The whistle of a common, unnoteworthy towhee isn't even given a glance. A flash of white skipping up from the trail is nothing more than a junco. You're starting to get bored, wondering what all the hype about birding Kennesaw is really about.

Suddenly the leader of the birders—almost certainly Giff Beaton—calls out the name of an unusual bird not frequently seen in the Atlanta area. The less knowledgeable birders quickly scurry closer to Giff, looking out over a slope into some scrubby habitat, their heads shifting back and forth, swiveling on

Figure 11. The brown-headed nuthatch is often a member of mixed-species flocks in southern forests. Photo by Giff Beaton.

their necks mechanically. One by one they sound off little calls of affection: oohs and aahs. Then the birders form a phalanx, as those with midrange experience step out in a star pattern and try to contribute by looking in different directions. They begin calling out names: Tennessee warbler, black-throated green warbler, black-throated blue warbler, blackpoll warbler. The less experienced birders stride over and cower under Giff's tall frame and broad shoulders, imploring him to point out the rarities. The scrub is alive with nearly a dozen species. The birds move fast, purposeful and jerky, and it seems every time you pinpoint one, it's just another red-eyed vireo. They flow in a living wave from the scrub and into the mature forest canopy, which is at eye level from the park road. Then, as quickly as they arrive, the birds disappear. This can be frustratingly overwhelming for novices, who have a hard enough time learning birds as it is without being swamped with large numbers of fast-moving birds of multiple species all at once. During spring, Kennesaw's mixed foraging flocks of Neotropical migrants are an exhilarating challenge.

The same thing happens at your feeder. Particularly during winter, you might look out the window and see only the occasional acrobatic squirrel robbing your seeds. Then, a tufted titmouse might appear, and within seconds the feeder is a mob of a half dozen species as the titmouse is joined by friends: along with the usual Carolina chickadees, there is a white-breasted nuthatch, brown-headed nuthatches, pine warblers, yellow-rumped warblers, and a downy woodpecker. Then the flock moves along, and your feeder becomes quiet save for the occasional mourning dove for the rest of the day. My father is convinced that the birds communicate with each other: he has noticed that as soon as the feeder is refilled a bird will show up ("one of those little gray ones"), and within seconds the whole gang appears. I try to tell him that it is equally likely that the birds have incorporated his feeding schedule into theirs, and that perhaps the few times that the birds chanced upon the feeder right away have left a lasting impression on him. While it is unlikely that birds have specific calls that alert other members of the flock to food, he is not too far off the mark about the nature of these flocks.

Mixed foraging flocks—bird flocks that include multiple species—are common in ecosystems throughout the world. They have been studied in Europe, India, Australia, tropical America, and here in the United States. During spring migration incredible mixed flocks of migrants move through the park. Since winter resident birds in Georgia also form mixed flocks, this is a phenomenon that can be observed at almost any time of year on Kennesaw Mountain. About the only time birds do not participate in these flocks is during breeding, when pairs set up and defend territories and raise a brood. Soon afterward they spread out, join mixed flocks, and prepare for migration or a long winter.

The most familiar mixed flocks on Kennesaw Mountain are those that form during winter and are led by Carolina chickadees and/or tufted titmice, which usually include attendant red-bellied, downy, or hairy woodpeckers, white-breasted nuthatches, and perhaps a yellow-bellied sapsucker. These flocks often include smaller followers such as brown-headed nuthatches, brown creepers, golden-crowned and ruby-crowned kinglets, yellow-rumped warblers, and often pine warblers. They travel in definite, cohesive groups on well-maintained foraging paths. Mixed flocks of blackbirds, including nonnative starlings and cowbirds, are also frequently seen in the park, especially in autumn. Historically these were probably composed mostly of common grackles, red-winged blackbirds, and perhaps an occasional rusty blackbird. These flocks are more nomadic and unpredictable than the mixed flocks of forest birds described above, and membership in them is perhaps more opportunistic. Finally, there are migratory mixed flocks of wood warblers and vireos, which form cohesive flocks that swarm the mountain to feed on caterpillars during spring; these kinds of flocks are very obvious on Kennesaw but not as well studied.

Birds are not the only animals that form mixed flocks. Monkeys, whales, fish, and hoofed mammals also join each other in mixed schools and herds. Perhaps the most famous mixed herds are those of the African savanna, where several kinds of antelope, ungulates, and zebras will graze together in tight social groups. The number and variety of species that form these groups hints that there must be great benefits to flocking together—perhaps even better benefits than can be obtained by simply flocking with their own species.

Mixed flocks have been studied extensively and the advantages to joining these flocks can be broadly summarized into two categories: feeding advantages and antipredatory advantages. Mixed flocks can more skillfully exploit certain foods by flocking together. For example, the movement of a large flock may flush small insects that certain members of the flock can snap up. Temporary members of the flock can also copy the leaders of the flock, using their superior knowledge of the terrain to find food. Perhaps having many eyes scouring the area allows mixed flocks to find food more effectively than feeding individually or in single-species flocks. This does require flock members to share the local resources, but as long as they find food better in these flocks than they would on their own, they might tend to join a mixed flock.

The flocks certainly have advantages when it comes to avoiding predators. Having many eyes and ears looking out for predators is a distinct advantage over a single individual or one small group looking out for predators. And each member of a group has a smaller chance of being singled out by a marauding hawk. All those rapidly shifting birds are as confusing to preda-tors as they are to a birder trying to pinpoint a single bird. If a hawk does at-tack, the scattering of a dozen colorful little birds can confuse the predator. And, mixed flocks often center on a bold member with very loud antipreda-tory calls, which the other members apparently understand. When spotted by their prey before an attack, birds of prey are not very effective as predators. Another remarkable aspect of mixed foraging flocks is that they are not afraid to turn the tables on would-be predators and attack them. As summarized by Sue Boinski and Paul Garber, ecologists have attempted to determine which of these factors—feeding or antipredatory advantages—are most important for the development of mixed flocks. As is often the case with ecological ques-tions, the best explanation appears be a combination of both.

Boinski and Garber's book notes that most flock leaders (referred to as the "nucleus" of the flock) are usually gregarious cooperative breeders—birds that move around in small family groups and use antipredator calls extensively to protect their own kin. The followers of these birds are usually smaller and in-sectivorous and are often the most vulnerable to predators. In most studies mixed flocks of birds spend less time individually looking out for predators than they would if they flocked by themselves. So, in mixed-species flocks in-dividual birds can spend more time feeding and less time looking over their shoulders, because some other bird has their back. The total amount of time spent looking for predators is greater, but it is divided among the individual members of the flock. On the whole, the flock can move quickly through a forest while foraging voraciously, and at the same time they are better able to detect lurking predators. The flock leaders probably don't mind the smaller birds who tag along, not only because the predators might target them but also because the smaller birds do their part in looking out for hawks.

This makes plenty of sense, but it doesn't provide an overwhelmingly compelling reason why different *kinds* of birds flock together. It seems they could gain the same benefits by flocking in single-species groups. One of the best possible explanations I've heard remains to this day untested: dif-ferent birds with overlapping or complementary sensory skills are the ones that form mixed-species flocks. It's not so much that they have more eyes and ears, it's that they have different kinds of eyes and ears. This seems like an excellent explanation for the birds that form the most common mixed flocks on Kennesaw. Perhaps smaller birds do take advantage of the tufted titmice and chickadees—the birds that most frequently lead mixed foraging flocks in the eastern deciduous forest. But the addition of downy woodpeckers, ruby-crowned kinglets, and brown-headed nuthatches adds overlapping sensory ca-pabilities to the flocks. Perhaps these flocks are a sort of avian A-Team, with each species bringing its own unique skills to the flock. Testing this would require a detailed study of the visual and auditory capabilities of each species, how they respond to predators, and how much overlap there is among their skills—a daunting task. But it would be well worth finding out which bird is the team's Hannibal, and certainly it would be fun to know which bird represents Murdock or B. A. Baracus.

More interesting still are the enormous mixed flocks of migrating warblers and vireos that arrive during Kennesaw's spring migration. These diverse flocks can easily number over a dozen species, and scattered nonflocking individuals seen along forest edges on the same day can lead to record daily counts—seeing as many as twenty species of wood warblers in a single day is not uncommon. High counts of eighteen to twenty-six wood warblers occur from mid-April to late May, and an all-time record of thirty wood warbler species was recorded on April 24, 1999. This spectacularly high number well exceeds the number needed, according to Giff Beaton, "to call your friends who had to work and torture them with tales of warblers dripping off trees." But to me the exciting thing about these flocks is not the total number of species you can see in a day, but how many birds are concentrated in large mixed flocks. Most of these birds hit you in big waves as you walk slowly up the mountain.

Studies conducted at other migratory stopover sites have shown similar patterns (summarized in John Rappole's excellent book *The Avian Migrant: The Biology of Bird Migration*), although the situation at Kennesaw may very well be unique. Migrants at sites on the Gulf Coast usually behave in one of two ways: some groups stop briefly and remain in their migratory flight state; they move restlessly through the available habitat briefly and then move on. These often forgo spending much time foraging, relying on energy from stored body fat, and actually lose weight during the stopover. Others remain for a few days in distinct habitats similar to their preferred breeding habitats, and they gain weight by gorging themselves on any food they can find. Rappole notes they can increase their feeding rate as much as 40 percent by compulsive eating, or "hyperphagia." Some even take the time to set up temporary territories. These distinctive groups leapfrog each other along their migratory route, exhibiting one or the other behavior depending on their fat reserves, some moving through the area just to rest for the day, while others remain at the site for a week or more to refuel.

These behaviors correspond to well-established physiological states determined from laboratory studies. Based on my experience observing Kennesaw's migrants, it seems as though these patterns also occur during spring migration in Georgia. Large multispecies flocks arrive before dawn, spend the day, and if weather permits, they are replaced by a new wave that arrives the next morning. Meanwhile, some individuals stay put and can be found day after day in reliable spots for up to a week. The only difference I've noticed between the published studies of migrants elsewhere and what I've seen at Kennesaw is that mixed migrating flocks on the mountain certainly spend a great deal of time feeding; this represents a third, poorly known physiological state known as "transit"—a happy medium between the migratory state and the refueling state observed elsewhere. Birds in this state probably maintain weight and then leave as soon as weather permits. Kennesaw would make an excellent study site to investigate these patterns; the mountain receives predictable visits from diverse assemblages of mixed migrating flocks. The relatively confined forested area, which is bisected by accessible trails, would allow a researcher to follow flocks around all day.

This would require following single mixed migratory flocks for a while, rather than taking the typical route that birders use along the main park road. The foraging path of Kennesaw's birders is standard—begin at dawn from the parking lot, walk across the main lawn near the maintenance shed (your shoes invariably become soaked with dew), over to the far corner where there is a wall of privet and honeysuckle. By then the sun is up and glows bright on this spot, and some of the warblers that stay for a few days take up residence in this thicket. The group by now has drawn most members, save perhaps one late tit who will intercept the flock at the Mountain Road gate. Then the group heads up the road, avoiding joggers and buses, and intersects one or two big mixed flocks on the way up. Unless someone reports a rarity after the group turns around, they are done for the day by 10:00 a.m., easily with over fifty birds ticked. After repeating this for nearly seven hundred days over twelve years, the king birder nucleus of the birding group Giff Beaton, along with several of the more die-hard flock members, has been able to produce an incredible summary of the movement and abundance patterns of migratory and resident birds of Kennesaw Mountain. The route they take each day maximizes the number of birds seen, and birders new to Kennesaw would be wise to seek out such a group and benefit from it. But after experiencing several exciting days along the usual park route, I wondered what it would be like to instead follow the birds, rather than the birders.

I am prone to think of such things, especially when I lose patience with birders walking up the Mountain Road. It is said that—as is the case with mixed flocks of birds—more eyes make for better birding. Here, too, there are nuclear species with the most skills, and if our humans are a good model for mixed flocks of birds, then the birders certainly demonstrate that followers benefit from the leaders more than the leaders benefit from the followers. The best groups of birders have a good mix of skill sets for maximum detection of the most kinds of birds, and perhaps the most birds are located by groups like this. It would be best if some were good at birding by ear, and others excellent at identifying tough little brown jobs in any molt. But this is rarely the case. Birders are almost always led by one expert who can do it all. I certainly never bring much to such a group, other than wry observations of the group itself.

I follow along watching the birders, noticing their bunching movements around the leader, their rapid striding to keep up, and their interesting scattering when the flock of birders intercepts a flock of birds. Occasionally strife breaks out. The nuclear birder becomes weary of the followers and ruffles his hackles at those who hassle him for help or get in the way of a good find. They are sometimes too eager, too enthusiastic, and occasionally very annoying. Their eyes bulge and twitch, their necks arch in sinewy curves, straining for good looks. Sometimes I can't stand it, and I allow the birders to slowly move away.

Instead I become a transient follower and stay with the birds, descending from the road down the Little Kennesaw trail to join them. They feed for a time among the catkins of oaks and hickories—dozens of little streamlined green birds that erupt with color upon closer inspection. There are always handfuls of black-throated green warblers bumping along, buzzing their edged consonant singsong. Every other bird I see is a red-eyed vireo fresh from its night flight of hundreds of miles, which has brought it here from Amazonia. The vireos must be either an important nucleus or the most common follower. A gorgeous Blackburnian warbler catches orange fire from a shaft of morning light high in the canopy, singing to me unfamiliar tunes, as it is here far from its breeding range. A yellow-throated warbler—slightly more at home here, but likely also headed much farther north—snatches up a juicy green caterpillar the size of its head and neck and chokes it down in a single gulp.

The flock swirls along the west slope and I double back up the trail to the road, keeping pace with the birds as they make their way among the vivid new green of the red oaks just leafing out. Then one by one or in small trios they fall out across the road, so I trot over to the trail intersection and up toward Big Kennesaw to keep up with them. I walk under stunted summit red oaks in a meadow of dainty white spring ephemerals and scarlet fire-pinks. The transitory flock pours through the trees, blackpolls and Cape May warblers forced to dwell at eye level, when they usually prefer to break my neck by staying high above in the canopy. They move directly overhead and east, away from the summit, and I struggle to keep up with them, counting the inchworms harvested, noting them eating a hairy caterpillar species that I imagine could be identified, until the birds descend the steep slope of the mountain more quickly than I wish to.

I huff it back up in time to rejoin the birders as they ascend the summit by the road from the other direction. They've seen a Nashville warbler in my absence, but in a sense I've seen much more.

# 11

# Bird Migration

I SHOULDN'T PICK ON BIRDERS TOO much—after all, they are among the people most likely to pick up this book in the first place—but sometimes it seems to me they are so focused on finding that next bird—the next one for their county, state, or life list—that they seem to lose sight of what birds actually are. I don't mean any disrespect. I hope that by considering an outsider's opinion, perhaps birders will come to appreciate the ecology of birds, rather than think of them as so many feathered postage stamps for their collection. I mean this only as a constructive critique. Think of it as gentle encouragement. I also get plenty excited when I spot a new bird, and I too have been known to go out of my way to see a "lifer"—a bird I've never seen before. I keep checklists of the birds I've seen at my favorite places. But I've never been content with simply listing birds and leaving it at that.

Of course, most birders never get this close to the edge of obsession either.

Figure 12. The bizarre migratory pathway of Swainson's thrush takes many individuals through the Atlanta area. Photo by Giff Beaton.

I think what motivates most of them is the beauty and excitement of pursuing and seeing birds. But knowing more about what birds do—their interactions with plant and animal communities, their behaviors, and their ancient history—should enrich this experience for birders. Sometimes it seems as if they hardly care. Perhaps an example might make my point: I talked to a birder over beers and pizza one time. He was a top-shelf birder and had been hired by a colleague of mine to run bird surveys for a big ecological restoration project in the Florida Panhandle. While munching on slices of pizza he rattled off lists of bird sightings new for the county without stopping to swallow: "Got a perpendicular stander-strider in Walton County, saw two yellow-beaked owls in Okaloosa County, along with red-eyed fairy-wrens, blue-patched blackpins, Winston's palmators, and green-backed needlebeaks. In one day I saw all seven species of crabdivers and had a masked bobwhite crane while driving along I-10."

You know the type. They use verbs like "got" or "had" when describing their experiences, as if enjoying birds was just like buying lunch. My eyes glazed over when I realized that if I let him, he was going to relate his entire bird list for every county in the Sunshine State. I glanced at my colleague, who rolled his eyes. He later confirmed that not only did this guy talk like this constantly, but his emails would ramble on for four pages just like this—I'm not exaggerating, I've seen them. I decided to butt in.

"Hey, so, one thing I've always thought about is migration in birds." I got a pause, so I pressed it to advantage. "Have you ever wondered why birds migrate? I've read that most migrants originate from the tropics, and having seen the rain forest down there, I wonder why they would ever leave? Especially considering that the first birds to leave wouldn't know where they were going and how far to go. What do you think?"

He munched a few more bites and then provided me with this thoughtful response: "I've seen most Neotropical migrants in Escambia County, but my list from Okaloosa County is weak. Still need striated sand-eaters, purple-margined blue-beaks, lacy parawackes, full-bodied caciques, and bell-bottomed periwinkles, not to mention the common flat-face and paramount bee-prodder."

Needless to say, I was unsatisfied with his explanation.

The riddle of bird migration is among the most fascinating questions in animal ecology and has vexed humanity for millennia. And incredibly, the reason birds migrate is not well understood, even today. We know how birds migrate; hundreds of experimental studies conducted on birds across the Northern Hemisphere have determined with minute clarity the physiological and instinctual underpinnings for migration. We understand in exquisite detail the various contrivances by which birds navigate—using the sun, the moon, and the stars, the earth's magnetic field, landforms, and onboard magnetic anomaly maps. We know the physiological feats of fat storage and cardiovascular flight endurance required to make the round trips. We also know with incredible certainly when birds arrive each year, and we are beginning to fully appreciate the routes they take, even though their flights cover thousands of miles and cross dozens of international boundaries. With the dawn of the internet birding age, nary a bird lands anywhere without scores of birders being aware of it, and Listservs, chat rooms, and blogs report the arrivals and departures of birds. This new technology and networks of enthusiastic birders allow novices to see up-to-the minute updates on the progress of the year's migration. Fine-scale radar images show blobs of approaching low-altitude migrants, and online forecasts of migration fallouts—weather conditions that induce large numbers of migrating birds to land temporarily— are becoming commonplace. Incredibly, despite this brave new world of information age technology, we are no closer to understanding the reasons birds ever developed migration in the first place.

We have vague and obvious notions of the adaptive value of migration, but these benefits do not explain why birds first began migrating—the step-by-step process that led from a permanent resident population to a fully migratory one. We largely assume that birds that arrive on their breeding grounds in spring take advantage of superabundant outbreaks of insects—mostly caterpillars for small wood warblers—and breed more successfully in North America than they would have if they'd stayed in the tropics. Likewise, the return to the tropics to escape the harsh approaching winter makes logical sense. Some of these observations are supported by hard evidence; in his book *The Ecology of Migrant Birds*, John Rappole notes the number of clutches and sizes of clutches are bigger for migrating birds than for their relatives in the tropics. But given the difficulty of migrating back and forth hundreds of miles—especially for new fledglings—it is possible that this benefit is counteracted by the serious trials involved in making the trip, leaving us without a good explanation for the value of migration. And the impetus for traveling hundreds of miles to get to these breeding areas in the first place remains vague.

Such is the mystery of bird migration, which has inspired thoughtful philosophizing since the time of the ancients. The Greeks noticed birds moving south during the fall and attempted to explain it, although their explanations were tainted by folklore and limited by the narrow scope of their observations. A constellation in the Northern Hemisphere listed by Ptolemy in the second century codifies migration in the heavens—the stars of Cygnus, the swan. Bird migration is even mentioned in the Bible, and the book of Job

(39:26) comes no closer to a natural explanation for the phenomenon: "Doth the hawk fly by Thy wisdom and stretch her wings toward the south?"

By the eighteenth century the timing of the arrival and departure of various bird species was becoming established, and at this time fantastical descriptions of hibernating swallows, migrations to the moon and back, and small birds riding on the backs of storks were finally debunked. Much of this progress was due to greater opportunity for naturalists to travel widely, as well as better communication between experts. The great eighteenth-century American naturalist William Bartram was very well traveled for his time. He spent much time botanizing in his native Pennsylvania and explored the Southeast at the time of the American Revolution. He observed the great flocks of swallows and martins moving up the Carolina coast during spring and moving the opposite direction in fall. He knew their arrival dates in Pennsylvania and knew that eastern phoebes were among the first arrivals in March. When they arrived, planting could begin, because although late frosts might still occur after this time, they would not be severe. Observations like this accumulated over the next century until a general picture of bird migration emerged.

A great stride was made in the 1880s when Wells W. Cooke, a schoolteacher who moved around the Midwest and Mississippi Valley, began keeping detailed records of the comings and goings of birds. He taught at Indian schools from Minnesota to the Oklahoma Territory, and in 1882 he published his observations in *Field and Stream*. He began correspondence with other ornithologists in the region and solicited their cooperation in an attempt to determine the patterns of arrival and departure of migrants up and down the Mississippi Valley. The results were the first of their kind in the United States and were published by the US Department of Agriculture. They seem remarkably crude by today's standards and read like an average birder's FOY (first of year) scribbles. But they were the first step toward a quantitative understanding of bird migration in America. In 1889, Witmer Stone—the early twentieth-century bird guru of Cape May, New Jersey—improved the interpretation of these patterns by proposing a graphical representation of Cooke's arrival and departure data, in what may possibly have been the very first horizontal bar graphs of bird seasonal abundance.

The next great improvement in migration studies would occur at the turn of the twentieth century, when a Swedish schoolteacher had the bright idea to begin systematically banding birds. His records of returning birds quickly convinced others of the value of the technique, and it spread throughout Europe. These studies began in earnest in the early twentieth century in the United States. Perhaps the first attempt was by none other than John James Audubon, who twisted metal wires around the legs of phoebes and confirmed that they returned to the same place the next year. Small bird-banding efforts began in New Haven, Connecticut, as early as 1909, and a more organized study was conducted beginning in 1914 by S. Prentiss Baldwin out of Cleveland, Ohio, who also banded at his winter home near Thomasville, Georgia. Methods and efforts were standardized by 1920 when the US Biological Survey, and then the US Fish and Wildlife Service, set up a band permitting system. When bird banding became standard practice among ornithologists, the incredible feats of bird migration became clear.

The basic setup for these studies is simple: catch birds and mark them, let them go, and leave a message on the band for the receiver to give you a buzz when they recapture the bird. At first the return addresses of the bands were simply the interested parties' names, but later, the message said: "Notify The Auk New York." The *Auk* was and still is the journal of the American Ornithologists' Union. The message eventually became "Notify U.S. Fish and Wildlife Service, Washington D.C." The early returns were usually from hunters who blasted the birds. One of these is both humorous and representative. He wrote, "Gentleman dear sirs your bird was shot here today by me Albert Bailey for which I was more than sorry when I found it had a ring on. I took it for a hawk as it flew several times over my yard as I thought after chickens and gentleman all I can say [is] that I am sorry if I did wrong in doing so and also beg pardon." The bird was a night heron.

My own understanding of bird migration advanced along similar lines. As a child I was vaguely aware of the comings and goings of ducks and other birds, and I learned from my parents that they flew south for the winter. When I first started out birding it took me some time to get the hang of which birds might be expected at certain seasons. Embarrassingly, I can remember searching in vain for Colima warblers in Big Bend National Park in December—a summer migrant that does not arrive until April. Eventually I learned which birds migrate, when, and where from, and their arrivals in spring have become as highly anticipated for me as any holiday or life event—I anticipate them as much as I look forward to blooming wildflowers, breeding pond salamanders, and basking snakes. But it was when I began traveling farther afield that the scale of bird migration finally hit home. One can fully appreciate the magnificence of migration by seeing these birds in their tropical wintering sites.

I first saw one of these birds at its tropical home in 2004. It was just a simple thing—a red-eyed vireo skulking in the canopy of a montane cloud forest in Panama. It was there along with some residents that certainly belonged there: an orange-bellied trogon, crowned wood nymph, bay-headed tanager, southern nightingale-wren, and olive-striped flycatcher. The vireo at first seemed so out of place, but I knew this was due only to my own bias. The strangest thing was that it actually belonged there. The rain forest was the most diverse place I'd ever seen: every day I saw a new set of various frogs, snakes, and lizards. It seemed as though every leaf housed a giant spiny katydid, a ridiculously camouflaged walking stick, or a hideous leaf-colored cockroach. Every single tree was some different, unidentifiable species from a strange family, teeming with fine encrustations of dripping mosses. The scale of living productivity was beyond comprehension. I wondered why any bird would need to leave such a place and undergo a thousand-mile migration, only to then exhaust itself further by singing and fighting over a territory, breeding, and raising a clutch of hungry young, only to then undertake the epic journey back.

More observations followed, and each time I noted with incredulity these birds where they seemed not to belong: a flock of warblers—redstarts, black-throated blues, black-and-whites, yellows, and palms—in a thicket on Grand Cayman Island in November; skinny, exhausted blackpolls in the British Virgin Islands, stopping over on their preposterous trans-Atlantic flight from the Canadian taiga to the Orinoco. I pointed out a kingbird on a power line to some local kids in Panama and tried to explain to them in broken Spanish that the bird would travel far north to Los Estados Unidos de América in the spring. They were skeptical.

I saw a flock of eastern kingbirds feeding voraciously on fruit in the lowland rain forest of Barro Colorado Island, Panama, in September. They were something to see: a mob of thirty or so, fluttering like giant butterflies around the top of a tree bursting with red berries. These were not the kingbirds of home, scanning from a solitary perch on a fence post at the edge of some old field, sallying forth for mayflies. They may as well have been a different species altogether. But they weren't. These birds had bred near somebody's cornfield in Ohio. Or in a pasture along a river in rural Pennsylvania. Perhaps one had even set up a territory in Kennesaw's old fields. For some reason I get more excited about seeing these old friends away from their summer range than I do about seeing a new tropical parrot for the first time. When I saw Neotropical migrants as parts of the tropical ecosystems from which they came, I stopped thinking of them as birds of home. Instead, I started considering the incredible connectivity between entire continents, and thinking of them instead as what they really are: tropical birds that breed in North America.

The birds that use Kennesaw Mountain as an important migration stopover are indeed just that. While many were once claimed as part of North America's fauna, our modern understanding of their biology suggests otherwise. These birds are more Neotropical than North American. First of all, they spend only a few months of their lives on the breeding grounds. Take the Kentucky and hooded warblers, two Neotropical migrants that nest within Kennesaw Mountain National Battlefield Park. They arrive in April and are gone by October. The earlier arrival dates and later departures are probably of birds that breed farther north. Kennesaw's birds probably spend only a few months vacationing in North America, and the rest of the year they are members of diverse bird assemblages in the Yucatán.

Most birds that migrate to North America, including the most common migrants that use Kennesaw as a stopover, belong to groups that are most numerous in Central and South America. The tyrant flycatchers—the bird family that includes the great crested flycatcher, Acadian flycatcher, eastern phoebe, eastern wood-pewee, and eastern kingbird—are represented by nearly four hundred species, most of which are found in tropical Central and South America. There are more than two hundred species of tanagers, and only a handful of these—like the beautiful scarlet and summer tanagers—migrate to North America. The rest are residents or short-distance migrants in the Neotropics. North America does have a large number of visiting wood warblers, and a few of these are permanent residents north of Mexico. Areas of the Southern Appalachians have very high numbers of breeding species, numbers comparable to those in the tropics. But the rest of the one hundred–plus species in this family are found in Central America and Mexico and do not migrate. Finally, most of the more than three hundred species of hummingbirds are spread from the Andes to Mexico and throughout the Caribbean, and only a tiny fraction of these spend any time at all in North America. These distribution patterns strongly suggest that these birds originated in the Neotropics and spread north for breeding. For some reason.

Many of the migrating species have either close relatives or separate populations that never leave the Neotropics. Almost 80 percent of the species that migrate to North America from south of the Tropic of Cancer have close relatives or subpopulations that breed in the Neotropics. It turns out that the answer to the question I first posed after seeing a red-eyed vireo down in the rain forest—why these birds would ever leave—is easy to answer: about half of them, including the vireo, have populations that never do. They are very much members of tropical bird communities, and only a small subset of the population undergoes migration. Some species that travel through Kennesaw on their way to northern breeding grounds have resident breeding populations in tropical America: red-eyed vireos, eastern wood-pewees, blue-gray gnatcatchers, yellow warblers, yellow-throated warblers, and many others. Some of these breed in the park, while their close relatives never leave their tropical homeland.

Understanding where these birds originated helps us narrow down the possibilities for how these birds developed migratory populations. Some reason to leave the warm, productive tropical regions is needed. Clues can be found by considering that Neotropical birds frequently fly north and arrive far outside their normal range. These birds light up bird Listservs with frantic activity, and people will race hundreds of miles down the interstate to get a glance at these vagrants, probably spending more money chasing down these rarities than they would if they simply saved up and took a trip to see them where they are common. Why do these birds show up in North America?

These are the "accidentals" listed in the back of field guides that occasionally turn up, especially in Florida: jacanas, Bahama swallows, fork-tailed flycatchers, kiskadees, and Cuban emeralds. Many more cases are known, and they often belong to the same groups that have established migratory populations in North America: tyrant flycatchers, vireos, warblers, orioles, and hummingbirds. These birds can occasionally arrive as a result of powerful hurricanes that blow them off course, but this is probably not important for establishing a foothold far to the north. Instead, some of these birds spread far outside their normal distribution through the simple and common process of juvenile dispersal.

During the breeding season, birds frequently produce more young than the available habitat can support. Tropical habitats are thought to be completely packed with birds that have carved out every available niche. The young of the year of most species must disperse in order to find new breeding territories of their own. Many of them disperse quite far. Many of them die trying. But some end up in unusual habitats far outside their normal range and set up new populations.

Short-distance postbreeding dispersal is exhibited by most birds; some species simply disperse to the edges of their parents' territories, while others might fly to separate postbreeding locations. In some species males stay on the breeding territory and females and juveniles disperse, returning the following year to the same site for breeding. Some birds make migratory flights when environmental conditions deteriorate in their usual habitats—these include nomadic desert birds, as well as Arctic birds that "irrupt" as far south as Georgia when their food sources dwindle. In other species the separate breeding and postbreeding habitats are pretty close together, and others might make a short migration down a mountain slope during winter.

Nearly all birds, whether they are migratory or sedentary, have some capacity to fly rather far if they need to. As well, many birds can rapidly lay down fat reserves for various needs other than migration: juveniles getting ready to disperse, females readying to lay a clutch, males preparing for territorial defense. Practically all birds examined have at least rudimentary navigation skills and homing abilities, which are probably useful for any animal that can fly. So, most birds have the basic hardware for long flight and exhibit various levels of postbreeding dispersal, many of which are not quite as impressive as transcontinental flights. But viewed as a continuum, birds show movements ranging from permanent residents with short-distance postbreeding dispersal all the way to the incredible transglobal flights of some seabirds. There are examples of birds that show all the necessary short steps between these extremes.

Long-distance migration develops in small steps from juvenile dispersal from ancestral tropical breeding grounds. There are enough juveniles leaving these areas that some of them head far away instead of staying to compete with resident birds, and these set up breeding territories in new locations. This can variously lead to range expansions, temporary vagrant populations, or—if the birds establish a beachhead in habitat that will support them—migratory populations. For this to work, thousands of spare juvenile birds must disperse away from their parents' territories looking for new homes randomly, and they must then double back to avoid the northern winters. Thousands migrate in all directions, but only the ones that find suitable habitat eventually develop migratory populations. They might disperse north, but if they lack the homing ability to return, they will get a rude surprise when winter arrives. This is why vagrants usually appear for only a short time, and usually only in subtropical locations like Florida and Texas. But we can infer that in the past, tropical birds were occasionally able to set up populations in the temperate zone.

For this scenario to lead to migratory populations, plenty of dispersing migrants must find good locations, set up territories, and be joined by other dispersing members of their own species, and all of these birds and their young must return to their point of origin (the young of these first migrants can inherit the route from their parents). Eventually more adaptations could lead to differences between these migratory populations and their ancestors that stayed behind. Perhaps also these tropical residents might be entirely replaced by the migratory ones, leaving a completely migratory species with no permanent roots.

These stages may at first appear to be quite a tall order and stretch credulity, especially considering the astonishingly long flights made by many of the Neotropical birds that migrate through Kennesaw. But many birds have established migratory populations, including rather long migratory flights, in very short periods. Consider the cattle egret, which arrived in the Western Hemisphere in the 1800s. In their native Africa, these birds are nonmigratory. After their arrival in South America in the mid-nineteenth century, they began establishing migratory populations throughout the Caribbean. These developed by our seemingly unlikely pathway—juvenile dispersal. Cattle egrets invaded North America by the 1940s, and these birds moved back south during the winter. The cattle egret, now a fully migratory wading bird, is found breeding throughout the Southeast and returns during winter to its tropical point of origin. This incredible expansion occurred stepwise through the simple process of juvenile dispersal in less than two hundred years. Other examples are known: the habitat destruction that wiped out the eastern deciduous forests at the turn of the century led to expansion of pasture birds into the eastern United States, and some of these, like Bewick's wren, quickly developed migratory populations. These have since disappeared as forests replaced second-growth scrub and pastures through ecological succession.

Given the frequency with which Neotropical birds disperse north, and the rapidity with which birds have developed migratory populations within historic times, it is likely that the process of long-distance dispersal led to migratory populations. The spectacular abundance of food in the form of emerging insects that develops in deciduous and coniferous forests of America and Canada enabled these birds to outbreed their southern nonmigratory ancestors, which eventually led (in some cases) to strictly migratory populations. Dispersal to these areas would give the pioneering birds an instant benefit. And the original impetus for leaving was to avoid competition with their parents and neighbors in their crowded tropical habitats.

But when you consider the migratory warblers, flycatchers, tanagers, and thrushes that breed far to the north of Kennesaw Mountain, and the incredible routes they must take to reach their breeding and wintering grounds, it seems that a piece of this puzzle is missing. For example, why on earth did they disperse so far? Why not simply migrate to northern Mexico? Why not stop in Georgia? Why go from the Amazon all the way to the boreal forests of Canada?

Birds that use Kennesaw Mountain as a stopover flaunt incredible migratory feats. Most migrate along a trans-Gulf migratory route—they fly over the Caribbean from locations in the West Indies, South America, or Mexico. Almost all of them continue on, moving up the Appalachians to breeding sites far to the north. Only a handful of species remain in the Atlanta area to breed—the pair of warblers already mentioned, plus a few flycatchers, tanagers, a hummingbird, and the wood thrush. Many species breed instead in the northeastern United States and as far as the boreal forests of Canada.

By late summer many of these species return by essentially the same path they took in the spring—examples include worm-eating warblers, yellow warblers, yellow-throated warblers, Nashville warblers, black-throated blue warblers, and black-throated green warblers. These are joined by some species whose spring trip was along a more westerly route that hugged the Gulf Coast, but whose return trip takes them through Kennesaw. These are more common during the fall than in the spring and include Tennessee warblers, chestnut-sided warblers, bay-breasted warblers, cerulean warblers, Swainson's thrush, purple martins, and broad-winged hawks. Others are more common in spring because their return route is along the Atlantic coast farther east than Atlanta—yellow-rumped warblers, Cape May warblers, Connecticut warblers, blackpoll warblers, great-crested flycatchers, and blue-headed vireos. Blackpoll and Connecticut warblers are the only Kennesaw migrants whose return flight takes them directly across the Atlantic Ocean to South America, with only breathless stopovers in the Caribbean. This last route in particular defies belief. How could such an incredibly long flight by such a tiny bird develop? Blackpolls winter in northern South America and fly across the Gulf of Mexico in spring, traveling in huge numbers through the Atlanta area in April. They are not seen again until the following April, because their return trip touches off in Nova Scotia and takes them directly home across the open Atlantic.

This seemingly impossible feat becomes more reasonable if you consider that the trip would have been much easier eighteen thousand years ago. During the late Pleistocene, at the end of the last ice age, much of the habitat now occupied by various Neotropical migrants was buried under a mile-thick layer of ice. At that time the breeding habitat currently preferred by blackpoll warblers was a thousand miles closer to the equator. Spruce-fir forests covered most of Georgia. Pollen samples analyzed by William Watts from a sag pond just west of Kennesaw Mountain in Bartow County show that this region was dominated by jack pine, spruce, and fir twenty thousand years ago. Deciduous forests were confined to sites along the Gulf Coast and northern Mexico. Coniferous forests were extensive throughout the heartland of America and stretched across the flatlands of the Southwest where deserts now occur. A thin strip of tundra ringed the glacial moraine, which was parked in New York and across the Midwest. At this time, the habitats now used by Neotropical migrants were much closer to their source in Central America, Mexico, and the West Indies. Sea level was over a hundred feet lower than it is now, so larger areas of the Caribbean and Gulf Coastal shelf were exposed, with less ocean separating them. Dispersal into prime temperate zone habitat could easily have occurred at this time, on a larger scale than the occasional accidentals that arrive today. A virtual ramp of tropical rain forest, tropical deciduous forest, and temperate coniferous and deciduous forest habitat led right up North America's back door from Mexico and the Caribbean. Thousands of birds dispersed from the tropics and established breeding populations along the thin rings of available habitat south of the glaciers.

At the end of the ice age, the glaciers began their long retreat. Slowly the ice moved back north, revealing millions of acres of bare land to be occupied by forests. The tundra and spruce-fir forests followed the ice north, filling the void through ecological succession. The diverse deciduous forests—the sanctuary of Asa Gray's disjunct plants—began to trickle out from refugia in the Florida Panhandle and Tunica Hills in Louisiana. Birds that set up migratory populations in these forests would return each year, only to find they had shifted a few hundred yards farther north. With each generation the forests and the birds would slowly expand their ranges until they finally occupied their present location. Through this incremental and gradual process, long-range migration developed. This explanation makes the bird's bewildering flights much more feasible. It would have allowed plenty of time for development of new adaptations and behaviors, and for birds to establish niches and locate novel, unused habitats. Only the birds with the best cardiovascular endurance and fat storage capacity left descendants that now make the most outrageous flights.

Evidence for this scenario comes from the modern distributions of wood warblers. Over a dozen species occupy cool temperate coniferous forests, which are currently positioned in the northernmost United States and Canada. Several more have ranges that center on these spruce-fir forests but also breed in deciduous forests of the Appalachians. Others are found in coniferous forests of the West. Although there are many warblers that breed strictly in deciduous forests, many of these prefer successional habitats—habitats that would have been very common during the last ten thousand years over much of the United States as new land became exposed where once there was ice. Their distributions reflect the habitat available during and just after the ice age better than they do the modern reality.

The legacy of the ice age is written in the DNA of Swainson's thrush. This small brown bird migrates in large numbers over Kennesaw Mountain during April and returns south from September through October. The winter range is in the Andes of Peru and Bolivia, and in Central America. Swainson's thrush is not as attractive as its close relative the wood thrush, which breeds in Kennesaw's forests and is a rich red-brown bird with a neat pattern of spots on its breast. Instead, Swainson's thrush is duller and its spots less bold. You can hear it sing its enchanting song from the far corner of a pine forest in the Rockies, but no closer to Georgia than the highlands of West Virginia. They sing the song hidden in the underbrush, and they are rather difficult to see.

Researchers Kristen Ruegg and Thomas Smith beat these odds, and using mist nets in likely breeding, stopover, and wintering sites from Alaska to Bolivia, they captured and obtained blood samples from 420 Swainson's thrushes. The analysis of these samples revealed a remarkable pattern: Swainson's thrushes migrate in two separate populations—a western coastal population that migrates from Mexico north along the Pacific coast to southeastern Alaska, and a continental population that migrates across the Gulf of Mexico and throughout the boreal forests as far west as Alaska. These populations reflect the known extent of coniferous forests during the ice age; at that time a desert separated an eastern and a western forested region. Ruegg and Smith's molecular clock estimate confirmed that these populations diverged over ten thousand years ago. Still more incredible was their finding that some thrushes in Alaska do not migrate by the most direct route south. Instead, they migrate east clear across Canada, funnel through the South, and fly back across the Caribbean. Such a pattern could occur only if these thrushes had spread in small steps during a time when the original spruce-fir forests were much farther to the south and east. The birds expanded incrementally northwest, just as the forest did. This set up the very unusual pattern whereby Swainson's thrushes breeding in Alaska take two very different routes back to separate wintering grounds: one that flies directly south, and another that flies east for quite a distance before turning south.

This route mirrors the proposed route of expansion for these northern forests from their ice age position. According to Evelyn Pielou, pollen analyses show that coniferous forests migrated northwest from the Great Lakes region into the Yukon and Alaska. The thrushes followed. A separate glacier would have kept the two populations from meeting in southeastern Alaska. Several other species of boreal forest–breeding birds show similar distributions. For example, the two kinds of yellow-rumped warblers—the myrtle warbler and Audubon's warbler—show a nearly identical distribution, with a contact zone in western Canada where the two expanding forests met.

It is amazing to think that some of the Swainson's thrushes that visit Kennesaw Mountain each fall are arriving from breeding sites in Alaska, after having flown east across Canada before turning south. They then fly across the Gulf of Mexico to wintering sites in the Andes. This bizarre and inefficient route is a legacy of the last ice age.

That's so much more interesting than simply ticking the paramount bee-prodder off your life list.

# 12

# Kennesaw's Bird Magnetism

O NE NOVEMBER I TOOK MY wife for a walk up Kennesaw. It was a cool, se-
rene, and cloudless day on the heels of a few days of low gray clouds and
rain, so the trail was crowded with many other walkers. The visitors' center
was a zoo so we drove down to the other side of the mountain off Burnt Hickory and parked near Pigeon Hill. We walked up the trail and approached the
summit of Little Kennesaw from the south, admiring the rock outcrops and
gnarled chestnut oaks. I had forgotten that from where we started, the hike to
the summit of Big Kennesaw is an affair requiring a rather substantial com-
mitment. We had eaten a big breakfast but brought no lunch. My wife doesn't
much like hiking anyway, so we were getting ready to turn around when I
heard distant, whimpering flutes. Over the booming of incoming passenger
aircraft and the persistent and ever-present hum of traffic it was like a faint
echo, ringing in my ears. Was it there or not? The sound was ventriloquis-
tic, arriving on the mountain seemingly from the southeast one second, then
apparently from the north. It was a high-pitched piccolo that rose, peaked,
and declined. The sounds repeated and sometimes overlapped, as if in angelic
conversation. Delighted, I told my wife she was in for a lucky treat. The cranes
were coming.

We scrambled up the side of Little Kennesaw for a better vantage point, the
sounds of the cranes distant and difficult to pinpoint. I feared we would not be
able to see the birds. I scanned off to the west and east to see whether I could
spot the dashed lines of a flock. Flocks of sandhill cranes are often enormous,
much larger than the fifteen-to-twenty-bird flocks of Canada geese. Instead,
over a hundred birds can cover big sections of sky, making up flocks in the
shape of an asymmetric wedge or even a W. They often fly incredibly high—
as high as twelve thousand feet—so that you must strain to see the individual
birds, and their calls truly travel down far from the heavens. By the time the
sounds reach you their flutelike notes collect in your ears like light snow.

The migration of sandhill cranes is an underappreciated natural specta-
cle that folks in the Atlanta area should always notice. It should brighten their
February and November like it has mine since I first noticed them tracing
across the sky above the Flint River floodplain when I was a teenager. Atlanta
falls right along their migratory path from the upper Midwest and Canada

to Florida, and each year thousands fly through over a period of a couple of weeks on their way south to winter in the marshes and swamps of the Panhandle and on their way north to breed among the lake-pocked Canadian muskeg. Sometimes on bright days, after a long week of bad weather, their appearance high in a cerulean sky will bring you back into soaring spirits, reminding you that the coming winter will be short, or that the short winter is nearly over. Under conditions like this dozens of flocks will pass in one day, so that hardly a minute is lacking their magical trumpeting.

According to Peter Matthiessen, cranes are among the most ancient birds, and fossils attributed to sandhill cranes have been found in nine-million-year-old deposits, making them among the oldest living bird species on earth. Standing at nearly four feet tall, the sandhill crane is a very large bird, among the largest in the state. Certainly it is our tallest bird, unless you count its relative, the critically endangered whooping crane, which has been reintroduced and now migrates through the East once again. Georgia has two populations of sandhill cranes: a permanent one that stays year-round in the Okefenokee Swamp, and a migratory one that winters in Florida, breeds in the wet prairies of the far north, and takes a direct path through Georgia each February and November. These are considered separate subspecies, the nonmigratory *Grus canadensis pratensis* being smaller than the migratory *G. c. tabida*, which we were presently scanning the horizon for. Sandhill cranes are considered "accidentals" at Kennesaw Mountain, because they are usually noted only once or twice per year—a status that possibly reflects their tendency to fly over Kennesaw when few birders visit the mountain, rather than their actual rarity.

Cranes are intimately tied to large, trackless marshes—their long legs and necks and bayonet beaks are well adapted for striding among tall reeds seeking cold-blooded prey and vegetable matter of almost any kind. From their tall stance sandhill cranes can scan far into the foggy depths of a Wisconsin morning for approaching danger. The wariness and anxiety they display at their nests were once great assets for surviving nest robbers like raccoons and predators like wolves. But this same caution and reliance on wilderness marshes has led to the drastic decline of nearly every crane species in the world. Sandhill cranes are a rare and happy exception—although by the early 1900s these birds were almost as rare as the whooping crane, they alone have made an incredible comeback. With the exception of the nonmigratory populations in Florida, Mississippi, and Cuba, which are small and in need of extreme conservation attention, migratory sandhill cranes number in the hundreds of thousands, possibly more individuals than all the other crane species combined.

The sounds became much closer than the intermittent and faint whispering ("tinkling bells," according to Aldo Leopold) we had heard all morning, and they began to fill the air around us as we wound up the flanks of Little Kennesaw. At this distance they sounded more like the desperate, breathless honking of some Pleistocene mammal. Writers have tried with difficulty to capture their stirring call with words. H. M. Laing (quoted by Arthur Cleveland Bent) thought it was a "hoarse, unnatural croak that rips from the throat, a vibrant puttering that seems to suggest something prehistoric—such a call as one might expect that our far-gone ancestors heard in the days when pterodactyls and their kind flew about the marshes." Leopold wrote that it contained a beauty "yet uncaptured by language," and that "when we hear his call we hear no mere bird. We hear the trumpet in the orchestra of evolution." Matthiessen considers cranes the greatest and most stirring birds, whose voices, "like clarion calls out of the farthest skies, summon our attention to our own swift passage on this precious earth." Cranes have a large, triply coiled trachea packed into their sternum, which amplifies sound vibrations and enables them to make their clamorous, penetrating calls. Matthiessen wrote that they can be heard from two and a half miles away.

The cranes were now directly overhead, the trilling honks noticeable to everyone on Kennesaw's trails. A fainter set of calls sounded from the west, and I looked and then pointed out a large flock of fifty or so birds in tight formation about a mile away. I handed my wife the binoculars and she looked at them, commenting that they looked much like the gray brolgas from her home in Australia. The flock continued on gracefully and within minutes it would be miles to the south, over near Powder Springs. To the east we could see another flock—this one a larger wedge of over a hundred birds trailing behind the apex bird—heading directly toward Atlanta. But the loudest flock, the closest flock, was still not in view.

Then they were directly overhead, so close we could easily see their eyes and red napes just peeking around the side of their heads from below. Their enormous cloud-gray wingspans could be heard swooshing over the sounds of their rattling *keeow! keeow! keeow!* Over the top of the mountain, the flock was no tightly composed *V*, wedge, or *W*. They were disorganized, flapping their wings far more frequently than the typical lazy put-putting of soaring cranes. The cranes called out almost angrily, circling like vultures, some close together in small packs crossing the paths of others who were off by themselves. About forty cranes swarmed clumsily around the summit for a couple of minutes, descending nearly to the height of the trees, as if the mountain were radiating an unseen force that confused and broke them up. They eventually floated a half mile south and re-formed an orderly wedge, continuing on toward Florida. One crane circled a few more times around the summit and moved off to the east before reorienting toward the now-distant flock. They became specks along the horizon before the soloist caught up.

In the early 1800s Philadelphia was the intellectual and scientific power-house of America, where men whose names still cling to plants and animals throughout our country laid the foundations for our understanding of the natural world. This circle of intellectual authority included some of the founding fathers of our political and social institutions, and these minds mingled and shared ideas with great gentlemen naturalists. Benjamin Franklin was a family friend of the pioneering botanists John and William Bartram, who named a rare flowering shrub after him. Alexander Wilson—considered the father of American ornithology—took illustration tips from William Bartram. Wilson was pals with John Bachman, who collected specimens in South Carolina and who is familiar to birders as the namesake of Bachman's sparrow—a rare visitor to Kennesaw Mountain—and the now-extinct Bachman's warbler. Wilson himself has a number of birds named after him, such as the Wilson's warbler, phalarope, and plover. Wilson became the patriarch of pioneering birders based in Philadelphia. But when they had the chance, these early birders would take a small watercraft out into Delaware Bay to the southernmost tip of New Jersey. Back in those days birding was accomplished using a shotgun rather than binoculars, and most birders were perhaps more appropriately referred to as gunners. And word had spread that there was good shooting to be had at Cape May, New Jersey.

Wilson's good friend George Ord was on a trip to Cape May when he blasted a small warbler he didn't recognize. He gave the specimen to Wilson, who described the bird as a new species in his classic *American Ornithology*, sanctifying the place with its own bird—the Cape May warbler. This is a common bird in the Atlanta area on spring migration, and it takes a more easterly route south during fall, so it is far less common on Kennesaw Mountain at that time. This easterly route takes small numbers through Cape May every fall, but it took some time for birders to find the best place to see them there. Some say the name is not fitting at all; the bird was not seen again at Cape May for another hundred years after its discovery, and it is rather uncommon during fall migration. But I think it's wholly appropriate if you look at the situation the other way around. Although Ord would have found dozens of specimens of the little bird if he'd traveled north into Canada's boreal forests, the fact that he shot it on migration at the southern tip of New Jersey is important. This bird is but one example of the birding superlatives of America's most famous migratory hot spot.

Over the next century, birders traded firearms for optics, and systematic study of this migration stopover led to a better understanding of its importance. Fall migration is especially exciting at Cape May, when birds overshoot the coast because of strong northwest winds, forcing them to double back to Cape May in the morning. Thousands of migrating robins, flickers, thrushes, and hawks are seen on occasion, sometimes dotting the lawns of the sleepy beach town like falling leaves. The sandy, piney habitat of southern New Jersey is suitable for some birds that do not otherwise occur this far north. Species that breed much farther north visit during spring migration. A perfect blend of climate, geography, coastline, and chance makes Cape May a hallowed destination for birders. And this is very important: Cape May's proximity to the northeastern megalopolis of Baltimore–Philadelphia–New York means it gets plenty of visits from a species that is certain to make apparent local bird numbers skyrocket. I'm talking, of course, about the birders themselves. There is no other birding destination with such a long and detailed pedigree of study—from Wilson himself all the way up to modern hourly web updates from platoons of die-hard birders scouring the cape for rarities. And birders are well known for picking out great sites and sticking with them. But who would know whether the birds were just as good in New Egypt, Tuckerton, Tabernacle, or Shamong, New Jersey?

Still, something about the place certainly got people's attention early on, and there is every indication that Cape May is an important stopover for migratory birds, even if we don't have comparative information about the rest of the Atlantic coast. Likewise, the Gulf Coast of Texas and Louisiana is a bottleneck for arriving trans- and intra-Gulf migrants moving north in the spring, and in this case there are radar data to prove it. Birds crossing the Gulf even correct themselves if a gale blows them too far east, so that they arrive consistently within a few dozen miles of these shores. Such an unnecessary waste of energy appears to be tied to their hardwired and ancient migratory instincts— during the last ice age that spot on the Gulf Coast may have been the best option for birds needing a nice stopover complete with deciduous trees bursting with fat inchworms on which to refuel.

Hot spots are locations with a reputation for good birding in several categories, including high numbers of species, numbers of individuals, and frequency of rare birds showing up where they seemingly don't belong. Migratory hot spots are now studied extensively by ecologists and are more appropriately referred to as stopovers—locations migratory birds use as staging and feeding areas on their way to and from wintering and breeding grounds. The importance of stopovers has only recently garnered attention, since initially the focus was understandably on their breeding or wintering habitats.

Several geographical factors appear to be responsible, at least in part, for the presence of an important migratory hot spot. Most well-known hot spots are along heavily vegetated coastlines, so that coastal birds, like sandpipers and terns, can be seen within a few minutes of forest dwellers, like wood thrushes and worm-eating warblers. Many are near important and broad biogeographic boundaries, as in Cape May's position at the midpoint between the southern and northern states. A similar and even greater admixture of species is seen along the southern coast of Texas, where otherwise Mexican species intermingle with more familiar North American birds.

A good migratory hot spot must also first be in the path of the birds. Any place can be good for birds if it has a good mix of habitats and if it falls between two major biogeographic zones—imagine a tall mountain range between two continents: it would have lots of birds because of the number of habitats along the elevation rise of the mountains, and possibly also an interesting mix of totally unrelated birds. But for such a place to have two seasonal highs of maximum bird abundance, it would have to lie along the migratory route of large numbers of birds moving during spring and fall. This is a key ingredient for a rich migratory bird hot spot.

Another important contributor is the availability of large, unbroken patches of forested habitat. In the Great Lakes region—an important choke point for Neotropical migrants on their way to and from the far north—more birds are seen via radar concentrating in large patches of forest, and they avoid agricultural fields. The birds appear to be attracted to forested natural landscapes and even heavily landscaped urban parks and yards. This is surely a simple result of the migrants' need to obtain food, which we have seen is heavily tied to spring outbreaks of caterpillars. We cannot expect our brave migrants to simply make do with cutover fields and useless grains, so they instead seek out large patches of forest. It's a good thing they also seem to make do with urban and suburban landscapes, because we have certainly provided them with plenty of those.

Finally, many migratory hot spots are often at geographic pinch points— peninsulas or isthmuses—protruding into a body of water. Point Pelee, Ontario, is a forested wedge sticking very much like a thorn into Lake Erie and accumulates large numbers of migrating birds in both spring and fall. It is assumed the fall rush is caused when the point funnels hundreds of birds to the very sharp tipping point before they make the decision to cross. Cape May is similarly tapered and appears to funnel migrants to the very end of the state, where they might linger for a time before they cross Delaware Bay and continue south. Since Cape May projects to the southern tip of New Jersey, it has this effect mostly in autumn. Many other birding hot spots are similarly shaped islands or peninsulas projecting from bigger landmasses all over the world—they are often along the major migratory routes on one or both sides of a large body of water and stud the coasts of the Mediterranean, Scandinavia, Central America, and Asia.

How does Kennesaw Mountain compare? First, and quite obviously, Kennesaw Mountain will never be placed on the A-list of migratory bird hot spots because it is too far inland. The number of breeding and visiting birds will always be embarrassingly puny compared to places along the coast. Our park rarely or never attracts sandpipers, terns, gulls, jaegers, diving ducks, sea ducks, or any ducks, really, save perhaps an occasional lost mallard. This is Kennesaw's greatest bird shortcoming, although it is understandably through no fault of its own.

Does Kennesaw Mountain lie in the path of migrating birds? The answer to this is an emphatic yes, although it could be positioned better for certain birds than it is. For birds that migrate directly across or along the Gulf of Mexico in spring, the Gulf Coast of Texas and Louisiana is better. If Kennesaw Mountain were there instead it would be incredible in spring. But plenty of trans-Gulf migrants also continue moving northeast from the Gulf Coast or migrate directly north through Georgia, so Kennesaw lies in their path and receives plenty of visits from such birds. During the fall, larger numbers of birds use the Atlantic coast as a return route to the Caribbean and South America, which is why Cape May is so much better than Kennesaw Mountain during that season, at least for some species. But Kennesaw is centrally located between these spring and fall extremes. It is neither hot nor cold, but a nice medium for both migration seasons, a Goldilocks situation that makes it pretty good for all migrating species. And as we shall soon see, for at least one important species it is among the best.

Kennesaw Mountain is also an undeniably large tract of mature forest, so much so that it is often described as "an island in a sea of urban sprawl." But objectively speaking, isn't Atlanta just as frequently referred to as "the city in the trees"? As we saw in chapter 3, regeneration occurs so quickly in the South that unless the landscape is completely paved over (which admittedly does happen in metro Atlanta far too frequently), a maturing forest will be present within a hundred years of abandonment. This has resulted in an urban landscape in and around Atlanta that is dominated by not only large numbers of buildings and dwellings but also thousands of trees. Many of them are large and beloved by city goers, and the old neighborhoods in Atlanta have giant old oaks teeming with squirrels, blue jays, and black rat snakes. Are the protected and largely intact forests of Kennesaw Mountain any better? Or more to the point, are they better from the point of view of a migrating bird looking for a bellyful of inchworms?

At first glance Kennesaw Mountain's inland location would seem to disqualify it as a geographic pinch point. But it could be argued, and in fact it has been argued, that Kennesaw Mountain is a peninsula of sorts. The Blue Ridge Mountains do indeed taper to a fine point not far from Kennesaw Mountain, so birds that migrate along the high elevations of the Appalachians might be expected to be funneled by the mountains before they melt away into the low hills of the Piedmont near Atlanta. The last high peak of much significance before the Gulf of Mexico is Kennesaw Mountain. Likewise, for birds approaching the mountains from the south, it is the first prominent peak, so it has been interpreted as a sort of beacon for the birds orienting themselves toward the spine of our eastern mountains.

But we should consider whether a large part of the park's magnetism for birds has nothing at all to do with the birds or the place. The final ingredient needed to make a bird hot spot is, of course, people. Nobody will ever know how many birds fly over any spot unless somebody is there to see them. And perhaps some places get a good reputation largely because birders have adopted them as easily accessible locations a short distance away from home with decent numbers of birds. In this category Kennesaw Mountain also excels. It is a large park within easy reach of most citizens of a large American city, and it receives visits from millions of tourists. Like Central Park, Jamaica Bay, and other notable urban bird hot spots, Kennesaw Mountain receives visits from plenty of birders. The more birders, the more likely it is that rarities will be located and noticed. Kennesaw Mountain can even be seen as a case in point: the mountain was not recognized for its importance to migrating wood warblers until the 1990s, when birders finally took notice. Surely the birds were there all along, but it took a dedicated effort by a handful of birders to document that the place was special.

The fact that Kennesaw Mountain is an important bird stopover was only recently discovered. But this also was not enough. Short of shooting a migrating warbler and naming it after the mountain, heralding the status of this inland site between two major migration flyways required a great deal of work, determination, enthusiasm, and no small amount of charm. Kennesaw needed a spokesperson. An advocate. A champion. Kennesaw needed a hero. Our hero certainly came in the physical guise that you'd expect for such a task, but he was also issued the prosaic name Giff Beaton.

If you look up the word "stud" in the dictionary, you'll find a picture of Giff Beaton in a crisp airline uniform, looking over his muscular shoulder grinning at you from the cockpit of a 737. He has intelligent but easy eyes and a big meaty jawline studded by a preposterously handsome chin dimple. He's tall and athletic. He is overwhelmingly confident but brimming with wit and enthusiasm, and if you really get to know him you'll find he's fast with an edgy sense of humor. He should have been the best man at your wedding. You send him in to negotiate any deal. He got picked first for all the clementary school recess kickball games. If your wife cheated on you with him you'd get over it fast. Did I mention he flies planes for Delta?

For the universe to accommodate such an outrageously great and masculine guy, there just had to be a catch. First, there's the name. I didn't have the courage to ask Giff where he got his interesting handle, so we'll have to leave it at that. But more importantly, Giff is an inveterate nerd. This flying beefcake is obsessed with daintily colorful winged creatures like wood warblers, butterflies, and tiger beetles. Words like "coral hairstreak butterfly," "superciliary," and "exquisite" have escaped his lips. When given the opportunity to explain his obsession with aerial nature in terms of some unfathomable, subconscious, and ultimately heroic connection to his ability to fly, he demurs, offering caterpillars as an example of something he's interested in that doesn't fly. Caterpillars! He's the acknowledged expert in Georgia for all of these animal groups, and he became so through no special scientific training. He taught himself everything he knows, which includes a considerable amount. Experience also played a role: because his job takes him all over the world, he has seen somewhere between three thousand and four thousand bird species. Plus, packed into the airline pilot physique is a bottomless steel trap of a brain—a hungry and unquenchable receptacle for processing biological shapes, colors, patterns, and sounds. This is not your ordinary Delta pilot, nor is he a standard academic biologist. Instead, think of Giff as a modern gentleman naturalist. With emphasis on "man."

In January 1991 Giff moved to Atlanta and quickly became a sort of Alexander Wilson of local ornithology, heading up a dedicated group of birders who began systematically studying the birdlife of Kennesaw Mountain. When Giff first moved in, his friend Bruce Dralle introduced him to some of the local birding spots around town and told him Kennesaw Mountain was a decent place to see early black-and-white warblers. At the time, the mountain was barely known as a birding spot, and none of the local guides mentioned it as anything special. Wanting to get an early start on his birding, Giff first visited Kennesaw Mountain one or two times in the spring of 1991 with Dralle. That first spring, the trips were nothing exciting; they did not go at peak migration times, and one can imagine it was not the same experience birders have now, because no reliable birding route had been blazed. The guys probably wandered fairly aimlessly looking for birds. I remember my first trip was like this—I walked up the main trail from the parking lot instead of the Mountain Road and had to crane my neck to look up in the canopy at anonymous birds I couldn't see much of, save their bellies.

Beaton and Dralle returned later for the fall migration, and according to Giff, one day in late August they "just killed it." They saw very large numbers of migrating birds much earlier than they would have otherwise expected. A few additional trips that year cinched it—they realized they were onto something. They decided to try again in the spring of 1992 to see whether it was just a fluke. They were not disappointed. Instead, as Giff remembers, "We decided collectively, Bruce Dralle and I, to hit it hard in 1992. We were astounded; it was better than any other Atlanta spot by far." A tight-knit group of regulars began birding with them. The great days and rarities started piling up. They saw two hundred broad-winged hawks on the same foggy day they witnessed a fallout of American coots, of all things—these normally aquatic birds were strangely perched in trees on the summit. They recorded a thousand thrushes flying overhead one September. They saw more than twenty-five species of warblers on nine separate days and experienced an all-time high and practically unthinkable count of thirty warbler species in one day. But it was the cerulean warbler that made them decide to start systematically birding Kennesaw in 1993 and keep detailed notes of everything they found.

Figure 13. Kennesaw Mountain is an important migratory stopover for the beautiful cerulean warbler. Photo by Giff Beaton.

The cerulean warbler is one of the prettiest birds in North America. Although not as gaudy as the painted bunting, and perhaps not as striking as the scarlet tanager or Blackburnian warbler, the subtler sky blue of the cerulean ranks it high on any list of coveted birds. Unlike some warblers accused of having inappropriate names—and there are many—the name "cerulean" (Latin for "blue") is quite fitting. And what a lovely blue it is: it has been described as "heavenly blue," "aqua," and even the curiously unimaginative "cerulean blue." The blue head and back of the bird contrasts with a lighter belly streaked with blue gray and interrupted by a handsome blue-black collar. However you attempt to describe it, its blue is unique among wood warblers and it is probably this extraordinary color scheme that makes it one of the most sought-after birds in the United States. The bird is also frequently very hard to see. And of course it is also rare and has become rarer still in the past few decades. By the time Beaton and Dralle started seeing predictable and rather large numbers of ceruleans on Kennesaw, the bird was being considered for listing under the Endangered Species Act.

The cerulean warbler was also first described by Alexander Wilson in his *American Ornithology*, from a male shot by yet another friend in eastern Pennsylvania. This warbler has always been a poorly known species by virtue of its highly arboreal habits—it feeds, breeds, and nests high in the canopy of large deciduous trees. For this reason it is often difficult to see. For years the only look I got was of the pale, nondescript underside of a bird pointed out to me in Kentucky. It can be maddeningly elusive on Kennesaw Mountain, and for years I would show up the day after the most recent sighting. The first one I got a decent look at required an hour of persistence and made my neck sore for a week. This was in western Pennsylvania; it took several more years before I finally saw a subtly beautiful female on Kennesaw Mountain. The males can be heard singing their buzzy song nearly constantly, but to see them doing anything requires patience. The cerulean warbler winters in northern South America and crosses the Gulf of Mexico to arrive on the Gulf Coast around mid-April. From there it is a rare migrant throughout the eastern United States until it arrives on its breeding grounds in mature riparian forests of the Ohio River valley around mid-May. Scattered breeding localities are known from as far south as North Georgia. On Kennesaw Mountain most cerulean warblers arrive in late April and a larger number pass through from late July through early September, with peak numbers arriving during the dreary dog days of August.

The bird prefers large tracts of forest and this is thought to be the reason the cerulean warbler is declining—forest fragmentation is rampant in the bird's wintering and breeding grounds. Part of the alarm over the cerulean warbler's status is due to how little we know about the bird; its migratory pathway is among the most poorly understood of any wood warbler. Its habitat requirements are only now becoming understood. Surveys conducted by canoe are far superior to the normal walking transect methods used by ornithologists—males call on evenly spaced territories along rivers in the heart of the species' distribution. Discovering large numbers of cerulean warblers at Kennesaw Mountain during spring and fall contributed a big piece of the puzzle about the bird's biology. In fact, Kennesaw is undisputedly one of the best places to see this bird on migration. In 1995 Beaton and Dralle saw thirty-three cerulean warblers in one morning—more than most birders see in their lives.

So with scientific zeal Beaton and company began documenting the pattern of bird migration on Kennesaw Mountain, but it was the importance of the place to this heavenly blue bird that made Giff realize that they somehow had to get the word out. Using the data he had collected up to that time, Giff published a paper in *Wingbars*, the newsletter of the American Birding Association. The report came out in June 1995 and made a big splash. Things started progressing quickly then, and as Giff remembers, "They took on a life of their own." In addition to the paper, Giff started giving talks at local, regional, and national bird conferences. Birders started showing up at Kennesaw from all over the country. When Giff organized local birding field trips, over a hundred people would show up. They came mostly to see the cerulean warbler, but local birders also started using Kennesaw as their prime go-to spot. I certainly did. So many birders came that the park historian became concerned that they would contribute to the erosion of important historical features. But the park superintendents loved it—always looking for anything to justify the need for already slim funds, they welcomed recognition of the importance of this historical park for rare birds. As the birders poured in, so too did the rarities—western birds like a black-throated gray warbler, MacGillivray's warbler, and Bell's vireo. Birds couldn't sneak through Kennesaw undetected anymore, and its reputation steadily grew larger and larger.

Eventually Giff published the results of his colleagues' twelve years of birding at Kennesaw in his exceptional regional guide, *Birds of Kennesaw Mountain*. By this time Kennesaw had become recognized as an internationally significant migratory bird hot spot and started showing up in regional and national birding guides. I first heard about its importance to birds around 2000 when I visited the mountain and saw a nice interpretive sign, which included a photo of a cerulean warbler. In just ten years the place had gone from a historical park known best for the heinous slaughter of three thousand Union soldiers to a birders' paradise on par with great birding hot spots like Point Reyes, Point Pelee, and Cape May. Giff doesn't try to hide his role in this transformation, nor should he. His charisma and energy are undeniable, and, in his own words, he's "a pretty decent cheerleader."

In his book, Giff answers the burning question everyone always asks him: "Why is Kennesaw so good?" He lists several factors, similar to those I mentioned for other bird hot spots that contribute to their importance as stopovers. The size, elevation, and location of Kennesaw Mountain as the last (or first, depending on your direction of approach) outpost of the Appalachians make it obvious to birds flying on migration, and it is a large patch of contiguous forest. Giff even recognizes that the number of birders covering Kennesaw has contributed to the number of birds noticed there. But this raises the unsavory possibility that it is the birders and not the birds who are truly responsible for the hot spot. Is it possible that the whole Atlanta area is similarly visited by large numbers of birds of all kinds, and because nobody has concentrated on another location to document them, they are able to fly through surreptitiously? In other words, could Giff just as easily choose any large tract of forest in the Atlanta area and find the same thing if he recruited twelve zealous birders and led bird walks of over a hundred people for a decade? Is Kennesaw good, or has Giff manufactured it through his own cult of personality? Is this hot spot biological or sociological?

Giff is convinced that he has documented a biological phenomenon, and his experience and naturalist instincts tell him that Kennesaw Mountain is special. Giff said, "To me, it is one of my favorite spots, and always will be. I have made well over a thousand birding trips up there! In terms of importance to birds, I don't think right now it's head and shoulders above every other local site like it was, but I think it's as important as anywhere else in Georgia. During the late 1990s and early 2000s, on any given day the Kennesaw Mountain Trail would always—or virtually always—have better birding than anywhere else."

But is Kennesaw really that good? In order to answer a question like this, you would have to conduct a study. Ideally you'd compare the number of birds seen by the same number of people at Kennesaw and some other location, perhaps one of the other small mountains nearby. To make things equal, you'd want each location to be about the same size. Certainly the area searched would have to be of a similar size. Unfortunately, since the same people can't be in two or more places at once, each group would have to have a similar level of birding skills. Or, you could have one person do all the birding, and this person could alternately search at random locations and compare the birds seen at those spots relative to those found on Kennesaw.

Exactly this kind of study was conducted in the late 1990s by a graduate student from Georgia Southern University. Surprisingly, the results do not strongly suggest that Kennesaw Mountain is any better than nearby Lost Mountain. This ornithological heresy was written by Andy Kinsey, who now lives near Gainesville and owns a nursery and tree farm. He's a super-nice guy and a family man. When he was a master's student he birded along defined trails on Kennesaw, Sweat, and Lost Mountain, all in the vicinity of the national battlefield park. He alternated where he birded on different days and compared the averages of several birding trips. Statistically speaking, the average number of species and average number of individual birds seen at Lost and Kennesaw Mountain were no different. Both were usually better than at Sweat Mountain. Kennesaw had a slight edge in all categories, but this was not enough for chance to be excluded as a possible explanation.

Such statistical tests are the bread and butter of ecologists; in order to convince us of a relevant pattern, you must first defeat the specter of chance. It's like this: if you had three Major Leaguers with batting averages of .330, .340, and .350, which one is the best? If you said the guy with a .350, you're using your gut. You might be right, but there's no way to be sure who is most likely to bat big in the next game. If you said that they are all too similar to really say, you're a scientist. What if the batter with the .350 had batted only once in his career, and the .330 was an average after hundreds of at-bats over a lifetime? I asked Giff what he thought of Kinsey's study, with the implication that part of Kennesaw's vaunted status is in fact due to the attention it has received, which of course he is nearly single-handedly responsible for. He accused me good-naturedly of "drinking too much of Andy's Kool-Aid."

But hidden in the pages of Kinsey's thesis is perhaps the most startling finding of all, relative to the allure of Kennesaw Mountain to birds. Kinsey found that birds seemed to arrive early in the morning on Kennesaw from the southeast, as if the prevailing winds had blown them off course and they were doubling back. Giff has noticed the same thing: even during the fall when birds might be expected to arrive from the north, they would arrive in the morning from all directions—and even from the south. On some mornings thrushes seemed to arrive from everywhere, their night calls ricocheting from every direction as they dripped down unseen into the trees. Moreover, Kinsey found an interesting difference in the birds' behavior during bad weather: birds would arrive just before dawn and stay longer, whereas during good weather most birds would disperse later in the day and move down the slopes of the mountain to feed in the nearby lowlands. Kinsey's study and Beaton's observations certainly suggest that the prominence of Kennesaw Mountain makes it a beacon for incoming birds. And since it is slightly more prominent than any of the other small peaks in the neighborhood, perhaps it receives a correspondingly higher number of visits from migrating birds. But why would Kennesaw beckon more during bad weather when birds don't see as well?

I think there is an additional, heretofore unmentioned element that may explain the strange patterns of abundance of Kennesaw's birds. Recall that Kennesaw Mountain was formed as a deep subsurface magma chamber long ago—it was injected under the crust and was later metamorphosed by massive pressures into a gneissic monolith, which has been eroding out for epochs, much more slowly than the softer rocks that overlay it. The slow cooling of the original magma chamber, plus its deep position in the earth, resulted in the modern solid rock outcrop of considerable prominence that we call Kennesaw Mountain. Strange minerals resulted from both the slow crystallization of the magma and its later metamorphosis. Since the texture of this rock can be quite coarse, some of these exotic crystals are quite large. And as we found in the first chapter of this book, large crystals of magnetite now exposed on Kennesaw's slopes emit a robust, anomalous magnetic signal.

Migrating birds can use several cues for navigation during migration, often in combination. Birds could potentially use the same range of senses that we possess for orientation and navigation: sight, smell, taste, hearing, and touch. However, like us, birds are visually oriented and perhaps their eyes are their most important navigational assets. But besides simply reading and memorizing the terrain below them as they fly, birds can also make use of polarized sunlight, the position of the sun, and even the position of the stars to orient themselves. But it is an additional sense—one not possessed by people—that birds rely on heavily for navigation. Birds can sense and make use of the earth's magnetic field.

Given that the earth's core is a rotating, solid mass of iron, it should be no surprise that it produces a powerful magnetic field—a field that is credited for protecting life forms from all sorts of powerful and dangerous radiation from the sun and outer space. This magnetic field can be imagined as a ball of invisible beams rising out from the planet like a grid. If this could actually be sensed, rather than imagined, you would have yourself a pretty good map of the whole earth and you could even determine your position with it. Early studies on bird navigation hinted that birds may indeed have an internal map used for migration. A deposit of magnetite in the ethmoid sinus of the beak—a region corresponding to the bridge of our nose—has a direct connection to the brain and appears to be involved in sensing magnetic signals. Homing pigeons are particularly adept at finding their home roosts during the day, but even in bad weather they aren't far off. But when Charles Walcott and Robert Green fitted them with curious little magnetic helmets, they flew all over the place, especially during bad weather. Pigeon fanciers notice that after solar flares their birds take longer to find their way home, if they ever return. Solar storms can interfere with the earth's magnetic field, interrupting its strength and creating the mysterious auroras. Based on these observations and a series of elegant experiments, animal behaviorist Kasper Thorup and his team showed that birds do indeed have an internal map of the earth based on the magnetic field: birds captured during migration and transported over two thousand miles off course did not continue flying in the same direction, nor did they double back to their capture position. Instead, they flew directly toward their destination from their release site, as if they knew exactly where they were.

But the earth's magnetic field is not the perfectly uniform, spherical globe often illustrated in science textbooks. The crust of the earth is pocked and piled with varying deposits of minerals that have their own unique magnetic signatures. In this way a magnetic map of the earth would probably be every bit as sculpted and detailed as the actual topography of the planet. Indeed, this is referred to as magnetic topography, and there is evidence that birds are influenced by the finer-scale local signatures of strongly magnetic mineral deposits. Many studies, including those by Walcott and others (summarized by Michael Freake and coauthors), have shown that homing pigeons and other birds become disoriented when flying over magnetic anomalies. Birds released near an iron mine flew erratically and stooped low for several minutes before clearing the mine, after which they resumed flying in straight lines in their intended directions.

Perhaps the reason Kennesaw Mountain appears to beckon birds is not only obvious ecological factors like forest cover, migration routes, and geography. Telling observations of birds arriving on Kennesaw Mountain may not be best explained in terms of its steep prominence, its luxurious forests, its proximity to the Appalachians, or its proximity to Atlanta and a dedicated pool of birders. Perhaps instead the flock of sandhill cranes I saw break up over the mountain and re-form beyond it were stymied by the dense magnetic field produced by thousands of large magnetite crystals that were forged deep in the earth's crust hundreds of millions of years ago. Perhaps the bizarre instance of American coots perched in trees one soggy morning was due to the unseen draw of the mountain's mineral aura, when these birds' usual navigational tools were of no use. Perhaps the night-calling thrushes arriving from all points of the compass are induced to land on Kennesaw not only by the mountain's physical presence but also by an unknowable force resulting from the same geological upheaval that produced the mountain itself. Perhaps the large numbers of wood warblers arriving from all-night flights across the South alight just a little longer on wet Kennesaw mornings because the mountain's magnetism draws their tiny internal compasses there in the dark, in the rain, and in the fog.

# 13

# Invaders

I VISITED THE SUMMIT OF BIG Kennesaw on April 10, 2005, and was surprised to find a strange plant I'd never seen, growing in abundance. It was about two feet tall and was spread everywhere along the summit and flanks of the mountain. A quick examination of its small white flowers revealed it to be a member of the mustard family. I had no idea what it was but suspected that it wasn't native. Very few native plants grow in what is known as a monoculture—a population of plants dominated by one species. If you ever see such a plant you can rightly conclude, probably nine times out of ten, that you are observing an alien species. I also didn't like the way this plant looked—it had a certain attitude—growing so tall for an herbaceous species, with leaves strangely shaped compared to those of native herbaceous plants. Another way to detect a nonnative plant, which works with less certainty than our first criterion, is growth habit—most native species have pretty similar growth habits. Since they all developed over long periods under similar environmental conditions, they've all converged on similar leaf sizes, shapes, and thicknesses.

Figure 14. Garlic mustard has taken over the herbaceous layer of this forest. Photo by Allie Fox.

This isn't always the case—witness a spruce pine growing within the swamp forests of South Georgia—but it can be a handy hint. This plant did not seem to belong, and indeed it doesn't. The plant is garlic mustard, *Alliaria petiolata*, a native of Europe that has become an invasive scourge in the United States.

Invasive species are plants, animals, or fungi that are not native to a region but aggressively and harmfully establish themselves and spread into new territory. Besides outright destruction of habitat by people, invasive species are the biggest threat to biodiversity in the world. And invasive species are our fault, too: most were introduced by humans. This can happen intentionally, such as by releasing wild animals for hunting, releasing unwanted pets, or planting nonnative plants for erosion measures, timber, or crops. Or it can happen unintentionally, as in releases or escapes from the pet trade, international shipments, or potted plants. A familiar example of an invasive species is the aggressive and smothering Asian vine kudzu, which can grow rapidly and envelop abandoned homesteads. Fire ants are another hated invasive species, and besides the painful and annoying stings that prevent Southerners from having a good, welcoming yard to play in, they cost billions of dollars in control efforts and in economic damage from crop losses. They can kill newborn calves and wipe out small native animals. Kennesaw Mountain National Battlefield Park is home to these and several other invasive species, most of which are plants. Some of them pollute the trails and were presumably planted in the past by the National Park Service for erosion control. Others arrived by more stealthy means.

Elsewhere invasive species have caused extinctions of native wildlife, especially in the Caribbean and Oceania where animal populations are small and restricted to tiny islands. On such islands mongooses, rats, cats, dogs, goats, and other animals introduced by people have wiped out native species, and the highest rates of extinction (so far) occur on islands. The diseases carried by nonnative species cause additional destruction, as I've described in the case of chestnut blight and the mighty American chestnut. But this crisis is not restricted to islands or to piecemeal losses of single tree species. The transport of species across continental boundaries and their arrival in new territories has led to a dramatic decline in the entire animal fauna of Australia. Emerging diseases arriving on the backs of invasive species have led to declines in all of the world's amphibians, and plummeting bat populations across the eastern United States. No fewer than four tree species in Georgia are currently threatened with extinction from introduced pathogens. In effect, humans are building bridges between the continents, allowing species without long associations to interact when they otherwise wouldn't. Disease and competition result in a dramatic loss of species diversity and the survival and spread of a few very adaptable species. The last time continental floras and faunas achieved such an intimate connection, the continents were quite literally connected in the giant supercontinent Pangaea. This was the event that brought Africa sliding into North America and incited the geological violence and tremendous pressure that metamorphosed Kennesaw Mountain's gabbro into gneiss. The greatest mass extinction in the history of the planet promptly ensued—one that made the extinction of the dinosaurs seem silly in comparison—and 90 percent of all life disappeared.

Although at first glance garlic mustard does not appear terribly sinister, and it possibly does not threaten Kennesaw Mountain as overtly as, say, overzealous relic hunters, this plant has the potential to harm the forests of the mountain with just as much potency. It can completely replace the herbaceous layer of a forest—the zone of greatest plant diversity in eastern deciduous forests—with a monoculture of garlic mustard. And garlic mustard grows best where garlic mustard has already grown, meaning that once it arrives it tends to stay. Meanwhile, native plants grow more slowly in areas that were previously occupied by garlic mustard. So even if the plant is removed, it leaves a lasting impact. Fortunately, when garlic mustard is completely removed, native plants will come back. But if left to its own devices, garlic mustard takes over, virtually completely, and stays in place forever. Garlic mustard not only outcompetes native herbaceous plants but also shades out and dominates saplings of overstory trees. In a forest invaded by garlic mustard, the very future of the forest is in question. The leaf litter layer often becomes thinner in forests invaded by garlic mustard, which leads to declines in salamanders. Without even considering what this could mean for the unique population of Webster's salamander on Kennesaw Mountain, remember that all those salamanders feed on the millions of insects involved in nutrient cycling in the forest floor decomposer food web. The widespread impact of garlic mustard is being intensively studied, but the complete extent of the problem cannot even be guessed.

Garlic mustard arrived in North America around 1860 from Europe. It is thought that it was intentionally introduced because parts of the plant are edible and make a decent garlic substitute. The economic instability caused by the Civil War made such substitutes appealing. According to Vikki Rodgers and colleagues, it quickly spread throughout the North and Midwest at an astonishing rate of 141 square miles (366 km$^2$) per year. One of the most alarming aspects of the spread is that the plant can invade perfectly pristine forests. Usually invasive plants do well only in sunny, disturbed habitats—weedy places. But this plant can penetrate the competitive environment of a mature hardwood forest packed with species that shrewdly divvy up the tiny amounts of sunlight that hit the forest floor, species that have been striving in such habitats for millions of years.

Several attributes of garlic mustard combine to give it its nasty competitive edge. Perhaps foremost is its toxicity. Like most plants, garlic mustard has a variety of compounds that discourage herbivores from feeding on it. This is because in its native range garlic mustard is harassed by no fewer than sixty-nine insect species, including weevils, bugs, and several kinds of caterpillars. None of these insects followed the plant to the United States, leaving it with not one enemy within its introduced range. Garlic mustard has developed defenses against its natural enemies to exaggerated extremes, and these make it nearly impervious to our native herbivores. Concentrations of toxins in the tissues make it dangerous for even large herbivores like white-tailed deer to eat it, and they will not touch it. This exacerbates the problem of garlic mustard's aggressive competitiveness—white-tailed deer will avoid the alien and selectively browse on the innocent native plants that it is replacing. The identity of one of the poisons that garlic mustard builds up in its tissues will ring familiar to fans of murder mysteries: it is nothing more obvious or less lethal than cyanide.

Garlic mustard uses its toxicity not only for self-defense but offense as well. Like the native broom sedge but on a much larger scale, garlic mustard poisons the soil around its roots. This inhibits the growth of native plants, microbes, and fungi and eliminates healthy decomposer communities. All of the beneficial interactions between plants and their fungal root associates are erased. Garlic mustard then stands alone, cruel king of its lonely domain. It is thought that this does not occur within its European range because the dozens of native herbivores keep the plant in check. We are not so lucky.

Garlic mustard also has a life cycle and growth habit not exhibited by any native plants. It is a biennial, meaning it grows for two years, reproduces the second year, and then dies. During the first year it sprouts as a small, ground-hugging rosette of crinkly, nearly octagonal leaves. At this time it competes with native plants with little enthusiasm. In Georgia, the young plant can obtain light during most winter days. Farther north it goes dormant under the snow. But it is only waiting. The first year of growth is only a ruse, a stratagem to assist what happens next. In the spring of its second year garlic mustard bolts up two or three feet in height, much taller than almost all of the spring-blooming wildflowers. It towers above them, easily outcompeting them for light. Around April it blooms, and it is not picky about what pollinators it will receive visits from. Solitary bees, bumblebees, and honeybees—species with few scruples—will visit this plant with just as much relish as they will any native mustard. This gives the plant ample cross-pollination, high genetic diversity, and a high rate of seed set. Then the real magic happens.

Garlic mustard is an unabashedly fertile and incredibly successful pro-
ducer of new garlic mustard plants. After cross-pollination the flowers soon
develop into multiple erect, rod-shaped seedpods (referred to as "siliques" in
the mustard family). These are packed with dozens of seeds. A small population of garlic mustard—one that could fit in your kitchen trash can—can produce one hundred thousand seeds, almost every one of which will be viable
and germinate. These are dispersed quite easily by wind, by animals, or on
clothing.

Eradication programs have failed disastrously in their attempts to control the plant. Herbicides can beat back but do not defeat garlic mustard, and
these chemicals also kill native plants. Pulling is effective but time consum-
ing and labor intensive, and it is not practical in most areas where infestations
are severe. It also increases soil erosion, something certainly not wanted near
the sensitive remains of earthworks on Kennesaw Mountain. However, garlic mustard itself causes increased soil erosion through its various impacts on
forest leaf litter and native plants, so this is a damned if you do, damned if you
don't proposition. Perhaps the only effective means of control is to pounce on
the plant as soon as it arrives in an area, eliminate it, and continue destroying it repeatedly every year before it sets seed. In a limited and well-delineated
area like Kennesaw Mountain, this is possible and necessary.

Scott Ranger first noticed the plant growing on Big Kennesaw back in 1989
right next to the parking area. Presumably, the tiny seeds of the plant hitched
a ride in somebody's shoes, tires, or clothes, and the invasion promptly began.
The oblivious park visitor who introduced garlic mustard had most likely just
arrived from somewhere in the Northeast or Midwest, where the plant has already conquered millions of acres. But this was the first case of the plant being
found in Georgia. Part of the reason is that garlic mustard prefers rich soils
with low acidity—the kind of soils that Kennesaw's mafic plants enjoy. The
plant also requires a cooling period before germination, which might sometimes be a tall order in southeastern winters. The plant's seeds have probably
been inadvertently sprinkled elsewhere in Georgia but have never taken off.
The cooler heights of Big Kennesaw provided a bridgehead for the plant.

Ranger was familiar with the danger this plant posed to the park, so he set
up an appointment with former park superintendent John Cissel. Cissel did
not seem the least bit concerned, and nothing happened. Based on an inter-
view Cissel gave to the *Civil War Times* at his retirement, we can with some
confidence conclude that Cissel thought he had bigger fish to fry. The park
was being overrun by thousands more visitors than it could handle, roads
were choked with traffic, and funds were scarce. And here some botanist was
claiming that some mustard plant was going to take over the mountain.

Years passed and only small-scale voluntary efforts to control the plant took place. A group of AmeriCorps volunteers dug up hundreds of pounds of garlic mustard and disposed of it (they were coincidentally led by a guy named Chris Hughes who I had known in college).

Sometime later Chris Evans, an exotic plant specialist, visited Kennesaw Mountain on a birding trip looking for cerulean warblers and noticed the plant. This time park officials responded. Current head park ranger Anthony Winegar considers invasive plants his "nemesis." Evans organized garlic mustard pulling days, and as many as forty volunteers arrived and began to wage war against the plant. The Kennesaw Mountain Trail Association joined in, and after each pulling they filled hundreds of garbage bags with the plants before they could set seed. The problem was bigger than anyone expected— seventeen acres on Kennesaw Mountain were infested with the plant. Chris intended to show how a rapid response to an invading species could halt its spread. Only later did he find out from Scott Ranger that the best opportunity had been squandered years before.

This plant and many other aliens remain established within the park, although the annual pulling appears to be holding garlic mustard in check. Anthony Winegar told me the park's current strategy for dealing with the plant is two pronged: the government sends its exotic plant management team in for a few weeks each year to work on garlic mustard and Asian privet (which is an even worse plant, to be honest, because it has taken over more of the state). The park is also actively seeking grant funds to help combat the invaders, but so far it has not been awarded these monies. The other tactic is continuing to organize and maintain volunteer efforts, and these sustained siege tactics appear to be working. I have never again seen garlic mustard as bold and dominant as that day in 2005. But the battle against this plant cannot relent, and vigilance must be maintained for years to win the war—the plant's seeds can remain viable in the soil for ten years.

# Epilogue

## The Future of Kennesaw Mountain

Monument, *n*. A structure intended to commemorate something which either needs no commemoration or cannot be commemorated.
—Ambrose Bierce, *The Devil's Dictionary*

O N JUNE 27, 1864, LANSING Dawdy, a former schoolteacher and adjutant of the Eighty-Sixth Illinois regiment, was shot and nearly killed as his Union column stormed the Dead Angle, site of perhaps the bloodiest assault on the Confederate stronghold during the Battle of Kennesaw Mountain. After the battle, rebel pickets were on patrol in the no-man's-land between the Dead Angle and the Union trenches and found him. When one of them realized he was still alive, he readied to bayonet him. Dawdy managed to give a Masonic hand signal, which the other rebel picket understood. A Mason himself, he intervened and dragged Dawdy over the rebel works. They carried him by night to a local enslaved woman's cabin, and she cared for him. To clean the wound, she pulled a silk handkerchief all the way through his body through the entrance and exit wound. Before Johnston evacuated the Kennesaw lines, Dawdy was transported to Atlanta as a prisoner. After a few weeks of recovery, a surgeon there recommended he be placed in the care of an Atlanta family. He was about to be put to bed in the spare room when one of Sherman's shells crashed through the roof and obliterated his intended quarters. He eventually convalesced with other Yankee prisoners in Macon. He received an honorable discharge on May 1, 1865. He survived the war.

Lansing Dawdy returned to Kennesaw Mountain several times after the war. According to the reminiscences of Margaret E. Jones, Dawdy was able to find and thank the kind woman who took care of him as well as the Confederate soldier who helped him over the rampart. In 1899, Dawdy purchased the sixty-acre farm that stood near the Dead Angle for $1,000. The plot was eventually transferred to the Colonel Dan McCook Brigade Association—named in honor of a Union colonel who was killed leading the attack on Cheatham Hill—in 1904. The small plot was intended as a quiet place for reflection and as a memorial

Figure 15. The Illinois soldiers' monument at the Dead Angle, Cheatham Hill. Photo by Wayne Hsieh.

for those who fought there, especially the Illinois boys who died within sight of the Dead Angle. A monument was erected as a tribute to Illinois troops on the fiftieth anniversary of the battle—June 27, 1914. Fittingly, this monument is made of Georgia marble and stands firm at Cheatham Hill to this day.

This small monument and the sixty-acre plot Dawdy bought formed the tiny nucleus from which today's Kennesaw Mountain National Battlefield Park grew. After being transferred to the ownership of the federal government in 1926, the park began to expand greatly and is now fully 2,965 acres in extent. It is still growing; a recent acquisition of a small hill west of the park added 42 new acres. The current stated purpose of the park is "to preserve, protect, and interpret, for the benefit and inspiration of the people, the historical and natural features of this major battle site in the American Civil War's 1864 Atlanta Campaign." Over a million tourists, history buffs, walkers, birders, and runners visit each year. For the past several decades Kennesaw was the second most frequently visited national battlefield or military park in the country, behind only Gettysburg. Since 2009 more people have visited Kennesaw Mountain every year than Gettysburg.

Not surprisingly, this level of visitation has led to trouble for the park. This is ironic given that, unquestionably, the most damage the mountain has ever endured was during the couple of weeks before, during, and after the battle that ultimately resulted in its establishment. During June and July 1864 thousands of soldiers felled trees, dug trenches, piled up earthworks, and rained countless bullets and explosive shells upon the mountain. One hundred and fifty years later, the land fares much better, even though the number of visitors each month is comparable to the number of soldiers that occupied the area in 1864. The trenches and earthworks are slowly healing as a result of erosion and reforestation, and only proactive, invasive, and ill-advised restoration measures will keep them from entirely disappearing. The forests are maturing after decades of succession. With a few notable exceptions, most plant and animal species present in 1864 are still here. And the modern Americans who visit the park—for the most part, anyway—are not firing cannons, shooting at each other, or digging holes.

But some folks just can't seem to follow the rules, so there have been cases where relic hunters have defaced the park. Collecting anything (including rocks, leaves, flowers, arrowheads, minié balls) or even killing snakes in a National Park Service site is illegal, which helps to preserve natural and historical features for all visitors to enjoy. A notable breach of this national etiquette happened in 2013 during the government shutdown, when most park employees were furloughed for weeks without pay. But a skeleton crew of rangers remained on duty, much to the surprise of a relic hunter from Cherokee County who thought he could take advantage of the lack of supervision to do a little prospecting. Fortunately, a local police officer noticed him walking toward Cheatham Hill with a metal detector. The officer alerted head park ranger Anthony Winegar, who set up an impromptu and rather simple sting operation by waiting for the man to return to his vehicle. When he returned, he was arrested and his ill-gotten artifacts were confiscated. The artifacts will join the park's educational collection. The man was convicted in federal court but received only a series of misdemeanor charges, even though he had been caught red-handed committing a felony.

Unfortunately, this sort of thing happens frequently at Kennesaw, and according to Winegar, rangers have a hard time patrolling because of a lack of workers and funding. But what they lack in a work force they make up for in gadgets and good old-fashioned police work: they have remote cameras set up all over the park, and on patrol they use thermal imagers, night vision goggles, and infrared illuminators to stalk their quarry. They often have no trouble obtaining convictions because they make it a point to catch criminals in the act. Still, Winegar suspects that in his sixteen-year career, they have caught only about 40 to 50 percent of them. The rest of the time they just find holes in the ground. Each year, they have to deal with three or four big cases (defined by Winegar as "thirty or more holes down to the mineral soil") in addition to a few smaller ones.

I just don't understand this. I suppose I can understand wanting to possess a piece of history, but I don't get the business side of it. The only motivation for defacing a National Park Service property in such a way is money. The artifacts the poachers find can be found for sale all over the internet. But how can you support such a trade if you know it involves a black market that destroys the very battlefields you are interested in?

To Winegar, the park's most valuable resources are the earthworks, which are easily seen all over the main trails. These trails follow the rebel defensive line quite closely. They are excellently preserved and quite observable, despite the passage of 150 years. He explains, "The placement of the earthworks is directly associated with the geography and topography of the park. But without the earthworks scarring the landscape, the topography would not matter so much. If one truly wants to understand the battle, they have to understand the land and why it was chosen as a defensive position." Winegar recognizes the importance of topographical features in understanding the outcome of battles, and he sees Kennesaw as William T. Sherman saw it: the tactical "key to the whole country." In addition, to Winegar, "the value of Kennesaw Mountain National Battlefield Park is that about two million people per year find their own unique value in it." However, while two million visitors a year prove the park's value, Winegar is concerned that it will be "loved to death."

Overcrowding of park roads and trails is another grave concern, although neither of these activities will necessarily lead directly to the destruction of park resources. One could argue that the thousands of feet walking, trotting, and running up and down Kennesaw's trails each year could wear down important artifacts like earthworks and trenches, but the inexorable pounding of rain and ice will do them in much more assuredly and effectively. The park trails are surprisingly well maintained and effective at keeping people from sensitive areas, and the years of wear and tear on these trails do not seem to me to be very harmful. New trails and switchback cuts worn by bushwhackers can be a problem and should be addressed by educational signs and natural barricades.

The real problem caused by all this volume instead affects the park's original purpose, which was to provide a fitting memorial—a peaceful place to reflect on what happened here. This is difficult to achieve when a running team is careening down a narrow path toward you. Running has become so popular at Kennesaw that it has been featured in the magazine *Runner's World* as a top US jogging destination. Several dozen high school and college teams swarm the mountain during cross-country season each fall, sometimes running the entire longitudinal trail from Big Kennesaw to Kolb's Farm and back. Although I think it is disingenuous for park personnel to claim that running shoes do any more damage to trails and archaeological features than ordinary hiking shoes, I would agree that these runners are not utilizing the place in the way intended by the National Park Service, and certainly not the way Lansing Dawdy would have preferred.

To me the fact that Kennesaw Mountain is overgrown with fine, ancient forests, that it is home to unique salamanders, that it is a refuge for the maligned and misunderstood copperhead, and that it is visited each year by nearly as many birds as people is the finest tribute that could be paid. I can't imagine a better monument.

Whether or not the soldiers would have agreed with this, the park would certainly not be here if they hadn't fought and died here. Given metro Atlanta's development track record, the land would no doubt all be in private ownership by now and would certainly be dotted with expensive homes. I would like to think that those who fought and died during the Battle of Kennesaw Mountain would have found the park a nice place to visit and a worthy memorial, and not just because it is quiet and preserves the trenches they dug. And not only because it houses a few human-made obelisks erected in their honor. I would like to think Lansing Dawdy would enjoy strolling up a trail with a pair of binoculars in the spring, admiring a cerulean warbler en route to breeding grounds in his home state.

Where some old battlefields will forever remain solely a memorial to the past, Kennesaw Mountain is that and so much more.

# References

Note: From chapter 2 on, references are grouped by subject matter.

**PREFACE**

Bierce, Ambrose. 2002. "On a Mountain," in *Phantoms of a Blood-Stained Period: The Complete Civil War Writings of Ambrose Bierce.* Edited by D. J. Klooster and R. Duncan. Boston: University of Massachusetts Press.

Castel, Albert. 1992. *Decision in the West: The Atlanta Campaign of 1864.* Lawrence: University Press of Kansas.

Hellman, Robert. 2003. "Kennesaw Mountain National Battlefield Park Cultural Overview." National Park Service. Accessed March 3, 2013. http://www.nps.gov/kemo.

Hess, E. J. 2013. *Kennesaw Mountain: Sherman, Johnston, and the Atlanta Campaign.* Chapel Hill: University of North Carolina Press.

Key, William. 1958. *The Battle of Atlanta and the Georgia Campaign.* New York: Twayne Publishers.

Sherman, William T. 1891. *Memoirs of William T. Sherman.* Vols. 1–2. New York: D. Appleton.

US War Department. 1880–1901. *The War of the Rebellion: A Compilation of the Official Records of the Union and Confederate Armies.* Vol. 38, parts 1–5. Washington, DC: US War Department.

**CHAPTER 1**

Abrams, C. E., and K. I. McConnell. 1984. "Geologic Setting of Volcanogenic Base and Precious Metal Deposits of the West Georgia Piedmont: A Multiply Deformed Metavolcanic Terrain." *Economic Geology* 79:1521–39.

Dietrich, R., and B. Skinner. 1979. *Rocks and Minerals.* Hoboken, NJ: John Wiley and Sons.

Grotzinger, J., T. H. Jordan, F. Press, and R. Siever. 2009. *Understanding Earth.* New York: Macmillan.

Hurst, J. V. 1952. "Geology of the Kennesaw Mountain-Sweat Mountain Area." Master's thesis, Emory University.

McConnell, K. I., and C. E. Abrams. 1984. *Geology of the Greater Atlanta Region.* Georgia Geologic Survey Bulletin 96.

**CHAPTER 2**

Asa Gray

Browne, J. 2010. "Asa Gray and Charles Darwin: Corresponding Naturalists." *Harvard Papers in Botany* 15 (2): 209–20.

Dupree, A. H. 1988. *Asa Gray: American Botanist, Friend of Darwin*. Baltimore: Johns Hopkins University Press.

ASIAN AND AMERICAN FLORAS

Dad, J. M., and A. B. Khan. 2011. "Threatened Medicinal Plants of Gurez Valley, Kashmir Himalayas: Distribution Pattern and Current Conservation Status." *International Journal of Biodiversity Science, Ecosystem Services & Management* 7 (1): 20–26.

Davis, M. B. 1983. "Quaternary History of Deciduous Forests of Eastern North America and Europe." *Annals of the Missouri Botanical Garden* 70:550–63.

Li, H. L. 1952. "Floristic Relationships between Eastern Asia and Eastern North America." *Transactions of the American Philosophical Society* 42 (2): 371–429.

Manchester, S. R. 1999. "Biogeographical Relationships of North American Tertiary Floras." *Annals of the Missouri Botanical Garden* 86:472–522.

Qian, H. 2002. "Floristic Relationships between Eastern Asia and North America: Test of Gray's hypothesis." *American Naturalist* 160 (3): 317–32.

Qian, H., and R. E. Ricklefs. 2004. "Geographical Distribution and Ecological Conservatism of Disjunct Genera of Vascular Plants in Eastern Asia and Eastern North America." *Journal of Ecology* 92 (2): 253–65.

Wen, J. 1999. "Evolution of Eastern Asian and Eastern North American Disjunct Distributions in Flowering Plants." *Annual Review of Ecology and Systematics* 30:421–55.

BAY STAR-VINE

Denk, T., and I. C. Oh. 2005. "Phylogeny of Schisandraceae Based on Morphological Data: Evidence from Modern Plants and the Fossil Record." *Plant Systematics and Evolution* 256:113–45.

Fan, J. H., L. B. Thien, and Y. B. Luo. 2011. "Pollination Systems, Biogeography, and Divergence Times of Three Allopatric Species of *Schisandra* in North America, China, and Japan." *Journal of Systematics and Evolution* 49 (4): 330–38.

Panossian, A., and G. Wikman. 2008. "Pharmacology of *Schisandra chinensis* Bail.: An Overview of Russian Research and Uses in Medicine." *Journal of Ethnopharmacology* 118 (2): 183–212.

Yuan, L. C., Y. B. Luo, L. B. Thien, J. H. Fan, H. L. Xu, and Z. D. Chen. 2007. "Pollination of *Schisandra henryi* (Schisandraceae) by Female, Pollen-Eating *Megommata* species (Cecidomyiidae, Diptera) in South-Central China." *Annals of Botany* 99 (3): 451–60.

CATALPA

Bowers, M. D. 2003. "Hostplant Suitability and Defensive Chemistry of the Catalpa Sphinx, *Ceratomia catalpae*." *Journal of Chemical Ecology* 29 (10): 2359–67.

Lampert, E. C., L. A. Dyer, and M. D. Bowers. 2011. "Chemical Defense across Three Trophic Levels: *Catalpa bignonioides*, the Caterpillar *Ceratomia catalpae*, and Its Endoparasitoid *Cotesia congregata*." *Journal of Chemical Ecology* 37 (10): 1063–70.

Ness, J. 2003. "*Catalpa bignonioides* Alters Extrafloral Nectar Production after Herbivory and Attracts Ant Bodyguards." *Oecologia* 134 (2): 210–18.

Stephenson, A. G. 1980. "Fruit Set, Herbivory, Fruit Reduction, and the Fruiting Strategy of *Catalpa speciosa* (Bignoniaceae)." *Ecology* 61 (1): 57–64.

———. 1981. "Toxic Nectar Deters Nectar Thieves of *Catalpa speciosa*." *American Midland Naturalist* 105:381–83.

———. 1982. "The Role of the Extrafloral Nectaries of *Catalpa speciosa* in Limiting Herbivory and Increasing Fruit Production." *Ecology* 63 (3): 663–69.

KENNESAW MOUNTAIN PLANT LIST

Zomlefer, W. B., D. E. Giannasi, and S. L. Echols. 2010. "Vascular Plant Flora of Kennesaw Mountain National Battlefield Park, Cobb County, Georgia." *Southeastern Naturalist* 9:129–64.

MAYAPPLE

Becker, H. 2000. "Mayapple's Cancer-Fighting Precursor." *Agricultural Research* 48 (7): 9.

Krochmal, A., L. Wilkins, D. Van Lear, and M. Chien. 1974. "Mayapple." USDA Forest Service Research Paper NE-296.

Maqbool, M. 2011. "Mayapple: A Review of the Literature from a Horticultural Perspective." *Journal of Medicinal Plants Research* 5 (7): 1037–45.

Moraes, R. M., C. Burandt, M. Ganzera, L. I. Xingli, I. Khan, and C. Canel. 2000. "The American Mayapple Revisited—*Podophyllum peltatum*—Still a Potential Cash Crop?" *Economic Botany* 54 (4): 471–76.

Moraes, R. M., H. Lata, E. Bedir, M. Maqbool, and K. Cushman. 2002. "The American Mayapple and Its Potential for Podophyllotoxin Production." In *Trends in New Crops and New Uses*, edited by J. Janick and A. Whipkey, 527–32. Alexandria, VA: American Society for Horticultural Science Press.

Rust, R. W., and R. R. Roth. 1981. "Seed Production and Seedling Establishment in the Mayapple, *Podophyllum peltatum* L." *American Midland Naturalist* 105:51–60.

Sohn, J. J., and D. Policansky. 1977. "The Costs of Reproduction in the Mayapple *Podophyllum peltatum* (Berberidaceae)." *Ecology* 58 (6): 1366–74.

Xiong, Y. Z., Q. Fang, and S. Q. Huang. 2013. "Pollinator Scarcity Drives the Shift to Delayed Selfing in Himalayan Mayapple *Podophyllum hexandrum* (Berberidaceae)." *AoB Plants* 5. doi:10.1093/aobpla/plt037.

POLLINATION

Luo, Y. B., J. H. Fan, L. C. Yuan, and J. H. Williams. 2009. "Pollination Biology of Basal Angiosperms." *American Journal of Botany* 96 (1): 166–82.

TULIP TREE

Parks, C. R., and J. F. Wendel. 1990. "Molecular Divergence between Asian and North American Species of *Liriodendron* (Magnoliaceae) with Implications for Interpretation of Fossil Floras." *American Journal of Botany* 77:1243–56.

Petrides, G. A. 1988. *Field Guide to Eastern Trees*. Boston: Houghton Mifflin.

Richardson, A. O., D. W. Rice, G. J. Young, A. J. Alverson, and J. D. Palmer. 2013. "The 'Fossilized' Mitochondrial Genome of *Liriodendron tulipifera*: Ancestral Gene

Content and Order, Ancestral Editing Sites, and Extraordinarily Low Mutation Rate." *BMC Biology* 11 (1): 11–29.

WITCH HAZEL

Anderson, G. J., and J. D. Hill. 2002. "Many to Flower, Few to Fruit: The Reproductive Biology of *Hamamelis virginiana* (Hamamelidaceae)." *American Journal of Botany* 89 (1): 67–78.

De Steven, D. 1982. "Seed Production and Seed Mortality in a Temperate Forest Shrub (Witch-Hazel, *Hamamelis virginiana*)." *Journal of Ecology* 70:437–43.

Fulling, E. H. 1953. "American Witch Hazel—History, Nomenclature and Modern Utilization." *Economic Botany* 7 (4): 359–81.

Sánchez-Tena, S., M. L. Fernández-Cachón, A. Carreras, M. L. Mateos-Martín, N. Costoya, M. P. Moyer, and M. Cascante. 2012. "Hamamelitannin from Witch Hazel (*Hamamelis virginiana*) Displays Specific Cytotoxic Activity against Colon Cancer Cells." *Journal of Natural Products* 75 (1): 26–33.

## CHAPTER 3

DISTURBANCE ECOLOGY

Hemstrom, M. A., and J. F. Franklin. 1982. "Fire and Other Disturbances of the Forests in Mount Rainier National Park." *Quaternary Research* 18:32–51.

McFarlane, R. W. 1994. *A Stillness in the Pines: The Ecology of the Red-Cockaded Woodpecker*. New York: W. W. Norton.

Runkle, J. R. 1981. "Gap Regeneration in Some Old-Growth Forests of the Eastern United States." *Ecology* 62:1041–51.

Thornton, I. W. B. 1996. *Krakatau: The Destruction and Reassembly of an Island Ecosystem*. Cambridge, MA: Harvard University Press.

GENERAL ECOLOGY

Smith, R. L., and T. M. Smith. 1994. *Ecology and Field Biology*. New York: Harper and Row.

KENNESAW AREA HISTORY

Castel, Albert. 1992. *Decision in the West: The Atlanta Campaign of 1864*. Lawrence: University Press of Kansas.

French, S. G. 1881. "Kennesaw Mountain." *Southern Historical Society Papers* 9:505–11.

Hess, E. J. 2013. *Kennesaw Mountain: Sherman, Johnston, and the Atlanta Campaign*. Chapel Hill: University of North Carolina Press.

Sherman, W. T. 1891. *Memoirs of William T. Sherman*. Vols. 1–2. New York: D. Appleton.

US War Department. 1880–1901. *The War of the Rebellion: A Compilation of the Official Records of the Union and Confederate Armies*. Vol. 38, parts 1–5. Washington, DC: US War Department.

Williams, D. 1993. *Georgia Gold Rush: Twenty-Niners, Cherokees, and Gold Fever.* Columbia: University of South Carolina Press.

KENNESAW MOUNTAIN NATIONAL BATTLEFIELD PARK

Hellman, Robert. 2003. "Kennesaw Mountain National Battlefield Park Cultural Overview." National Park Service. Accessed March 3, 2013. http://www.nps.gov/kemo.

KENNESAW MOUNTAIN PLANT LIST

Zomlefer, W. B., D. E. Giannasi, and S. L. Echols. 2010. "Vascular Plant Flora of Kennesaw Mountain National Battlefield Park, Cobb County, Georgia." *Southeastern Naturalist* 9:129–64.

MOUNT ST. HELENS

Baross, J. A., C. N. Dahm, A. K. Ward, M. D. Lilley, and J. R. Sedell. 1982. "Initial Microbiological Response in Lakes to the Mt St Helens Eruption." *Nature* 296:49–52.
Merrill, E. H. 1994. "Summer Foraging Ecology of Wapiti (*Cervus elaphus roosevelti*) in the Mount St. Helens Blast Zone." *Canadian Journal of Zoology* 72:303–11.
Wood, D. M., and R. Del Moral. 1987. "Mechanisms of Early Primary Succession in Subalpine Habitats on Mount St. Helens." *Ecology* 68:780–90.

PIEDMONT NATURAL HISTORY

Barden, L. S. 1997. "Historic Prairies in the Piedmont of North and South Carolina, USA." *Natural Areas Journal* 17:149–52.
Burbanck, M. P., and D. L. Phillips. 1987. "Evidence of Plant Succession on Granite Outcrops of the Georgia Piedmont." *American Midland Naturalist* 109:94–104.
Burbanck, M. P., and R. B. Platt. 1964. "Granite Outcrop Communities of the Piedmont Plateau in Georgia." *Ecology* 45:292–306.
Davis, J. E., C. McRae, B. L. Estep, L. S. Barden, and J. F. Matthews. 2002. "Vascular Flora of Piedmont Prairies: Evidence from Seral Prairie Remnants." *Castanea* 67:1–12.
Godfrey, M. A. 1997. *Field Guide to the Piedmont.* 2nd ed. Chapel Hill, NC: Chapel Hill Books.
Johnston, D. W., and E. P. Odum. 1956. "Breeding Bird Populations in Relation to Plant Succession of the Piedmont of Georgia." *Ecology* 37:50–62.
Leslie, K. A., and M. P. Burbanck. 1979. "Vegetation of Granitic Outcroppings at Kennesaw Mountain, Cobb County, Georgia." *Castanea* 44:80–87.
Murdy, W. H., and M. E. B. Carter. 2000. *Guide to the Plants of Granite Outcrops.* Athens: University of Georgia Press.
Nicholson, S. A., and C. D. Monk. 1974. "Plant Species Diversity in Old-Field Succession on the Georgia Piedmont." *Ecology* 55 (5): 1075–85.
Wharton, C. H. 1978. "The Natural Environments of Georgia." *Georgia Department of Natural Resources Bulletin* 119.

## CHAPTER 4

### AMERICAN CHESTNUT

Dalgleish, H. J., and R. K. Swihart. 2012. "American Chestnut Past and Future: Implications of Restoration for Resource Pulses and Consumer Populations of Eastern US Forests." *Restoration Ecology* 20 (4): 490–97.

Diamond, S. J., R. H. Giles, R. L. Kirkpatrick, and G. J. Griffin. 2000. "Hard Mast Production before and after the Chestnut Blight." *Southern Journal of Applied Forestry* 24 (4): 196–201.

Popkin, G. 2018. "Can a Transgenic Chestnut Restore a Forest Icon?" *Science* 361:830–31.

### FOREST COMPOSITION

Keever, C. 1953. "Present Composition of Some Stands of the Former Oak-Chestnut Forest in the Southern Blue Ridge Mountains." *Ecology* 34 (1): 44–54.

United States Geological Survey [USGS]. 1992. *Marietta Quadrangle.* 7.5 minute series. Reston, VA: US Department of the Interior.

### FUNGI

Selosse, M. A., F. Richard, X. He, and S. W. Simard. 2006. "Mycorrhizal Networks: Des Liaisons Dangereuses?" *Trends in Ecology & Evolution* 21 (11): 621–28.

Whitfield J. 2007. "Fungal Roles in Soil Ecology: Underground Networking." *Nature* 449:136–38.

### GENERAL ECOLOGY

Kricher, J. C., and G. Morrison. 1988. *Ecology of Eastern Forests.* New York: Houghton Mifflin.

Smith, R. L., and T. M. Smith. 1994. *Ecology and Field Biology.* New York: Harper and Row.

### NUTS

Barnett, R. J. 1977. "The Effect of Burial by Squirrels on Germination and Survival of Oak and Hickory Nuts." *American Midland Naturalist* 98:319–30.

Greenberg, C. H. 2000. "Individual Variation in Acorn Production by Five Species of Southern Appalachian Oaks." *Forest Ecology and Management* 132 (2): 199–210.

Lewis, A. R. 1982. "Selection of Nuts by Gray Squirrels and Optimal Foraging Theory." *American Midland Naturalist* 107 (2): 250–57.

Rose, A. K., C. H. Greenberg, and T. M. Fearer. 2012. "Acorn Production Prediction Models for Five Common Oak Species of the Eastern United States." *Journal of Wildlife Management* 76 (4): 750–58.

Vander Wall, S. B. 2001. "The Evolutionary Ecology of Nut Dispersal." *Botanical Review* 67 (1): 74–117.

### PIEDMONT NATURAL HISTORY

Godfrey, M. A. 1997. *Field Guide to the Piedmont.* Chapel Hill: University of North Carolina Press.

Salamanders

Burton, T. M., and G. E. Likens. 1975. "Salamander Populations and Biomass in the Hubbard Brook Experimental Forest, New Hampshire." *Copeia* 1975:541–46.


## CHAPTER 5

Evolution of deciduousness

Axelrod, D. I. 1966. "Origin of Deciduous and Evergreen Habits in Temperate Forests." *Evolution* 20 (1): 1–15.

Wolfe, J. A. 1987. "Late Cretaceous-Cenozoic History of Deciduousness and the Terminal Cretaceous Event." *Paleobiology* 13 (2): 215–26.

Forest ecology

Bierzychudek, P. 1982. "Life Histories and Demography of Shade-Tolerant Temperate Forest Herbs: A Review." *New Phytologist* 90 (4): 757–76.

Chazdon, R. L., and R. W. Pearcy. 1991. "The Importance of Sun Flecks for Forest Understory Plants." *Bioscience* 41:760–66.

Gilliam, F. S. 2007. "The Ecological Significance of the Herbaceous Layer in Temperate Forest Ecosystems." *Bioscience* 57 (10): 845–58.

———. 2014. *The Herbaceous Layer in Forests of Eastern North America.* Oxford: Oxford University Press.

Shefferson, R. P. 2009. "The Evolutionary Ecology of Vegetative Dormancy in Mature Herbaceous Perennial Plants." *Journal of Ecology* 97 (5): 1000–1009.

Stiles, E. W. 1980. "Patterns of Fruit Presentation and Seed Dispersal in Bird-Disseminated Woody Plants in the Eastern Deciduous Forest." *American Naturalist* 116 (5): 670–88.

Terborgh, J. 1985. "The Vertical Component of Plant Species Diversity in Temperate and Tropical Forests." *American Naturalist* 126 (6): 760–76.

Whigham, D. F. 2004. "Ecology of Woodland Herbs in Temperate Deciduous Forests." *Annual Review of Ecology, Evolution, and Systematics* 35:583–621.

General ecology

Smith, R. L., and T. M. Smith. 1994. *Ecology and Field Biology.* New York: Harper and Row.

Georgia climate data

Griffith, G. E., J. M. Omernik, J. A. Comstock, S. Lawrence, G. Martin, A. Goddard, V. J. Hulcher, and T. Foster. 2001. "Ecoregions of Alabama and Georgia." Poster with map (scale 1:1,700,000), descriptive text, summary tables, and photographs. Reston, VA: US Geological Survey.

Leaf form

Givnish, T. J. 1987. "Comparative Studies of Leaf Form: Assessing the Relative Roles of Selective Pressures and Phylogenetic Constraints." *New Phytologist* 106:131–60.

MAFIC AREAS

Oakley, S. C., H. E. LeGrand, and M. P. Schafale. 1995. *An Inventory of Mafic Natural Areas in the North Carolina Piedmont.* North Carolina Natural Heritage Program. Accessed May 8, 2020. https://digital.ncdcr.gov/digital/collection/p249901coll22/id/658738.

OAK HYBRIDS

Petrides, G. A. 1988. *Field Guide to Eastern Trees.* Boston: Houghton Mifflin.

SEED DISPERSAL

Stamp, N. E., and J. R. Lucas. 1983. "Ecological Correlates of Explosive Seed Dispersal." *Oecologia* 59:272–78.
Zettler, Jennifer A., Timothy P. Spira, and Craig R. Allen. 2001. "Yellow jackets (*Vespula* spp.) disperse *Trillium* (spp.) seeds in eastern North America." *American Midland Naturalist* 146 (2): 444–46.

SERPENTINE SOIL

Brady, K. U., A. R. Kruckeberg, and H. D. Bradshaw Jr. 2005. "Evolutionary Ecology of Plant Adaptation to Serpentine Soils." *Annual Review of Ecology, Evolution, and Systematics* 36:243–66.

## CHAPTER 6

ASIAN PLETHODONTID

Min, M. S., S. Y. Yang, R. M. Bonett, D. R. Vieites, R. A. Brandon, and D. B. Wake. 2005. "Discovery of the First Asian Lungless Salamander." *Nature* 435:87–90.

BIRD LIFE HISTORIES

Bent, A. C. 1968. *Life Histories of North American Cardinals, Grosbeaks, Buntings, Towhees, Finches, Sparrows, and Allies.* New York: Dover.

BIRD TAXONOMY

Ball, R. M., and J. C. Avise. 1992. "Mitochondrial DNA Phylogeographic Differentiation among Avian Populations and the Evolutionary Significance of Subspecies." *Auk* 109:626–36.

GENERAL BIOLOGY OF AMPHIBIANS

Duellman, W. E., and L. Trueb. 1986. *Biology of Amphibians.* Baltimore: Johns Hopkins University Press.

KENNESAW MOUNTAIN PLANT LIST

Zomlefer, W. B., D. E. Giannasi, and S. L. Echols. 2010. "Vascular Plant Flora of Kennesaw Mountain National Battlefield Park, Cobb County, Georgia." *Southeastern Naturalist* 9:129–64.

RED HILLS SALAMANDER

Highton, R. 1961. "A New Genus of Lungless Salamander from the Coastal Plain of Alabama." *Copeia* 1961:65–68.

SALAMANDER ANATOMY

Buckley, D., M. H. Wake, and D. B. Wake. 2010. "Comparative Skull Osteology of *Karsenia koreana* (Amphibia, Caudata, Plethodontidae)." *Journal of Morphology* 271:533–58.

SALAMANDER BEHAVIOR

Camp, C. 1999. "Intraspecific Aggressive Behavior in Southeastern Small Species of *Plethodon*: Inferences for the Evolution of Aggression in Terrestrial Salamanders." *Herpetologica* 55:248–54.

Jaeger, R. G. 1984. "Agonistic Behavior of the Red-Backed Salamander." *Copeia* 1984:309–14.

———. 1988. "A Comparison of Territorial and Non-territorial Behaviour in Two Species of Salamanders." *Animal Behaviour* 36:307–10.

SALAMANDER COURTSHIP

Arnold, S. J. 1977. "The Evolution of Courtship Behavior in New World Salamanders with Some Comments on Old World Salamanders." In *The Reproductive Biology of Amphibians*, edited by D. H. Taylor and S. I. Guttman, 141–83. New York: Plenum Press.

Houck, L. D., and S. J. Arnold. 2003. "Courtship and Mating Behavior." In *Reproductive Biology and Phylogeny of Urodela*, edited by D. M. Sever, 383–424. Enfield, NH: Science Publishers.

Houck, L. D., and N. L. Reagan. 1990. "Male Courtship Pheromones Increase Female Receptivity in a Lungless Salamander." *Animal Behaviour* 39:729–34.

SALAMANDER DISTRIBUTIONS

Conant, R., and J. T. Collins, 1991. *A Field Guide to Reptiles and Amphibians of Eastern and Central North America*. 3rd ed. New York: Houghton Mifflin Harcourt.

SALAMANDER DIVERSITY

Amphibiaweb. Accessed July 25, 2013. www.amphibiaweb.com.

SALAMANDER ECOLOGY

Walker, D. M., C. M. Murray, D. Talbert, P. Tinker, S. P. Graham, and T. W. Crowther. 2018. "A Salamander's Top Down Effect on Fungal Communities in a Detritivore Ecosystem." *FEMS Microbiology Ecology* 94 (12). doi:10.1093/femsec/fiy168.

SALAMANDER EVOLUTION

Carstens, B. C., A. L. Stevenson, J. D. Degenhardt, and J. Sullivan. 2004. "Testing Nested Phylogenetic and Phylogeographic Hypotheses in the *Plethodon vandykei* Species Group." *Systematic Biology* 53:781–92.

Feist, S., T. Mann, S. Graham, J. Wooten, C. Toyota, D. Mann, M. Balius, J. Polanco, and P. Wolwehender. 2019. "A Morphologically Cryptic Salamander Reveals Additional Hidden Diversity: Evidence for Ancient Genetic Divergence in Webster's Salamander, *Plethodon websteri*." *Conservation Genetics* 20:1–14.

Highton, R 1989. "Geographic Protein Variation." In *Biochemical Evolution in the Slimy Salamanders of the* Plethodon glutinosus *Complex in the Eastern United States,* edited by R. Highton, G. C. Maha, and L. R. Maxson, 1–78. Illinois Biological Monographs, Number 57. Urbana: University of Illinois Press.

———. 1995. "Speciation in Eastern North American Salamanders of the Genus *Plethodon*." *Annual Review of Ecology and Systematics* 26:579–600.

———. 1997. "Geographic Protein Variation and Speciation in the *Plethodon dorsalis* Complex." *Herpetologica* 53 (3): 345–56.

———. 1999. "Geographic Protein Variation and Speciation in the Salamanders of the *Plethodon cinereus* Group with the Description of Two New Species." *Herpetologica* 55:43–90.

Highton, R., and T. P. Webster. 1976. "Geographic Protein Variation and Divergence in Populations of the Salamander *Plethodon cinereus*." *Evolution* 30 (1): 33–45.

Wake, D. B. 2009. "What Salamanders Have Taught Us about Evolution." *Annual Review of Ecology and Evolutionary Systematics* 40:333–52.

Wake, D. B., G. Roth, and M. H. Wake. 1983. "On the Problem of Stasis in Organismal Evolution." *Journal of Theoretical Biology* 101:211–24.

SALAMANDER POPULATION ECOLOGY

Burton, T. M., and G. E. Likens. 1975. "Salamander Populations and Biomass in the Hubbard Brook Experimental Forest, New Hampshire." *Copeia* 1975:541–46.

SOUTHEASTERN RELICT HABITAT

Delcourt, H. R. 1974. "Primeval Magnolia-Holly-Beech Climax in Louisiana." *Ecology* 55 (3): 638–44.

SPECIFIC SALAMANDER SPECIES

Highton, R. 1985. "The Width of the Contact Zone between *Plethodon dorsalis* and *P. websteri* in Jefferson County, Alabama." *Journal of Herpetology* 19:544–46.

Valentine, B. D. 1963. "The Lungless Salamander *Phaeognathus*: Collecting Techniques and Habits." *Journal of the Ohio Herpetological Society* 4:49–54.

US SALAMANDER STANDARD REFERENCE

Petranka, J. W. 1998. *Salamanders of the United States and Canada.* Washington DC: Smithsonian Institution Press.

WEBSTER'S SALAMANDER

Highton, R. 1979. "A New Cryptic Species of Salamander of the Genus *Plethodon* from the Southeastern United States (Amphibia: Plethodontidae)." *Brimleyana* 1:31–36.

## CHAPTER 7

AGKISTRODON SNAKES

Gloyd, H. K., and R. Conant. 1990. *Snakes of the* Agkistrodon *Complex: A Monographic Review*. St. Louis: Society for the Study of Amphibians and Reptiles.

COPPERHEADS (CIVIL WAR CONTEXT)

Klement, F. K. 1970. *The Limits of Dissent: Clement L. Vallandigham and the Civil War*. Lexington: University of Kentucky Press.

Weber, J. L. 2004. *Copperheads: The Rise and Fall of Lincoln's Opponents in the North*. Oxford: Oxford University Press.

HORMONES OF WINNERS AND LOSERS

Bernhardt, P. C., J. M. Dabbs Jr., J. A. Fielden, and C. D. Lutter. 1998. "Testosterone Changes during Vicarious Experiences of Winning and Losing among Fans at Sporting Events." *Physiology & Behavior* 65 (1): 59–62.

Schuett, G. W., and M. S. Grober. 2000. "Post-Fight Levels of Plasma Lactate and Corticosterone in Male Copperheads, *Agkistrodon contortrix* (Serpentes, Viperidae): Differences between Winners and Losers." *Physiology & Behavior* 71 (3): 335–41.

SNAKE BEHAVIOR

Cundall, D. A., and H. W. Greene. 2000. "Feeding in Snakes." In *Feeding: Form, Function, and Evolution in Tetrapod Vertebrates*, edited by K. Schwenk, 293–333. Amsterdam: Elsevier.

Schuett, G. W., and D. Duvall. 1996. "Head Lifting by Female Copperheads, *Agkistrodon contortrix*, during Courtship: Potential Mate Choice." *Animal Behaviour* 51 (2): 367–73.

SNAKE ECOLOGY

Duvall, D., G. W. Schuett, and S. J. Arnold. 1993. "Ecology and Evolution of Snake Mating Systems." In *Snakes: Ecology and Behavior*, edited by R. A. Seigel and J. T. Collins, 165–200. New York: McGraw-Hill.

Shine, R. 1994. "Sexual Dimorphism in Snakes Revisited." *Copeia* 1994 (2): 326–46.

Smith, C. F., G. W. Schuett, R. L. Earley, and K. Schwenk. 2009. "The Spatial and Reproductive Ecology of the Copperhead (*Agkistrodon contortrix*) at the Northeastern Extreme of its Range." *Herpetological Monographs* 23 (1): 45–73.

## CHAPTER 8

BIRD MIGRATION

Hedenström, A. 2010. "Extreme Endurance Migration: What Is the Limit to Non-stop Flight?" *PloS Biology* 8 (5): e10000362.

Lasiewski, R. C. 1962. "The Energetics of Migrating Hummingbirds." *Condor* 64 (4): 324.

### Buckeye ecology

Bertin, R. I. 1982. "The Ecology of Sex Expression in Red Buckeye." *Ecology* 63:445–56.

### Buckeye hybridization

DePamphilis, C. W., and R. Wyatt. "Electrophoretic Confirmation of Interspecific Hybridization in *Aesculus* (Hippocastanaceae) and the Genetic Structure of a Broad Hybrid Zone." *Evolution* 44:1295–1317.

Modliszewski, J. L., D. T. Thomas, C. Fan, D. J. Crawford, C. W. DePamphilis, and J. Xiang. 2006. "Ancestral Chloroplast Polymorphism and Historical Secondary Contact in a Broad Hybrid Zone of *Aesculus* (Sapindaceae)." *American Journal of Botany* 93:377–88.

Thomas, D. T., A. R. Ahedor, C. F. Williams, C. DePamphilis, D. J. Crawford, and J. Xiang. 2008. "Genetic Analysis of a Broad Hybrid Zone in *Aesculus* (Sapindaceae): Is There Evidence of Long-Distance Pollen Dispersal?" *International Journal of Plant Science* 169:647–57.

### Hummingbird color preference

Bené, F. 1941. "Experiments on the Color Preferences of Black-Chinned Hummingbirds." *Condor* 43:237–42.

### Hummingbird ecology

Bertin, R. I. 1982. "The Ruby-Throated Hummingbird and Its Major Food Plants: Ranges, Phenology, and Migration." *Canadian Journal of Zoology* 60:210–19.

Carpenter, F. L., M. A. Hixon, C. A. Beuchat, R. W. Russell, and D. C. Paton. 1993. "Biphasic Mass Gain in Migrant Hummingbirds: Body Composition Changes, Torpor, and Ecological Significance." *Ecology* 74:1173–82.

Fenster, C. B., and M. R. Dudash. 2001. "Spatiotemporal Variation in the Role of Hummingbirds as Pollinators of *Silene virginica*." *Ecology* 82:844–51.

Grant, K. A., and V. Grant. 1968. *Hummingbirds and Their Flowers*. New York: Columbia University Press.

### Hummingbird field guide

Williamson, S. L. 2001. *A Field Guide to Hummingbirds of North America*. New York: Houghton Mifflin Harcourt.

### Hummingbird flight

Clark, C. J. 2009. "Courtship Dives of Anna's Hummingbird Offer Insights into Flight Performance Limits." *Proceedings of the Royal Society B* 276:3047–52.

### Kennesaw Mountain birds

Beaton, G. 2004. "Birds of Kennesaw Mountain: An Annotated Checklist." *Georgia Ornithological Society Occasional Publication* 16:1–150.

### Pollination ecology

Armbruster, W. S., and B. G. Baldwin. 1998. "Switch from Specialized to Generalized Pollination." *Nature* 394:632.

Bascompte, J. P., C. J. Jordano, J. M. Melian, and J. M. Olesen. 2003. "The Nested Assembly of Plant-Pollinator Networks." *Proceedings of the National Academy of Sciences USA* 104:19891–96.

Graham, S. P. 2010. "Visitors to Southeastern Wildflowers." *Southeastern Naturalist* 9:413–26.

Irwin, R. E., and L. S. Adler. 2006. "Correlations among Traits Associated with Herbivore Resistance and Pollination: Implications for Pollination and Nectar Robbing in a Distylous Plant." *Ecology* 93:64–72.

Kremen, C., and T. Ricketts. 2000. "Global Perspectives on Pollination Disruptions." *Conservation Biology* 14:1226–28.

Motten, A. F. 1986. "Pollination Ecology of the Spring Wildflower Community of a Temperate Deciduous Forest." *Ecology* 56:21–42.

Olesen, J. M., J. Bascompte, Y. L. Dupont, and P. Jordano. 2007. "The Modularity of Pollination Networks." *Proceedings of the National Academy of Sciences USA* 104:19891–96.

Pellmyr, O., J. N. Thompson, J. M. Brown, and R. G. Harrison. 1996. "Evolution of Pollination and Mutualism in the Yucca Moth Lineage." *American Naturalist* 148:827–47.

Proctor, M., P. Yeo, and A. Lack. 1996. *The Natural History of Pollination.* Portland, OR: Timber Press.

Raguso, R. A., and M. A. Willis. 2003. "Hawkmoth Pollination in Arizona's Sonoran Desert: Behavioral Responses to Floral Traits." In *Butterflies: Ecology and Evolution Taking Flight,* edited by C. L. Boggs, W. B. Watts, and P. R. Ehrlich, 43–66. Chicago: University of Chicago Press.

———. 2005. "Synergy between Visual and Olfactory Cues in Nectar Feeding by Wild Hawkmoths, *Manduca sexta.*" *Animal Behaviour* 69:407–18.

Raven, P. H. 1973. "Why Are Bird-Visited Flowers Predominantly Red?" *Evolution* 26:674.

Waser, N. M. 1988. "Comparative Pollen and Dye Transfer by Pollinators of *Delphinium nelsonii.*" *Functional Ecology* 2:41–48.

Waser, N. M., L. Chittka, M. V. Price, N. M. Williams, and J. Ollerton. 1996. "Generalization in Pollination Systems, and Why It Matters." *Ecology* 77:1043–60.

Wilson, P., M. C. Castellanos, A. D. Wolfe, and J. D. Thomson. 2006. "Shifts between Bee and Bird Pollination in Penstemons." In *Plant-Pollinator Interactions: From Specialization to Generalization,* edited by N. M. Waser and J. Ollerton, 47–68. Chicago: University of Chicago Press.

POLLINATOR DECLINE

Cane, J. H., and V. J. Tepedino. 2001. "Causes and Extent of Declines among Native North American Invertebrate Pollinators: Detection, Evidence, and Consequences." *Conservation Ecology* 5:1–7.

National Research Council. 2007. *Status of Pollinators in North America.* Washington, DC: National Academies Press.

SAPSUCKER TREES

Foster, W. L., and J. Tate. 1966. "The Activities and Coactions of Animals at Sapsucker Trees." *Living Bird* 5:87–113.

Southwick, E. E., and A. K. Southwick. 1980. "Energetics of Feeding on Tree Sap by Ruby-Throated Hummingbirds in Michigan." *American Midland Naturalist* 104:328–34.

## CHAPTER 9

### Forest/bird ecology

MacArthur, R. H. 1958. "Population Ecology of Some Warblers of Northeastern Coniferous Forests." *Ecology* 3 (94): 599–619.

Marquis, R. J., and C. J. Whelan. 1994. "Insectivorous Birds Increase Growth of White Oak through Consumption of Leaf-Chewing Insects. *Ecology* 75 (7): 2007–14.

Patten, M. A., and J. C. Burger. 1998. "Spruce Budworm Outbreaks and the Incidence of Vagrancy in Eastern North American Wood-Warblers. *Canadian Journal of Zoology* 76:433–39.

### Forest/insect ecology

Berryman, A. A. 1996. "What Causes Population Cycles of Forest Lepidoptera?" *Trends in Ecology & Evolution* 11 (1): 28–32.

Bray, J. R. 1964. "Primary Consumption in Three Forest Canopies." *Ecology* 45 (1): 165–67.

Butler, L., and J. Strazanac. 2000. "Occurrence of Lepidoptera on Selected Host Trees in Two Central Appalachian National Forests." *Annals of the Entomological Society of America* 93 (3): 500–511.

Landsber, J., and C. Ohmart. 1989. "Levels of Insect Defoliation in Forests: Patterns and Concepts." *Trends in Ecology & Evolution* 4 (4): 96–100.

Mattson, W. J., and N. D. Addy. 1975. "Phytophagous Insects as Regulators of Forest Primary Production." *Science* 190:515–22.

Myers, J. H. 1993. "Population Outbreaks in Forest Lepidoptera." *American Scientist* 81 (3): 240–51.

Summerville, K. S., M. J. Boulware, J. A. Veech, and T. O. Crist. 2003. "Spatial Variation in Species Diversity and Composition in Eastern Deciduous Forests of North America." *Conservation Biology* 17: 1045–57.

Summerville, K. S., and T. O. Crist. 2003. "Determinants of Lepidopteran Community Composition and Species Diversity in Eastern Deciduous Forests: Roles of Season, Eco-region, and Patch Size." *Oikos* 100:134–48.

Summerville, K. S., T. O. Crist, J. K. Kahn, and J. C. Gering. 2003. "Community Structure of Arboreal Caterpillars within and among Four Tree Species of the Eastern Deciduous Forest." *Ecological Entomology* 28 (6): 747–57.

### Lepidoptera ecology

Forsberg, J. 1987. "A Model for Male Mate Discrimination in Butterflies." *Oikos* 49 (1): 46–54.

Futuyma, D. J. 1976. "Food Plant Specialization and Environmental Predictability in Lepidoptera." *American Naturalist* 110:285–92.

Mutanen, M., N. Wahlberg, and L. Kaila. 2010. "Comprehensive Gene and Taxon Coverage Elucidates Radiation Patterns in Moths and Butterflies." *Proceedings of the Royal Society of London B: Biological Sciences* 277:2839–48.

Pe'er, G., D. Saltz, T. Münkemüller, Y. G. Matsinos, and H. H. Thulke. 2013. "Simple Rules for Complex Landscapes: The Case of Hilltopping Movements and Topography." *Oikos* 122 (10): 1483–95.

Pe'er, G., D. Saltz, H. H. Thulke, and U. Motro. 2004. "Response to Topography in a Hilltopping Butterfly and Implications for Modelling Nonrandom Dispersal." *Animal Behaviour* 68 (4): 825–39.

Rutowski, R. L. 1991. "The Evolution of Male Mate-Locating Behavior in Butterflies." *American Naturalist* 138 (5): 1121–39.

Vane-Wright, D. 2015. *Butterflies: A Complete Guide to Their Biology and Behavior.* London: Natural History Museum.

LEPIDOPTERA EVOLUTION

Thompson, J. N., and O. Pellmyr. 1991. "Evolution of Oviposition Behavior and Host Preference in Lepidoptera." *Annual Review of Entomology* 36 (1): 65–89.

MACROEVOLUTION

Futuyma, D. J., and A. A. Agrawal. 2009. "Macroevolution and the Biological Diversity of Plants and Herbivores." *Proceedings of the National Academy of Sciences* 106:18054–61.

PLANT DEFENSE COMPOUNDS

Cohen, M. B., M. A. Schuler, and M. R. Berenbaum. 1992. "A Host-Inducible Cytochrome P-450 from a Host-Specific Caterpillar: Molecular Cloning and Evolution." *Proceedings of the National Academy of Sciences* 89 (22): 10920–24.

Nishida, R. 2002. "Sequestration of Defensive Substances from Plants by Lepidoptera." *Annual Review of Entomology* 47 (1): 57–92.

TOP-DOWN ECOSYSTEM EFFECTS

Schmitz, O. J., P. A. Hambäck, and A. P. Beckerman. 2000. "Trophic Cascades in Terrestrial Systems: A Review of the Effects of Carnivore Removals on Plants." *American Naturalist* 155 (2): 141–53.

**CHAPTER 10**

ANIMAL MIGRATION

Boinski, S., and P. A. Garber. 2000. *On the Move: How and Why Animals Travel in Groups.* Chicago: University of Chicago Press.

Rappole, J. H. 2013. *The Avian Migrant: The Biology of Bird Migration.* New York: Columbia University Press.

FOREST ECOLOGY

Kricher, J. C., and G. Morrison. 1988. *Ecology of Eastern Forests.* New York: Houghton Mifflin.

KENNESAW MOUNTAIN BIRDS

Beaton, G. 2004. "Birds of Kennesaw Mountain: An Annotated Checklist." *Georgia Ornithological Society Occasional Publication* 16:1–150.

## CHAPTER 11

ANIMAL MIGRATION

Boinski, S., and P. A. Garber. 2000. *On the Move: How and Why Animals Travel in Groups.* Chicago: University of Chicago Press.

BIRD BANDING

Cole, L. J. 1910. "The Tagging of Wild Birds: Report of Progress in 1909." *Auk* 27 (2): 153–68.
———. 1922. "The Early History of Bird Banding in America." *Wilson Bulletin* 34 (2): 108–14.

BIRD MIGRATION

Moore, F., and P. Kerlinger. 1987. "Stopover and Fat Deposition by North American Wood-Warblers (Parulinae) following Spring Migration over the Gulf of Mexico. *Oecologia* 74 (1): 47–54.
Rappole, J. H. 1995. *The Ecology of Migrant Birds: A Neotropical Perspective.* Washington, DC: Smithsonian Institution Press.
———. 2013. *The Avian Migrant: The Biology of Bird Migration.* New York: Columbia University Press.
Ruegg, K. C., and T. B. Smith. 2002. "Not as the Crow Flies: A Historical Explanation for Circuitous Migration in Swainson's Thrush (*Catharus ustulatus*)." *Proceedings of the Royal Society of London B: Biological Sciences* 269:1375–81.
Stevenson, H. M. 1957. "The Relative Magnitude of the Trans-Gulf and Circum-Gulf Spring Migrations." *Wilson Bulletin* 69 (1): 39–77.
Stone, W. 1889. "Graphic Representation of Bird Migration." *Auk* 6 (2): 139–44.

ICE AGE IN NORTH AMERICA

Pielou, E. C. 2008. *After the Ice Age: The Return of Life to Glaciated North America.* Chicago: University of Chicago Press.
Watts, W. A. 1970. "The Full-Glacial Vegetation of Northwestern Georgia." *Ecology* 51 (1): 17–33.

KENNESAW MOUNTAIN BIRDS

Beaton, G. 2004. "Birds of Kennesaw Mountain: An Annotated Checklist." *Georgia Ornithological Society Occasional Publication* 16:1–150.

ORNITHOLOGY

Birkhead, T. 2011. *The Wisdom of Birds: An Illustrated History of Ornithology.* London: Bloomsbury.

## CHAPTER 12

### ALEXANDER WILSON

Cantwell, R. 1961. *Alexander Wilson: Naturalist and Pioneer; A Biography*. Philadelphia: Lippincott.

### BIRD LIFE HISTORIES

Bent, A. C. 1953. *Life Histories of North American Wood Warblers*. New York: Dover.

### BIRD MIGRATION

Bonter, D. N., and T. M. Donovan. 2009. "Characteristics of Important Stopover Locations for Migrating Birds: Remote Sensing with Radar in the Great Lakes Basin." *Conservation Biology* 23 (2): 440–48.

Gauthreaux, S. A., Jr., C. G. Belser, and C. M. Welch. 2006. "Atmospheric Trajectories and Spring Bird Migration across the Gulf of Mexico." *Journal of Ornithology* 147 (2): 317–25.

Harris, T. 2016. *Migration Hotspots: The World's Best Bird Migration Sites*. London: Bloomsbury.

Hutto, R. L. 1998. "On the Importance of Stopover Sites to Migrating Birds." *Auk* 115 (4): 823–25.

Rappole, J. H. 2013. *The Avian Migrant: The Biology of Bird Migration*. New York: Columbia University Press.

Thorup, K., I. Bisson, M. S. Bowlin, R. A. Holland, J. C. Wingfield, M. Ramenofsky, and M. Wikelski. 2007. "Evidence for Navigational Map Stretching across the Continental U.S. in a Migratory Songbird." *Proceedings of the National Academy of Sciences* 104 (46): 18115–19.

### BIRD POPULATION ASSESSMENT

Robbins, M. B., Á. S. Nyári, M. Papes, B. W. Benz, and B. R. Barber. 2010. "River-Based Surveys for Assessing Riparian Bird Populations: Cerulean Warbler as a Test Case." *Southeastern Naturalist* 9 (1): 95–104.

### CERULEAN WARBLER

Ruley, D. A. 2000. *Petition under the Endangered Species Act to List the Cerulean Warbler, Dendroica cerulea, as a Threatened Species*. Asheville, NC: Southern Environmental Law Center.

US Fish and Wildlife Service. 2006. "Endangered and Threatened Wildlife and Plants: 12-Month Finding on a Petition to List the Cerulean Warbler (*Dendroica cerulea*) as Threatened with Critical Habitat." *Federal Register* 71 (234): 70717–33.

### CRANES

Leopold, Aldo. 1949. *A Sand County Almanac: With Other Essays on Conservation from Round River*. New York, New York. Ballantine Books.

Matthiessen, P. 2001. *The Birds of Heaven: Travels with Cranes*. New York: Macmillan.

Tacha, T. C., P. A. Vohs, and G. C. Iverson. 1984. "Migration Routes of Sandhill Cranes from Mid-Continental North America." *Journal of Wildlife Management* 48 (3): 1028–33.

Williams, L. E., and R. W. Phillips. 1972. "North Florida Sandhill Crane Populations." *Auk* 89 (3): 541–48.

HISTORIC BIRD HOT SPOT

Stone, W. 1937. *Bird Studies at Old Cape May.* New York: Dover.

KENNESAW MOUNTAIN BIRDS

Beaton, G. 2004. "Birds of Kennesaw Mountain: An Annotated Checklist." *Georgia Ornithological Society Occasional Publication* 16:1–150.

Kinsey, A. A. 1999. "Temporal and Spatial Variation in Abundance of Migratory Birds at Kennesaw Mountain, Georgia." Master's thesis, Georgia Southern University.

MAGNETISM AND ANIMALS

Alerstam, T. 1987. "Bird Migration across a Strong Magnetic Anomaly." *Journal of Experimental Biology* 130 (1): 63–86.

Freake, M. J., R. Muheim, and J. B. Phillips. 2006. "Magnetic Maps in Animals: A Theory Comes of Age?" *Quarterly Review of Biology* 81 (4): 327–47.

Lohmann, K. J., C. M. Lohmann, and N. F. Putman. 2007. "Magnetic Maps in Animals: Nature's GPS." *Journal of Experimental Biology* 210 (21): 3697–705.

Walcott, C., and R. P. Green. 1974. "Orientation of homing pigeons altered by a change in the direction of an applied magnetic field." *Science* 184 (4133): 180–82.

WARBLER FIELD GUIDE

Dunn, J., and K. Garrett. 1997. *A Field Guide to Warblers of North America.* New York: Houghton Mifflin Harcourt.

## CHAPTER 13

GARLIC MUSTARD

Blossey, B., V. Nuzzo, H. Hinz, and E. Gerber. 2001. "Developing Biological Control of *Alliaria petiolata* (M. Bieb.) Cavara and Grande (Garlic Mustard)." *Natural Areas Journal* 21 (4): 357–67.

Carlson, A. M., and D. L. Gorchov. 2004. "Effects of Herbicide on the Invasive Biennial *Alliaria petiolata* (Garlic Mustard) and Initial Responses of Native Plants in a Southwestern Ohio Forest." *Restoration Ecology* 12 (4): 559–67.

Cipollini, D., and B. Gruner. 2007. "Cyanide in the Chemical Arsenal of Garlic Mustard, *Alliaria petiolata.*" *Journal of Chemical Ecology* 33 (1): 85–94.

Davis, A. S., D. A. Landis, V. Nuzzo, B. Blossey, E. Gerber, and H. L. Hinz. 2006. "Demographic Models Inform Selection of Biocontrol Agents for Garlic Mustard (*Alliaria petiolata*)." *Ecological Applications* 16 (6): 2399–410.

Meekins, J. F., and B. C. McCarthy. 1999. "Competitive Ability of *Alliaria petiolata* (Garlic Mustard, Brassicaceae), an Invasive, Nonindigenous Forest Herb." *International Journal of Plant Sciences* 160 (4): 743–52.

Nuzzo, V. 1999. "Invasion Pattern of Herb Garlic Mustard (*Alliaria petiolata*) in High Quality Forests." *Biological Invasions* 1 (2–3): 169–79.

Nuzzo, V., and B. N. McKnight. 1993. "Distribution and Spread of the Invasive Biennial *Alliaria petiolata* (Garlic Mustard) in North America." In *Biological Pollution: The Control and Impact of Invasive Exotic Species. Proceedings of a Symposium Held at Indianapolis, Indiana, USA, 25–26 October 1991,* 137–45. Indiana Academy of Science.

Roberts, K. J., and R. C. Anderson. 2001. "Effect of Garlic Mustard [*Alliaria petiolata* (Beib. Cavara & Grande)] Extracts on Plants and Arbuscular Mycorrhizal (AM) Fungi." *American Midland Naturalist* 146 (1): 146–52.

Rodgers, V. L., K. A. Stinson, and A. C. Finzi. 2008. "Ready or Not, Garlic Mustard Is Moving In: *Alliaria petiolata* as a Member of Eastern North American Forests." *Bioscience* 58 (5): 426–36.

Stinson, K., S. Kaufman, L. Durbin, and F. Lowenstein. 2007. "Impacts of Garlic Mustard Invasion on a Forest Understory Community." *Northeastern Naturalist* 14 (1): 73–88.

## KENNESAW MOUNTAIN PLANT LIST, INCLUDING ALIEN SPECIES

Zomlefer, W. B., D. E. Giannasi, and S. L. Echols. 2010. "Vascular Plant Flora of Kennesaw Mountain National Battlefield Park, Cobb County, Georgia." *Southeastern Naturalist* 9 (1): 129–64.

## EPILOGUE

Bierce, Ambrose. 2001. *The Unabridged Devil's Dictionary.* Athens. University of Georgia Press.

## KENNESAW MOUNTAIN HISTORY

Alexander, M. E. Jones. 1925. "Autobiographical Notes." Knox County ILGenWeb. Accessed March 21, 2013. http://knox.illinoisgenweb.org.

Blythe, R. W., M. A. Carroll, and S. H. Moffson. 1995. *Kennesaw Mountain National Battlefield Park Historic Resource Study.* National Park Service, Cultural Resources Planning Division.

Hellman, Robert. 2003. "Kennesaw Mountain National Battlefield Park Cultural Overview." National Park Service. Accessed March 3, 2013. http://www.nps.gov/kemo.

Hess, E. J. 2013. *Kennesaw Mountain: Sherman, Johnston, and the Atlanta Campaign.* Chapel Hill: University of North Carolina Press.

## KENNESAW MOUNTAIN NATIONAL BATTLEFIELD PARK

Lindley, J. 2013. "Local Man Arrested in Kennesaw Park." *Canton (GA) Cherokee Ledger,* October 16, 2013.

Strack, J. A., and C. A. Miller. 2007. "Running Uphill: Urbanization, Conflict, and Visitor Use at Kennesaw Mountain National Battlefield Park." *Proceedings of the 2007 Northeastern Recreation Research Symposium.* NRS-P-23

# Index